STATE OF THE ARTS

TURNING POINT Christian Worldview Series
Marvin Olasky, General Editor

Turning Point: A Christian Worldview Declaration
by Herbert Schlossberg and Marvin Olasky

Prodigal Press: The Anti-Christian Bias of the American News Media
by Marvin Olasky

Freedom, Justice, and Hope: Toward a Strategy for the Poor and the Oppressed
by Marvin Olasky, Herbert Schlossberg, Pierre Berthoud, and Clark H. Pinnock

Beyond Good Intentions: A Biblical View of Politics
by Doug Bandow

Prosperity and Poverty: The Compassionate Use of Resources in a World of Scarcity
by E. Calvin Beisner

The Seductive Image: A Christian Critique of the World of Film
by K. L. Billingsley

All God's Children and Blue Suede Shoes: Christians and Popular Culture
by Kenneth A. Myers

A World Without Tyranny: Christian Faith and International Politics
by Dean C. Curry

Prospects for Growth: A Biblical View of Population, Resources and the Future
by E. Calvin Beisner

More Than Kindness: A Compassionate Approach to Crisis Childbearing
by Susan Olasky and Marvin Olasky

Reading Between the Lines: A Christian Guide to Literature
by Gene Edward Veith, Jr.

State of the Arts: From Bezalel to Mapplethorpe
by Gene Edward Veith, Jr.

Recovering the Lost Tools of Learning: An Approach to Distinctively Christian Education
by Douglas Wilson

STATE OF THE ARTS

From Bezalel to Mapplethorpe

Gene Edward Veith, Jr.

CROSSWAY BOOKS • WHEATON, ILLINOIS
A DIVISION OF GOOD NEWS PUBLISHERS

75528
(9-95)

State of the Arts: From Bezalel to Mapplethorpe

Copyright © 1991 by Gene Edward Veith, Jr.

Published by Crossway Books, a division of
Good News Publishers, Wheaton, Illinois 60187.

 Published in association with the
Fieldstead Institute
P.O. Box 19061,
Irvine, California 92713

Cover illustration: Bonnie Timmons / The Image Bank

First printing, 1991

Printed in the United States of America

Unless otherwise noted, Bible quotations are taken from *Holy Bible: New
International Version*, copyright © 1978 by the New York International Bible
Society. Used by permission of Zondervan Bible Publishers.

Scripture quotations taken from the *Revised Standard Version* are identified
RSV. Copyright 1946, 1953 © 1971, 1973 by the Division of Christian
Education of the National Council of Churches in the USA.

Scripture quotations taken from the *King James Version* are identified KJV.

Library of Congress Cataloging-in-Publication Data
Veith, Gene Edward, 1951-
    State of the arts : from Bezalel to Mapplethorpe /
Gene Edward Veith, Jr.
        p. cm. — (Turning point Christian worldview series)
Includes bibliographical references and index
    1. Arts and society. 2. Arts and religion. 3. Christianity and the arts. I.
Title. II. Series.
NX180.S6V4 1991   700'.1'04—dc20   90-25447
ISBN 0-89107-608-5

99		98		97		96		95		94		93		92		91
15	14	13	12	11	10	9	8	7	6	5	4	3	2	1

The author and the publisher gratefully acknowledge permission to use material from the following:

Bierstadt, *The Rocky Mountains, Lander's Peak*. All rights reserved by The Metropolitan Museum of Art, New York, Rogers Fund, 1907.

Bowden, Sandra, *Tel Megiddo* and *Aaron's Breastplate*, courtesy of Sandra Bowden, 237 Moe Road, Clifton Park, New York 12065.

Cézanne, *Mont Sainte-Victoire Seen from Bibemure Quarry*, The Baltimore Museum of Art: The Cone Collection, formed by Dr. Claribel Cone and Miss Etta Cone of Baltimore, MD. BMA 1950.196

Cranach, *The Repose in Egypt*, National Museum, Berlin. Courtesy of Marburg/Art Resource.

The Discus Thrower, The Vatican, Rome. Courtesy of Alinari/Art Resource.

Duccio, *Temptation of Christ on the Mountain*, copyright The Frick Collection, New York.

El Greco, *The Agony in the Garden*, The Toledo Museum of Art, Toledo, OH; gift of Edward Drummond Libbey.

Gainsborough, *Robert Andrews and His Wife, Mary*, reproduced by courtesy of the Trustees, The National Gallery, London.

Ivory Pomegranate, photograph by André Lemaire. Courtesy of André Lemaire and *Biblical Archaeology Review*.

Jerusalem painted pottery, Israel Department of Antiquities. Photograph by Nahman Avigad in *Discovering Jerusalem: Recent Archaeological Excavations in the Upper City* (Nashville: Thomas Nelson, 1983). Courtesy of Nahman Avigad and Thomas Nelson Pubs.

Knippers, Edward, *The Gift (Sacrifice of Isaac)* and *The Pest House (Christ Heals the Sick)*, courtesy of Edward Knippers, 2408 Washington Blvd., Arlington, VA 22201.

Initial page (*"Christi Autum Generatio . . ."*), Lindisfarne Gospels, British Library, London.

McReynolds, Cliff, *A New Earth (2 Peter 3:13)* and detail from *A New Earth (2 Peter 3:13)*, courtesy of Cliff McReynolds, Pomegranate Publishers, P. O. Box 808022, Petaluma, CA 94925.

Monet, *Water-Lily Pond*, reproduced by courtesy of the Trustees, The National Gallery, London.

Mosque of Shaykh Lutfullah, Isfahan, Iran. Photograph by Arthur Upham Pope, courtesy of Asian Art Photographic Distribution, University of Michigan.

Munch, Edvard, B-11106, *Geschrei (The Scream)*, 1895, National Gallery of Art, Washington, DC, Rosenwald Collection

Picasso, *Girl Before a Mirror*, Boisgeloup, March 1932. Oil on canvas, 64 x 51 1/4 inches. Collection, The Museum of Modern Art, New York. Gift of Mrs. Simon Guggenheim.

Prescott, Theodore, *Descent from the Cross*, *Annunciation*, and *Icon*, courtesy of Theodore Prescott, Messiah College, Grantham, Pennsylvania 17207.

Raphael, *The School of Athens*, Vatican, Rome. Courtesy of Alinari/Art Resource.

Rembrandt, *The Adoration of the Shepherds*, reproduced by courtesy of the Trustees, The National Gallery, London. *The Storm on the Sea of Galilee*, Isabella Stewart Gardner Museum, Boston. *Family Group*, Herzog Anton Ulrich Museum, Brunswick, Germany. Courtesy of Marburg/Art Resource.

For
Philip Griffith and Karen Mulder
Ezekiel 37:1-10

TABLE OF

CONTENTS

ILLUSTRATIONS

ACKNOWLEDGMENTS

When I first started writing about Christianity and the arts some time ago, my knowledge was only theoretical. Because of Philip Griffith and Karen Mulder, founders of Christians in the Arts Networking, this would change. Philip, Karen, their board members (with whom I was privileged to serve), and others whom I met through the network are real artists. Knowing them and becoming involved in a small way with their ministry has deepened my appreciation for Christian artists—for their bold faithfulness, their God-given creativity, and their capacity for service. I salute them all, with special thanks to Philip and Karen, to whom this book is dedicated.

The book itself owes its existence to James Sire, who encouraged me through an earlier and related book on the subject, *The Gift of Art*. Marvin Olasky, editor of the Turning Point Series, asked me to write this book, and his ideas greatly influenced the outcome. Thanks also go to Dr. R. John Buuck, President of Concordia University-Wisconsin, and to the Board of Regents, for granting me a sabbatical to complete this project.

Thanks too to my wife Jackquelyn—not, as the conventions of Acknowledgments usually go, for typing the manuscript. I now compose on a computer. Rather, I thank her for other things too numerous to mention. I am also grateful to and for Paul, Joanna, and Mary.

INTRODUCTION

*T*he arts today are a study in paradox. Although we are told that more people patronize the arts—by attending museums, galleries, concerts, and plays—than attend sporting events, very few people seem to understand what they are seeing. Although a painting by Van Gogh sells for $82.5 million, the artist himself died in poverty. Although exhibitors of Robert Mapplethorpe's pornographic photographs openly scorn the values and tastes of the "bourgeois low-brow American public," they demand to be funded by these same taxpayers. As art has become a big business, a political issue, and a fashion statement, it has grown more and more superficial (witness the decline from Van Gogh to Mapplethorpe).

Appreciating the arts has become a sign of social status and intellectual sophistication. This great prestige, ironically, comes at a time when art is at its most obscure. People ashamed of their ignorance uncritically accept bad art—even against their personal tastes—while remaining blind to art of genuine merit.

Art has become intimidating. Corporations are pouring money into the arts, going so far as to hire expensive consultants to tell them what they should like. Wealthy and powerful executives, whose decisions are law in the board room, become almost comically insecure and submissive before the gurus of artistic fashion. Some people are so terrified of being thought uncultured or unprogressive that they are ashamed of their secret preference for wildlife paintings over Jackson Pollock's random paint drippings.

Despite their unprecedented success and prestige, the arts are in a bad way. Art has become elitist, cut off from actual human life. Consequently, ordinary people are left with ugliness, and artistic circles are left with esoteric experiments. Aesthetic excellence becomes less important than commercialism, social climbing, and novelty for novelty's sake. Bad art drives out good art.

Christians might think that the confusions in the art world are no concern to them, simply another example of the vanity of this world. The arts, though, are important. We cannot escape them. They permeate our lives and our culture. The decor of our surroundings; the music we listen to; the entertainment we enjoy in books, television, and films are all manifestations of the arts. They influence us and our children whether we are aware of it or not. For good or for evil, the ideas, the concerns, and the imagination of the age are expressed and communicated throughout the culture by the arts. The question is not whether we will live with the arts; the question is whether we will live with good art or bad art.

Properly considered, the arts are inestimable gifts of God. They can enrich our lives. They have a spiritual dimension and can enhance our relationship to God and to our neighbors. The Bible itself sanctions the arts, describing the gifts God has given to artists and recounting in loving detail works of art that were ordained by God to manifest His glory and to enrich His people.

That the arts can be corrupt does not mean that Christians should abandon them. On the contrary, the corruption of the arts means that Christians dare not abandon them any longer. Art—like all things human—needs to be redeemed.

In every dimension of our lives, including the arts, we need to be able to discern between good and evil, truth and falsehood. Art calls also for another level of discernment—between the aesthetically good and the aesthetically bad. If much of art is tasteless or idolatrous, much is excellent. This book is designed to help Christians tell the difference.

A further purpose is to help Christians recover their own artistic heritage, which extends from the time of Bezalel, who was empowered by God to make the art of the Tabernacle, to the exciting work of contemporary Christian artists. In short, this book is designed to help Christians develop an informed and sophisticated taste, one that is open yet critical, discerning yet appreciative of what is truly excellent.

AN OVERVIEW OF THE BOOK

This book is an expansion of an earlier much-smaller volume entitled *The Gift of Art: The Place of the Arts in Scripture* (Downers Grove, IL: InterVarsity Press, 1983). The present volume includes, often in expanded form, the material from that book (mostly in the section "The Biblical Foundations"). This new book also includes chapters on understanding art, surveys of art history, discussions of current trends and controversies, treatments of contemporary Christian artists, and—fittingly in a book on art—illustrations.

My earlier book was primarily addressed to artists, exploring how artistry can be a Biblical vocation. This new book, which should still prove useful to Christians with artistic gifts, is also addressed to nonartists, to Christians who wish to learn about the arts and to develop discernment and appreciation. Artists alone cannot revive the arts. Their works must find an audience. If Christians can develop a taste for artistic excellence and spiritual depth, if they can learn to reject the superficialities of both the pop culture and the established art world, and if they will patronize artists of merit, then they will strengthen both the church and the arts and leaven the entire culture.

The first chapter looks at some travesties that now pass for art and argues that the art world itself is in desperate need for a conceptual framework that can justify art—such as Christianity. The chapter also surveys different ways Christians have responded to the arts and suggests how to put together and balance the views of both the iconophiles and the iconoclasts.

Then follows a section entitled "Comprehending the Arts." Its purpose is to show what art is and to explain how to approach a work of art with both appreciation and understanding. This section also surveys the history of art, showing the significance of its manifold styles and exploring how art reflects the worldviews of its creators. The section goes on to examine the spiritual and aesthetic malaise that plagues the contemporary art world.

The next section explores what the Bible says about the arts. Its focus is on the gifts God gave to Bezalel, on the specific works of art which God ordained for the Tabernacle and the Temple, and on the two ancient concepts of creation and imitation which continue to energize the arts. While the Bible sanctions the arts, it also warns against idolatry, of worshiping art, whether in primitive nature religions or in the more sophisticated venues of secular aestheticism. Throughout the discussions of Biblical history and archeological discoveries, we will draw from the Bible practical applications related to the artist's vocation and the nature of God-pleasing art.

The final section addresses the relationship between Christianity and the arts, focusing upon the contemporary Christian artists and upon the role of art in worship and in evangelism. Today Christian artists are proving that one can be contemporary and stylistically original without succumbing to the godlessness of modern art. They are also proving that a Biblical worldview retains its power to inspire art of depth and beauty. While the various theological traditions have differed in the way art may be used in worship, each provides for a legitimate use of the arts. Evangelistically, art can function as signs of God's Word, communicating the moral law, the human need for salvation, and the good news of redemption through Jesus Christ.

The Lord told Bezalel, the artist of the Tabernacle, to make the garments of the high priest, with their dazzling gems and elaborate design, "for glory and for beauty" (Exodus 28:2 KJV). God's purpose for these particular works of Bezalel suggests a purpose for all of the arts—to glorify God and to manifest beauty.

While art that fails in these purposes can be problematic, art that fulfills them has enormous value. Art that does not glorify God—through immorality or idolatry—can be thought of as bad art. Art that falls short of the purpose of beauty—work that fails aesthetically—is also bad art. They are, however, "bad" in different senses: The former is spiritually bad in its effect, while the latter is aesthetically bad in its form. Scripture also suggests how art can be good. Art may glorify God directly by expressing His Word or indirectly by celebrating His creation. Art may also fulfill its purpose, apart from any explicit religious meaning, simply by being beautiful. The purposes of glory and beauty enable the arts to fulfill their own nature and to enrich human life. The Bible, even in its prohibitions, liberates the arts.

O N E

THE STATE OF THE ARTS

*R*ecovering a Christian sensibility towards the arts is particularly urgent today, both for the sake of Christians and for the sake of the arts. While the art world has acquired unparalleled status and influence, its aesthetic achievements are undercut by a philosophical and spiritual bankruptcy. Christians need the arts, but the arts are in desperate need of Christianity, or at least of some conceptual framework that can justify beauty and inspire artistic excellence.

TRAVESTIES OF THE ARTS

Consider some items from the annals of the contemporary art world:

> AIDS-martyr Robert Mapplethorpe's exhibition causes a furor. His photographs of homosexual erotica include sadism, masochism, pedophilia, and scatology. One photograph, for example, depicts a man urinating into the mouth of another man. The public is outraged, especially since the exhibit was financed by tax dollars, but the artistic establishment self-righteously rallies to its defense.

> A new art form has emerged that is supplanting painting and sculpture for many artists—performance art. In one such work, the artist comes in and verbally abuses the people who have come to his show. As the tension builds, the artist, demonstrating how creative people suffer for the sake of their audiences, lacerates himself with fishhooks and razor blades.

A sculptor displays a cube made of sterling silver. He takes pictures of it at regular intervals as it corrodes. The photographs are exhibited along with the decaying piece of metal.

Andy Warhol, the late art world celebrity, has made a fashion of borrowing images from the popular culture (Brillo boxes, Campbell Soup cans, Marilyn Monroe, and, eventually, himself) into the high-culture realm of fine art. Among his creations is a movie that depicts an actor sleeping. It lasts eight hours.

Such work does not represent all contemporary art, which includes works of genuine merit and artistic skill. Still, examples of the inane, the outrageous, and the repulsive in contemporary art could be multiplied. Andrés Serrano experiments with what has been labeled "postmodern blasphemy." He displays a photograph of a crucifix immersed in his urine. The artistry of Annie Sprinkle, performance artist and "feminine porn activist," consists of masturbating in public.

     Let us set aside for the moment questions about censorship and aesthetics, whether such work should be supported by tax dollars and whether it merits the name of art (questions this book will address later). I am intrigued by the art establishment's uncritical acceptance of such art. Defenders often express a personal distaste for it, but then they raise questions that reveal their own aesthetic uncertainties: Who is to say what is art? Who are we to question the work of a creative artist? Great art has often seemed shocking and controversial. Who is to say that these works might not be great? The concept of relativism, that moral values and truth itself have no objective basis and are "only relative," is paralyzing the intellectual world, which finds itself without content that can be learned or taught. Relativism in the aesthetic realm is similarly dominating and confusing the art world, which has lost its criteria for making aesthetic judgments.

     The major purpose of artists such as Mapplethorpe and Serrano is to shock people. In this regard, public revulsion is an appropriate and intended aesthetic response. And yet, many of the most dedicated art patrons refuse to be shocked. They smile and nod knowingly. They think, *How interesting.* They experience the exquisite pleasure of feeling sophisticated, of belonging to an elite group who "gets it," while looking down on those who do not. The outrage or bewilderment of those outside the art world only increases their smugness at being on the cutting edge.

     Those who subject themselves to the performance artist's derision and who sit through the entire Andy Warhol movie exhibit an almost ascetic devotion. Their self-flagellating zeal and their air of self-righteousness all suggest that, for them, art has become a religion. Art is considered sacred, the source of their values and their means of transcendence. This is a sophisticated manifestation of what the Bible terms idolatry. Today, among the educated elite, the religion of art may be Christianity's most serious competitor.

Although this book will attack idolatry in its various forms, its purpose is to champion the arts. Art needs to be defended, not only from its usual detractors, but from some of its most ardent advocates and practitioners. Christianity with its Biblical worldview provides a stronger, more vital basis for the arts than the competing worldviews of materialism, existentialism, and humanism, which today are proving themselves artistic dead ends.

None of the works of art cited above are beautiful, ennobling, thought-provoking, human, or well-crafted. Mapplethorpe's photographs and Serrano's crucifix are defended on the grounds that "great art often shocks people." (Even if that were true, of course, it would not follow that whatever shocks people must be great art.)[1] The implication is revealing—the standard of shock replaces the standard of beauty. Concepts such as beauty, order, and meaning are being challenged by the new aesthetic theories in favor of ugliness, randomness, and irrationalism. The purpose is not to give the audience pleasure, but to assault them with a "decentering" experience. Art becomes defined as "whatever an artist does." As a result, the work of art becomes less important than the artist, a view which encourages posturing, egotism, and self-indulgence instead of artistic excellence. These new assumptions about art have been catastrophic for true creativity.

Compare the works of Mapplethorpe and Warhol to those of other modern artists such as Chagall, or to those of Van Gogh or Goya or Michelangelo or Giotto, or as far back as the cave paintings of Lascaux. Something valuable has been lost. Just as the current intellectual establishment has lost its conceptual basis for truth, the artistic establishment has lost its conceptual basis for beauty. A Christian view of the arts can supply both.

CHRISTIAN RESPONSES TO THE ARTS

Christianity has taken two extreme positions in regard to the arts. Some Christians, the "iconophiles," have exalted art, going so far as to make works of art central to their religious and devotional lives. Other Christians, the iconoclasts, have rejected art, going so far as to destroy works of art considered idolatrous. Some Christians have expressed their piety by making pilgrimages to the Black Madonna in Poland or by lighting candles to an icon of Christ. Others have expressed their piety by smashing stained glass windows and burning religious images.

Some of the world's greatest paintings, sculptures, architecture, and music have been inspired by the Christian faith. It might be said that no other philosophical or religious system has nourished the arts as Christianity has. Yet Christians have also mistrusted the arts. Scriptural warnings against idolatry imply that works of art can undermine faith, whether by promoting false religion or by the confusion of aesthetic experience for true worship. Christians have often seen nonreligious art as insidiously worldly.

The theological debates between the iconophiles (lovers of religious images) and the iconoclasts (destroyers of religious images) began in the earliest days of the Christian church, erupted again during the Reformation, and they continue today. That both icon makers and icon breakers have been part of the history of the church suggests that both may have a certain grounding in Biblical truth. The iconophiles may well be correct in valuing art (although they perhaps take this value to an unbiblical extreme). The iconoclasts are also correct in refusing to worship it (although they perhaps take this fear of images to an unbiblical extreme). By putting the views together and allowing them to correct each other, we can learn from both factions.

Many Christians today, however, are neither iconophiles nor iconoclasts, both of whom at least took art seriously. Many accept art, but uncritically, without considering its quality or significance. They welcome it solely as decoration, as part of the background, needing no attention or scrutiny. They listen to music that makes the top-forty chart, and they watch hours of television, without giving these works of art and their meaning a second thought. Many collect religious knickknacks because they are "cute" or for other emotional associations and never worry about their theological implications. Works of art that are more demanding (and thus could be more rewarding) are passed over. The aesthetic quality or the meaning of a work of art is seldom considered.

From no fault of their own, many Christians—like most people in our culture today—simply know little about art. They may know what they like, but that is nothing more than knowledge about themselves. They do not know what to look for or how to read a visual image. Part of the blame, no doubt, lies with the current artistic establishment, which has turned art into an elite and esoteric mystery, segregating the arts from ordinary people and everyday life. Those who are oblivious to the arts, or those who have had the arts stolen from them, are shut out of a realm that, for better or worse, is a critical dimension of human culture.

The indifference of the contemporary church to the arts has traumatized many of its Christian artists. Boldly defying the dictates of the non-Christian "art world," which, however, determines an artist's professional success, these artists look to fellow Christians for support. Often, they do not find it, encountering rejection from both the art establishment and the church. Christians have become content with institutional ugliness—bland, mass-produced decorations, prefabricated church buildings, tacky knickknacks, artifacts of the dominant mass culture—rather than patronizing the significant creative efforts of their fellow Christians.

On a personal level, Christian artists often are not understood in their own fellowships. Artists, in some ways, are a peculiar breed, by nature sensitive and driven by their gifts. People who sell insurance or work in a factory or serve hamburgers in a fast-food restaurant find ready acceptance in the church, but when a new member says, "I'm an artist," people shift uneasily. Vague associations of bizarre behavior, a sense of disapproval (Why don't you do something *practical*?), combined with a feeling of cultural inferiority, color many people's reactions to artists.

Artists are quick to pick up this reaction. Furthermore, they may feel suffocated by the unrelieved ugliness of their worship surroundings. *There is so much linoleum*, they think, *so much bad music, so little aesthetic stimulation, and none of these people seem to care.* While the purpose of going to church is to feed on the Word of God, not to satisfy one's aesthetic sensibility, many Christian artists feel utter isolation in church. They may have sacrificed professional success in their loyalty to Christ. Yet their local church neither supports them in their work nor affirms their gifts.

Franky Schaeffer, an artist and the son of the eminent theologian and cultural critic Francis Schaeffer, expresses this frustration somewhat bitterly, yet plaintively:

Loneliness is a constant reality for Christians who seriously pursue an artistic career. We are caught on the horns of a miserable dilemma. On the one hand is the church; on the other is the larger world and its art community. The nonbelieving art community, be it in the field of painting, theater, writing, film, music, or dance, has little interest in those who would express orthodox Jewish-Christian themes through their personal lives or their art-works. Yet the church is no better; it has lost vital contact with art and culture and has even lost the cultural vocabulary to discuss art and the humanities, let alone encourage artists. . . .

In the most unfortunate reaction possible, many Christians find false security through collective ignorance and deny rather than affirm, run rather than shape, endlessly say no rather than present good alternatives. The Christian who is serious about being an artist occupies, in this reactionary ghetto [of the church], a place as comfortable as that of a live fish placed in boiling water.[2]

Most of us are probably surprised that the artists in our midst feel this way. They do. These feelings not only can jeopardize artists' involvement in a local church, but, if they continue to fester, also can jeopardize their faith.

And yet artists need the discipling of the church. They need its dogmas, its moral authority, its pastoral care, and its community support. The church also needs its artists, both for the sake of its own spiritual life and for the sake of its larger mission in the world. This book is, among other things, an attempt to show the church how to understand what artists do, to explain the "cultural vocabulary," so that the church can not only join in solidarity with its artists but also join them in engaging the cultural landscape that is in urgent need of Christ.

Many scholars have shown that ours is an increasingly visual age.[3] The visual images of television dominate our popular culture. Entertainment, information, politics, and sometimes even religion are visualized, a process which sometimes changes their very nature. Christians, who must be centered on the Word, must be cautious lest they surrender language to the graven images of the mass culture and the neopagan thought forms that they breed. The new graven images must be recognized and understood. This requires positive knowledge about art and something of the spirit of the iconoclasts.

Just as the art forms of the popular culture—music, videos, and film, as well as television—are unsurpassed in their influence, the art of the high culture has a profound effect on the intellectual climate. The decadence and nihilism of much contemporary art is part of the texture of our culture. To engage those for whom art has taken the place of religion and potentially to reach them with the gospel, Christians need to become both critics and makers of art. This requires a critical sensibility and something of the spirit of the iconophiles.

TOWARDS A BIBLICAL VIEW OF THE ARTS

In navigating through all of these issues, Christians have recourse to the Scriptures. The Bible has a great deal to say about the arts. It recounts the commissioning and empowering of Bezalel to create the art of the Tabernacle. It goes on to describe, in exhausting but loving detail, the specifications for that art and, later, for the crafting of the Temple. The Bible mentions or offers examples of nearly every art form—painting, sculpture, music, architecture, crafts, poetry. The Temple alone included both abstract art and representational art, works that were purely decorative and works that were complexly symbolic. Clearly God, the ultimate Artist who created every detail of the universe purely from His own imagination, values the arts.

Yet the Bible also warns against their misuse. While Bezalel was empowered to build the Tabernacle for worship of the true God, Aaron used his artistic talents to manufacture an idol, a work of art that displaced the true faith and led the people into the grossest sin. Biblical sanctions for art are intermingled with radical condemnations of idolatry. Art can express falsehood as well as truth. Aesthetic experience can easily be confused with religious experience. We are often tempted to abandon the Biblical faith based upon the self-consuming revelation of God for an aesthetic faith based upon our own pleasure and self-gratification.

That Christianity has inspired both icon makers and icon breakers suggests that both extremes may have seized upon an aspect of Biblical truth. Those who honor icons are correct in valuing works of art, in using art to express God's Word, and in recognizing the God-given value of aesthetic experience. The iconoclasts are also correct in insisting that human beings must never worship their own creations, that the gospel must involve casting down idols of all kinds even if they are aesthetically beautiful.

A fully Biblical view must find a way of affirming both the artist Bezalel and the idol-smashing Hezekiah. This will mean finding the sense in which the arts are inestimable gifts of God and encouraging Christians to enjoy and create them. At the same time, a Biblical view must include a critical stance towards the arts, a willingness to question and a refusal to overmystify.

In carefully setting forth the boundaries of art, the Bible creates a space for beauty. Aesthetic experience, the perception of beauty, is valuable for its own sake and can also profoundly enrich our lives. Art can open our eyes to the beauties of the created order. A painting or a song or a poem can spark a flash of illumination.

Art can even disclose spiritual truths and express them in a penetrating way. It is little wonder that the church has always employed art in one way or another. From the majestic symbolism of the cathedrals to the universal practice of using music to praise and worship God, Christians have always expressed their faith in aesthetic forms. The tradition of Christian art is a magnificent legacy, one contemporary Christians should draw upon and maintain.

While the secular aesthetes of the high culture need the message of iconoclasm, most Christians today should value art more than they do. This book is designed to help Christians learn to enjoy and understand works of art. I also hope to introduce contemporary Christians to the continuing tradition of Christian art. This includes the legacy of the past and also the work of contemporary Christian artists, who are, in the tradition of Bezalel, crafting works of glory and beauty (Exodus 28:2).

COMPREHENDING THE ARTS

T W O

THE SCOPE OF THE ARTS

When we think of art, we usually think of paintings hanging on museum walls. Art, though, as a faculty God gave to the human race, involves much more than the "fine art" that exists sheerly for contemplation. The universal habit of decoration, for example, draws on our innate artistic concerns. We wear clothes in colors and designs we find attractive. We decorate our homes with paint, wallpaper, and carefully chosen furniture. We choose our automobiles, houses, restaurants, and packaged goods partly because of their aesthetic appeal.

Aesthetics, the perception of beauty in all its forms, is at the essence of the arts and imparts richness to everyday life. Some objects are created solely for their aesthetic and intellectual appeal; these are the works which end up in museums. Others appeal to our sense of beauty but also have another function, or they fade into the background to become a part of a pleasing environment. Anything designed to give pleasure to an audience partakes of art, including nearly every form of entertainment. We listen to music, watch actors perform on television, get swept up by the photography of a motion picture—all of this is art. Many people say that they are completely uninterested in art, yet they listen to the radio, watch television, go shopping for new clothes or a new car, and fix up the house. Our lives are permeated with art.

A tree or a mountain range may also have an aesthetic appeal, yet the beauties of nature are not considered art. The term art is usually reserved for something made by human beings. A painting of the tree or the mountain range would be art. The God-given capacity of human beings to make things is at the essence of art. A carpenter building a house is, in this sense, just as much an artist as the

painter. Both use their talents, their minds, and their skill with their
hands to make something valuable. To consider art is to contemplate
human creativity in all of its forms.

We are accustomed to think about art too narrowly, as something for museums and experts rather than as part of the texture of
life. This limited view is almost unique to modern Western culture.
The ancient Hebrews, the Greeks, the medieval craftsmen, the
Renaissance painters, or the tribes of Africa or South America did
not have museums. Art was integrated with life. Museums were not
invented until the eighteenth-century Enlightenment, an era that
marked the fragmentation of human life in other ways as well.

The segregation of art from life is especially evident today, having been heightened by the contemporary art world and its quasi-
religious philosophy of art. The result is impoverishment of both art,
which has become abstrusely theoretical and elitist, and ordinary
life, which has increasingly fallen prey to the ugly and the tasteless.

Although we will focus later on how to understand the fine art
of the museums, it might prove helpful first to consider art in its
broader dimensions. The larger perspective will clarify the place of
the arts in human nature and in God's design. By breaking out of
the narrow boundaries prescribed by modern art, we might also see
possibilities for the restoration of the arts.[1]

ART AS WORK

Aristotle defined art as the capacity to make.[2] For the ancients, any
exercise of human creativity—building ships, making shoes, healing
the sick, governing the state—is described as an art. In this sense,
whenever we exercise our minds or our hands to make something
that was not there before, we are functioning as artists. Painters and
sculptors are not the only artists; all honest occupations involve art.

Dante imagined the Seventh Circle of Hell as a barren plain
upon which flakes of fire eternally rain down upon three groups of
sinners—those who have committed violence against God, against
nature, and against art.[3] Violence against God, futile as it is, would
be the sin of blasphemy. Violence against nature, according to
Dante, includes sexual perversion. Dante's third category of sinners
on the burning plain is doubly baffling for a modern reader. Violence
against art, according to his system, is usury, the lending out of
money at exorbitant interest.

Although some may take pleasure at the thought of credit card
companies and investment bankers being consigned to the Seventh
Circle of Hell, most do not see what is so sinful about using money

to make money. Clearly, Dante is writing in terms of an antiquated medieval economic theory. But what does any of this have to do with *art*?

Lest we dismiss the passage as a quaint medievalism, we should remember that Dante is himself one of the greatest Christian artists and that he usually rewards close attention:

> By Art and Nature, if thou well recall
> How Genesis begins, man ought to get
> His bread, and make prosperity for all.
>
> But the usurer contrives a third way yet,
> And in herself and in her follower, Art,
> Scorns Nature, for his hope is elsewhere set.[4]

According to Dante and medieval thought, human beings are to earn their living in two ways—by means of nature and by means of art. The allusion to Genesis underscores the point that the earth with its bounty was given to Adam (earning a living by nature). Yet Adam is also told that he must "work it and take care of it" (Genesis 2:15) (earning a living by art). After the fall, Adam is told that he must struggle with nature to produce food and that he must labor by the sweat of his brow (Genesis 3:19). To survive, human beings must depend upon both the resources of nature and their own creative abilities.

Our food comes from the abundance of nature, and yet farmers must apply the "art" of agriculture in order to grow the crops nature makes possible. Every occupation, therefore, involves an art. Shoemakers, physicians, soldiers, merchants, rulers—all are artists in that they exercise their skills creatively to make a product or perform a service for others.

Under this view, dishonest ways to earn a living—robbery, embezzlement, exploitation, fraud—are sinful because they generate wealth apart from both nature and art. Criminals, who produce nothing, acquire money by seizing what others produce. By this reasoning, usury was considered sinful because a usurer does not create anything. In using money to breed more money, a loan shark exploits other people's labor and their art, making a profit without making a product. In defense of our credit-driven economy, we might argue that lending money for interest *is* productive because such investment enables others to build houses, factories, and other "artistic" enterprises. We do not have to agree with medieval economics to appreciate Dante's point: Art is inherent in every true vocation; creativity is at the essence of the human capacity to work, to be productive, and to serve society.

What we think of as art—sculpture, painting, literature, music—was valued in the Middle Ages, but in the medieval mind, it existed on the same plane as every other kind of human labor. Medieval artists, with only a few exceptions, did not sign their work. (Dante, Chaucer, and Giotto did, but they were part of a proto-Renaissance that anticipated what was to come.) We do not know who designed the dazzling stained glass windows at Chartres, nor do we know who illuminated the Book of Kells or who wrote "Sir Gawaine and the Green Knight." The thought of attaching their names to what they made never occurred to medieval artists, any more than the factory workers who put together my car or the carpenters who built my house would have thought to sign their work. They were all simply plying their craft. Their concern was not to express their egos, but to make something well.

To fully comprehend the scope of art and its place in the human scene, we need to recover the view of art as pertaining to any creative human labor. Such a view frees art from the elitist associations that often separate the arts from ordinary life. Conversely, this view of art restores dignity to the whole range of human work. Running a business, working on an assembly line, framing a house, serving a client, teaching a class—such vocations, and indeed all vocations, involve a God-given creative faculty that is different only in kind from that of the greatest painters, writers, and musicians.

To see one's work as an art form is to rediscover its satisfactions. It should be possible to find the same fulfillment in one's job that a painter finds in executing a beautiful landscape. The worker, thinking in these terms, can also develop the artist's obsession with excellence.

FUNCTIONAL ARTS

Aristotle and Dante felt that all human work involves artistry. More modern definitions of art stress its aesthetic dimension—that is, the making of beauty. Here too artistry goes beyond the objects in a museum.

An architect is in every sense an artist. Incorporating engineering specifications, efficient utilization of space, and other practical requirements, architects work all elements into an aesthetic design. The building must be appealing as well as functional. The building is a work of art.

Art can be functional. That is, the aesthetic can be joined with the practical. What is true of architecture is also true of industrial design, packaging, marketing, and communications. Even engineering, that most technical and scientifically based profession, can be seen as a creative art. A scientist considering a problem and devising an invention or an "elegant" solution is drawing upon the creative imagination no less than the poet or sculptor.

The beauty that inheres in the functional is in fact a profound testimony to the artistry that underlies all existence—that of God Himself. Francis Schaeffer has commented upon the beauty of aircraft. Though designed solely for flight according to the laws of nature, their form is at once functional and aesthetic. Schaeffer quotes Sir Archibald Russel, the designer of the supersonic transport, the Concorde:

> When one designs an airplane, he must stay as close as possible to the laws of nature. You are really playing with the laws of nature and trying not to offend them. . . . Every shape and curve of the Concorde is arranged so it will conform with the natural flow as conditioned by the laws of nature.[5]

"It so happens," Russel concludes, "that our ideas of beauty are those of nature."[6] We might go further: Our ideas of beauty are those of God.

Artistry and aesthetics can thus apply to every vocation in which human beings exercise their ingenuity in productive ways. In ordinary occupations and in artifacts which we use every day, we come face to face with creation. God's creation encompasses and makes possible the creativity of human beings made in His image.

DECORATIVE ARTS

Although the functional can be beautiful in itself, human beings have always had the impulse to add beauty to their environment. Not content with pottery that was merely functional—although it often displayed remarkable symmetry and grace—the ancients adorned their vessels with bright colors, intricate pictures, and abstract designs. For the same reason, we paint our houses, wear brightly colored patterned clothing, and hang pictures on the wall. Our need for decoration is another testimony to the pervasiveness of art and the importance of the aesthetic dimension in ordinary human life.

The art world today tends to scorn art that is "merely decorative." Choosing a painting because it matches the furniture does tend to minimize the work of art. The meaning of the work and its self-contained identity is neglected, giving the object of art no more status than the coffee table or the wallpaper. Decorative art fades into the background.

And yet, decoration is a legitimate function of the arts. When we decorate our homes, we are, in effect, turning where we live into a work of art. This is not simply a matter of aesthetic perfection—as in the flawless but impersonal interiors shown in interior design magazines. Decoration, like all art, is a form of self-expression, a way of projecting ourselves into the space where we live. When we put up a child's drawing on the refrigerator or arrange a tattered but comfortable easy chair next to the end table that has been in the family for generations or place a cross on a wall, we affirm what is important to us in a tangible way. Decoration is not merely a matter of aesthetic arrangement; like all art, it works with highly personal associations and has meaning.

The impulse to create art that touches and enriches everyday life should be nurtured.[7] We should value highly crafts such as quilting, cooking, woodworking, embroidery, the making of clothing and of other useful and decorative artifacts. Cultivation of beauty as a part of life is a way to counter the ugliness that pervades contemporary secular culture. The concrete slabs, the featureless metal buildings, the sterile high-tech look, and the mass production of impersonal consumer products are all signs of how modern materialism, in turning away from God, has also turned away from what is human.

If decoration is art (which is not the same as saying that art is decoration), it follows that we should be sensitive to the quality and meaning of decoration no less than of the art of the museums. In other words, we might ask what is expressed by the decoration of our environment.

When I walk into a certain bank building, I feel dwarfed by its colossal scale, its high ceilings, and the sheer number of tellers' windows. Everything is off-white, trimmed in stainless steel. The furniture consists of upholstered cubes and angular metallic tubes. This particular bank conspicuously proclaims itself a patron of the arts by its free-standing sculptures in the lobby and its paintings on the walls—all are abstract, massive, and ostentatiously expensive. Art is used as a sign of social status and high finance rather than as a mark of humanity. There is scarcely a bright color or an earth tone in the entire building, except for what the customers might wear (the bank employees, both men and women, wear the corporate uniform—navy blue pin-striped power suits).

The whole atmosphere, scrupulously designed and aesthetically sophisticated as it may be, intimidates, or, at best, awes the customer by the efficiency, the wealth, and the grand scale of the world of high finance. Understandably, many people consider such a monument to the corporate economy a safe and reliable place to keep their money.

I started going to another bank with ornate, rather Victorian-looking wallpaper, dark wood paneling, and flowers in the lobby. The wall behind the tellers' windows consists almost entirely of a large picture window through which one can see the river that runs behind the building. (The bank employees face the customers; the people who wait in line can enjoy the view.) While customers wait to apply for a loan, they, no less than the bank executives, have access to comfortable leather furniture and a newspaper (*The Wall Street Journal*, of course) on the coffee table. The atmosphere is opulent, but rather old-fashioned, making me think of nineteenth-century robber barons, who for all of their faults seem to have had more character than contemporary corporate raiders. More significantly, the decor of this bank centers around the customer, who is made to feel important, even honored.

Perhaps the first bank is more honest or more appropriate in its expression of bottom-line corporate power, where the individual depositor plays only a small role in a vast economic network. The second bank, with its human scale and its obvious catering to customers with broadly accessible, nostalgic aesthetic touches, may only be using a shrewd marketing ploy to lure in new depositors. The point is, decor conveys meaning. It even conveys a philosophy.

Today we have shopping malls that rival the Hanging Gardens of Babylon in their luxurious ostentation. We have church buildings, oddly enough, that resemble shopping malls, with atriums and fountains and vast parking lots. What do such structures mean?

Our commercial buildings, with their spaciousness and elaborate symbolic ornamentation, ironically, emulate the church buildings of old. A cathedral marks off a vast space as a way to elevate the mind to God; a mall marks off a vast space as a way to elevate the mind to shopping. In both cases, the individual human being is made to feel very small. Gothic cathedrals, with their ceilings vaulting upwards into space, make human beings feel insignificant, just as the bank building does, although to a different purpose. The churches made worshipers feel their smallness in the presence of a holy, infinite God. The banks, malls, and skyscrapers reduce the unique individual into a faceless component of the mass culture—an economic statistic, a follower of fashions, a consumer.

A further difference is that the cathedrals displace the worshiper's self-consciousness and pride with a sense of awe at the sub-limity and grandeur of God. The place of human beings in the universe is clarified, but ultimately affirmed, so that even secularist visitors to the cathedrals feel oddly exalted and satisfied. Skyscrapers, on the other hand, make human beings feel small, but offer nothing to reaffirm their significance. We may be impressed by their engineering, by the corporate power they represent, and by the vitality of the city, but, like the Tower of Babel, they isolate us. Paradoxically, the vast shopping malls are impersonal, but in a more comforting way—we lose our often painful individuality in the crowds, in the pleasant surroundings, in the community of mass marketing.

Churches designed like commercial buildings cater to "church shopping," an exquisitely precise metaphor. Faith today is often packaged and sold as a matter of consumer preference rather than proclaimed as all-consuming truth. Churches today are often designed for the comfort of their worshipers—the pews are cushioned in soft velour, the colors are soothing, the pulpit and the choir loft are on a stage as in a theater or television studio. The danger is that the church's message might likewise come across as comfortable, cushioned, soothing, and entertaining.

Romanesque and Gothic churches, on the other hand, were designed in the shape of the cross. Such a floor plan, with its two wings shooting off in opposite directions completely out of sight of the main altar, was extravagantly impractical. The building, though, existed to express the cross, not the convenience of the parishioners. Every detail of a Gothic church—the doors, the windows, even the gutter pipes—expressed the church's message.

I am not saying that contemporary churches should necessarily emulate past designs. To do nothing more than reproduce medieval art forms may imply that Christianity is nothing more than a medieval faith. Many contemporary church buildings successfully draw on centuries of Christian tradition and symbolism (declaring that Christianity is a historical, universal faith) while expressing Christian truth in contemporary ways. Massive materials can express the solidity of God's Word and the materiality of the Incarnation. Floor plans that seat people facing each other can express and encourage Christian community. Skylights can bathe the altar in light (a symbol from both nature and the Bible). Banners, crosses, and other historic symbols rendered in terms of the modern imagination can bridge the present to the past and convey the continuity of the church throughout time and eternity. Mere simplicity can seem eloquent in a church building. On the other hand, tackiness, gaudy luxury, and uncritical appeals to the lowest common denominator can unwittingly interfere with the message of Scripture and the credibility of the church.

In speaking of decoration at such length, I do not wish to exaggerate its importance. It is true that decoration is only decoration and, to a large measure, indifferent. The quality of one's worship does not depend upon the beauty or the tastefulness of the facilities. As Luther observes, worship is made holy, not by human efforts, but by God's Word.[8] This means that wherever the Word of God is proclaimed—in a centuries-old chapel or in a sheet metal prefabricated building, in a home or in a prison—the Holy Spirit is present with power. It is also true that the sheerly functional and the sheerly personal can have an aesthetic appeal of their own. I like my messy office with its apparent chaos and its clutter of papers and objects which only I appreciate.

We should realize, however, that tastelessness, inappropriateness, and ugliness can debase our surroundings and deaden our sensibilities. The bombed-out tenements and garbage-strewn neighborhoods reflect and reinforce the despair of the inner city. The gargantuan glass and metal boxes that dominate the skylines can crush the individuality of those who use them. The tangle of billboards, neon signs, fast-food restaurants, and concrete block shopping centers threatens to fill up every human or natural space. All of this sprawl wears on people and becomes both a symptom and a cause of the impersonal, dehumanized culture.

Christians, unlike the secular culture, have a basis for affirming the personal and the beautiful—a personal God who created structures of beauty in the very texture of the universe. Christians, therefore, ought to cultivate what is aesthetically worthy.

FINE ARTS

Although the decorative and the functional can have aesthetic meaning, some works are made for their aesthetic meaning alone. These are the "fine arts." A quilt may be beautiful, but its purpose is to keep someone warm. A house may have a striking design and an attractive decor, but it exists not merely to be attractive but to provide shelter. A painting in a museum, on the other hand, exists in its own right, with no other purpose than to be beautiful and to be meaningful. It is an object for contemplation.

Most of what we think of as art falls into this category: painting, sculpture, music, drama, literature. In the fine arts, aesthetics and meaning are expressed in their most intense and purposeful way. Fine art demands close attention. Whereas the musak played in the grocery store is only soothing background noise, a Beethoven symphony should be listened to in its own right.

The line between the fine arts and the functional or decorative arts is not always static or easy to draw. If a well-crafted quilt is removed from the guest bedroom—that is, taken out of its context of ordinary use—and displayed upon a wall, it becomes "an object of art."[9] Portraying the quilt as fine art in this way shifts attention away from its function (how warm it keeps one at night) to its aesthetic design (the intricacy and visual appeal of its patterning). Tribal crafts and archaeological artifacts are today treated as fine art, even though their original purpose may have been decorative or functional. Certainly a Canaanite idol was never thought of as art. To a Greek Orthodox Christian, an icon is a vehicle for meditation regardless of any aesthetic appeal. Still, the idols and the icons can be judged and interpreted aesthetically, although such evaluation may have to put aside their original function.

This book will now turn to consideration of the fine arts, but the broader applications of artistry—the human impulse to work, make, and beautify—should be kept in mind throughout the discussions to come. Many people say that they have no interest in art, and yet they do appreciate quality, excellence, and craftsmanship in their own labor. They do not realize that they too are artists. They warmly perceive the beauties of nature and of their surroundings. They do not realize that the faculty that enables them to appreciate nature can be stimulated also by art made by human hands.

The following chapters will show how to become an art critic. This skill, if used well, should heighten awareness, not only of the art that hangs in the museums but of the art that, for better or worse, is all around us.

THREE

UNDERSTANDING ART

*M*any people admit that they do not understand art, much less appreciate it. They might respond to the *content* of a work of art—a picture of Jesus or a sunset—but they do not know how to respond to the artistry of the work. They are unable to interpret or to evaluate what they see. What is this picture *saying* about Jesus or the sunset? Is this a good picture of Jesus or a bad picture of Jesus? Christians need to be able to answer such questions.

THE LIKEABLE AND THE GOOD

"I don't know much about art, but I know what I like." Actually, there is some wisdom in this standard declaration of taste. "What I like" may involve some sort of aesthetic response, a perception of beauty. On the other hand, the statement often obscures the important distinction between "what I like" and "what is good."

A moviegoer says of the latest slasher film, "That was a really good movie!" What was good about it? Was the acting or the directing or the cinematography especially skillful? "No," even the most enthusiastic fan will usually admit. Did it have a good plot? "Well, no . . . the plot was actually kind of stupid." Did it have a profound theme, giving us new insights into the human condition? "Of course not." Why did you like it? "Because it was really gross."

The moviegoer *liked* the film, but not because it was good. Some people enjoy being scared; others enjoy the spectacle of people getting butchered. Visceral reactions—to sex, violence, shock, or dazzling special effects—are relatively easy to induce, and much popular art is only entertaining rather than done well. The point is, there is a difference between the likeable and the good.

There are many reasons why, subjectively, we might like a work of art apart from its objective merit. A black velvet painting of Elvis will have its ardent defenders—not because of its exquisite technique or profound significance, but because true fans will like *anything* that reminds them of Elvis. "What they like" is the subject matter, or perhaps the emotional associations provoked by the image (those large "love-me-tender" eyes deepened by the velvet). Their gut-level response has little to do with the quality of the work. Occasionally, I will indulge myself by reading a murder mystery or a spy thriller for sheer entertainment and escape. As I read, I often find stereotyped characters, an utterly predictable plot, and a clumsy style, yet I enjoy the book. We can like what is not good.

We can also dislike what is good. My daughters do not like any dish that has onions in it. They may say, "This isn't any good," but what they mean is that they have an idiosyncratic prejudice against certain vegetables. I acknowledge the greatness of Thomas Hardy's novels, but I do not particularly enjoy reading them. They are brilliantly written, with masterfully drawn characters, skillful plots, and profound, thought-provoking themes. And yet, I find them too depressing. Perhaps more to the point, I find them too long. This aversion to monumental pessimistic fiction is a weakness in me, not in the novels. I do not like them although they are good.

To say we like something is to describe ourselves; to say something is good is to describe the object. We can like something for a wide range of personal and highly subjective reasons. Tastes vary. To say something is good is to make an objective judgment about its quality. For this we need knowledge.

The teenager who thinks Ozzy Osbourne writes better music than Beethoven is not only confusing the likeable with the good. He is also revealing his ignorance about music. Beethoven may be less accessible than rock music, just as anything complex is more difficult than anything simple. But the more one knows about music, the higher Beethoven will rate. (Strictly speaking, of course, comparing Beethoven to rock music or Shakespeare to "I Love Lucy" is not fair. Each art form has its own standards of excellence, so that some rock musicians and some situation comedies are better than others. Still, to judge an art form requires knowledge about it.)

Developing "good taste" means learning how to "like" what is "good." Taking pleasure (subjectively) in what is excellent (objectively) is the definition of good taste. Even though our likings can vary with our personalities and our moods, we can grow in our tastes. Just as we can mature spiritually and intellectually, we can mature aesthetically. Such maturity requires both experience and knowledge (some of which this book will attempt to supply).

FORM AND CONTENT

To better understand a work of art and our reaction to it, we might distinguish between the subject matter and the artistry of the work, between its content and its form. (Granted, the distinction is problematic, and I myself will be blurring the distinction, but for now let us speak of them separately.) The content would refer to what the work is about or what it is depicting—a bowl of fruit, a landscape, the face of Christ. The form would refer to the artfulness of the work—its technique, its composition, the skill of its artist. In the case of a painting, form would involve its visual effect—the arrangement of color, mass, and light. Musical form would involve the ordering of sound, while poetic form would involve the use of language.

To understand a work of art, we should probably first see it as an object of beauty; that is, we should notice its form. The beauty of a work of art is more than subjective pleasure; beauty also has to do with objective qualities in the work. The interplay of colors, the relationship between the shapes, the sense of the unity of the whole—such formal characteristics convey a sense of beauty.

An artist's skill and genius can be apparent even in a painting whose content we might find inconsequential. A still-life painting of a bowl of onions can be startlingly beautiful because of the brush strokes, the harmony in the colors, the sharpness of the imitation, the sense of weight, the play of the light (even for those who do not like onions). Most of us react powerfully to the beauties of nature (dogwood trees, the Grand Canyon, peacocks) without worrying about what they mean. Our senses take them in, and it requires no reflection or analysis for us to perceive their beauty. In the same way, we should approach a work of art as an object of beauty before interpreting it further. A still life, a landscape, or an abstract painting can be visually rewarding in the same way that the branches of a tree can form a design of beautiful intricacy.

The beauty of a work of art involves more than being attractive or pleasant to look at. Even natural beauty involves a wide range of complex and varied perceptions. A dogwood blossom charms us because of its delicacy. Standing on the brink of the Grand Canyon we may feel dizzy, perhaps even afraid, yet exalted at its grandeur. The awe one feels at the Grand Canyon is a very different sensation from enjoying a flower, yet both are types of aesthetic experience.[1]

The aesthetic dimension of a work of art can likewise stimulate the viewer in many different ways, not all of them superficially pleasant. A painting of the Crucifixion may be purposefully ugly, designed to jar us into a recognition of the horrors of Christ's execution. If it does so, it is because of its careful aesthetic design, and it will be aesthetically and objectively "good." Although the subject matter may not be pleasant, the aesthetic design that communicates that unpleasantness with such force will still be a source of aesthetic satisfaction and even pleasure.

This is why we can "enjoy" a movie that made us cry. In real life, we do not want to be sad, but a sad story can be entertaining because of the special experience rendered by the aesthetic form. Aristotle in fact considered tragedy to be the highest form of literature because of its magnitude, its unity, and the emotional catharsis of pity and fear that it creates, all of which constitute a special kind of pleasure.[2] Edgar Allan Poe argued that since great beauty can move a person to tears, the quickest route to beauty is to write about a melancholy subject.[3] One need not accept Poe's logic nor his nineteenth-century sentimentality to recognize that beauty can embrace more than the superficially gratifying, and that the most satisfying art through its aesthetic form can engage the deepest, most complex, and even most painful human emotions.

What makes a work of art good *as a work of art* is its form. Augustine believed that all form in nature and in art comes from God, the source of all creation. Everything that exists has its origin in God, and its form and its order rest upon God's design. Mathematics, music, and aesthetic laws all manifest the *logos*, God's divine Word, which undergirds every aspect of the created order. Human beings, radically sinful as we are, tend to rebel against God's good creation, preferring the dark void of nonbeing that is evil; yet whatever exists objectively partakes in God's created order and is therefore good.

According to Augustine, a poet may be a lost sinner, yet insofar as the verse manifests order in the design of its metrics, in the harmony of its music—in short, in its aesthetic form—the poem partakes of the divine *logos* and for that reason is valuable. Such unwitting participation in God's design does not excuse the sinfulness of the poet, the reader, or the content of the poem. Augustine, a stern critic of the arts, attacks the way sinners use the arts to draw people away from God, the true source of beauty. At the same time, he defends the artfulness of art. Criticizing its content and its use, he upholds its form, grounding its aesthetic dimension in God's creation.[4]

If Augustine is right, this helps explain why a work of art that is truly excellent aesthetically, even though its maker may not be a Christian, can present something of value to a Christian and can be interpreted in the framework of the Christian revelation. Picasso's anguished cry at the cruelty of war in his *Guernica*, the ethereal loveliness of an impressionistic landscape, the haunting misery of a novel by Kafka—such works can resonate deeply for Christians. Even though the artist's philosophy must be rejected, something in these works rings true, something that is beautiful.

The reason, Augustine might say, is that somehow in their quest for aesthetic excellence and intellectual integrity, these artists unknowingly stumbled upon some aspect of the divine *logos* that underlies all beauty and all truth. This would also explain why art that is pornographic or inhuman or otherwise worthless in what it conveys is generally worthless aesthetically as well.

At any rate, Augustine could excoriate the sinful content of a work of art while praising its beautiful form, a complex double judgment that may be a good model for Christian critics. To be sure, when people evaluate a work of art, whether praising or condemning it, they sometimes are responding to its form, to its aesthetic merits; sometimes they are responding to its content, to what it communicates. Both kinds of criticism are legitimate, but they should be kept distinct.

An excellent work of art may convey a theme that we reject. We may acknowledge the artistic skill of a work, possibly even finding great value in its aesthetic dimension, while disagreeing with its overt message. Conversely, we may agree with the theme of a work, finding it theologically impeccable, while criticizing the work's lack of artistic merit. Fully comprehending a work of art, though, requires attention to both form and content and to how the two relate to each other.

GOOD ART

While it is possible to consider the form and the content of a piece of art separately, full understanding comes only when they are joined again. Many people see only the content and neglect the form—in doing so they miss the aesthetic dimension of the work of art. Others, including many in the art world, see only the form and neglect the content—they see the work as only colors and shapes on a canvas as if all art were abstract art. This perspective does see the beauty and the artfulness of the work, but it is oblivious to its meaning, to what the colors and the shapes signify. In the best works of art and in the best responses to art, the form and the content fuse.

To say Rembrandt is a great painter refers to his mastery of his medium, his command of aesthetic form in all its dimensions. The difference between a painting of Christ by Rembrandt and a typical Sunday school illustration of Christ is a matter of form. Rembrandt's paintings will typically have a complexity, a richness, that lesser artists seldom even aspire to. Besides flawless drawing and use of color, Rembrandt will use light expressively and symbolically. The composition of the painting will determine how the viewer focuses on its parts and will give a sense of aesthetic unity to the whole.

Rembrandt's paintings reward close attention in a way that Sunday school illustrations usually do not. There is literally more to them. This does not minimize the Sunday school illustrations—their purpose is to help the reader briefly visualize a scene or perhaps to express some quality of Christ (His love, for example, by portraying a loving look on His face). A more restricted purpose means they will usually be simpler. Knowing there will be little time for sustained attention to the work of art, the Sunday school illustrator will go for immediate instead of complex effects. The appeal will be to the emotions of the viewers, emotional reactions being easier to provoke than theological reflection. The colors will be pleasant and decorative (soft pastels), rather than the violent clashes between lights and darks of a Rembrandt work.

Of course, for Christians any painting of Christ demands special interest because of its content. The religious or devotional use of a work of art does not depend upon its aesthetic merit. Even an aesthetically inferior depiction of Christ can stir us to prayer.

In the hands of a great artist, however, form is intimately related to meaning. Consider Rembrandt's *The Adoration of the Shepherds* (Fig. 3.1).

The colors are dark and subdued, the earth tones and shadows of a stable. The composition is such that all of the lines in the painting, from the rafter beams to the shepherds' staffs, draw our eyes to the Christ-child. As our eyes zero in on the baby Jesus, along with the eyes of everyone else in the painting, we see something astonishing. The warm, ethereal light that suffuses all of the faces and that is strong enough to cast a shadow behind the Virgin Mary is coming from the baby Jesus. In fact, as our eyes are drawn to the Christ-child, the effect is something like gazing at the sun. The details of the child's appearance are nearly lost in the splendor of His light.

Rembrandt is not only illustrating Luke's Christmas story (Luke 2:8-20), but also John's: "The true light that gives light to every man was coming into the world" (John 1:9). Rembrandt is not

FIG 3.1   REMBRANDT, *The Adoration of the Shepherds*
             Reproduced by courtesy of the Trustees, The National Gallery, London

simply showing what the Bethlehem stable looked like (actually, the
Christ-child must have looked like any other baby); rather he is
using his artistic medium to proclaim the meaning of that event. He
is able to do so while capturing the down-to-earth texture of that
stable—the realistic barn with its dirt floor and muted colors; the
ordinary people crowding around with a range of animated expressions; and vivid, lively details (such as the little boy bringing along
his dog). Rembrandt is depicting nothing less than the Incarnation,
the Third Person of the Trinity coming down to our physical, human

FIG 3.2   REMBRANDT, *The Storm on the Sea of Galilee*

world, scattering our darkness with the light of His grace (Isaiah 9:2).

   This is all communicated by the visual form of the painting—its colors, composition, and drafting. By close attention to the aesthetic design of the work, the viewer is led to a deeper contemplation of its subject matter. Consider Rembrandt's *The Storm on the Sea of Galilee* (Fig. 3.2), a depiction of Jesus calming the storm as recorded in Luke 8:22-25. Rembrandt's painting is more than a photographic rendition of what Jesus' miracle might have looked like. Rather, the painting, by its formal composition and technique, becomes a profound meditation on the meaning of that miracle.

In this painting, the eye is drawn in two different directions. The left half of the painting is full of turmoil—the violent crashing of the waves overwhelming the boat, the frenetic activity of the disciples facing every which way in an effort to control the sail. In contrast, the right half of the painting, where Jesus is, conveys a sense of calm, with its cool darkness and order.

The eye is drawn first to the storm, then, inexorably, by the lines of the painting and the tilted curve of the boat, to Jesus in the back of the boat. He is not at the center of the painting; rather He is at the lower right-hand corner, a small figure in the painting as a whole. Nor is He bathed in light; the storm is what is most apparent visually. The disciples who are facing the storm are desperate (and, in one case, sick). However, the disciples who are facing Jesus are secure. The figure of Jesus is framed in darkness, but once the eye makes Him out, we see light emanating from His face.

The turmoil of the storm is balanced and countered by the peace of Christ. The storm is depicted with frenetic movement and evocations of destructive power. The space around Christ, bathed by His light, conveys serenity. Those who turn to Jesus, Rembrandt is showing, can have peace in the midst of turmoil and suffering. Just as He calmed the storm on the Sea of Galilee, His presence can calm the storms in our lives.

As our eyes play over the painting, we become involved in a spiritual meditation. The theme, in all of its contrasts and complexity, emerges from the composition of the painting (the balancing of light and dark, motion and rest, the power of the sea and the power of Jesus Christ). The meaning of Rembrandt's painting comes from the merging of its content and its form.

BAD ART

If good art exhibits a unity of form and content, bad art exhibits disunity. The black velvet painting of Elvis is aesthetically bad, among other reasons, because the form and the content simply do not go together. To make a quasi-religious icon to a rock and roll star is incongruous to begin with. Such grandiose, reverential treatment for the singer of "You Ain't Nothin' but a Hound Dog" is intrinsically comical (with all due respects to Elvis Presley, whose music I *like*). Further, the attempt to praise Elvis is subverted by the material, which, for all of black velvet's pretensions to elegance, is actually cheap and tawdry. The mass-produced, manufactured image also undercuts the personal quality that the work attempts to convey. The idealization of the image, the larger-than-life soulful eyes, the stylized sexiness jarringly combined with other-worldly reverence, the whitewashing of the real Elvis (with his obsessions, drug addictions, and human complexity), also subvert the effort to honor a real person. The other faults of the work—its sentimentality, clumsy drawing, washed-out coloring, and superficiality of detail—are failures of form.

There is a type of art known as "kitsch." In addition to paintings of Elvis on black velvet, this category would include plaster lawn ornaments, vacation souvenirs purchased in "tourist traps," and "cute" knickknacks on the mantle. Kitsch is art of poor quality, which nevertheless manages to be enormously popular by appealing to some sentiment or association. Kitsch does provoke a response—it is more than background decoration—but the response is one-dimensional. Kitsch may trivialize what is great (as in an ashtray modeled after the Cathedral of Cologne). Perhaps more often, it magnifies what is trivial (as in gold-plated bathroom fixtures or solemnly adorned shrines to Liberace). In either case, the tackiness, gaudiness, and vulgarity of kitsch is a parody or perversion of true art.

Calvin Seerveld has written tellingly about kitsch and its incompatibility with a Christian aesthetic. "It is hard to talk with Christian care about kitsch," he observes, "because those who love it are naive about it, unaware that they are identifying with something fake and inferior, and those people deserve supportive help, not a sophisticated put-down."[5] A taste for kitsch is not a moral or spiritual failing, and those with more knowledge of art and a more sophisticated aesthetic sensibility should not be too harsh with those who collect sentimental figurines or tourist-trap souvenirs.

Having made this important point, Seerveld goes on to describe what is wrong with kitsch:

> Kitsch accepts the technocratic denaturing of ordinary life, but pretends to lift you above it, nostalgically. Kitsch is willing to be slick; it always glitters somehow, bewitching the simple with illusions of grandeur. Kitsch is emotionally cheap, whether it be expensive tinsel and Christmas tree baubles or a technically flawless, effulgent painting by Bouguereau, whether it be an ornate beer stein from the corner variety store, a dirty joke graffito lacquered to its sides, or a sunset with palm trees painted by a native on a piece of black velvet brought back from the

Barbados. Kitsch never enlarges experience; it blandly affects a show to stimulate feelings of exquisiteness or a mood of supernal tenderness, but it flops into bathos simply because it is ersatz, like a seven-inch-high, silver-plated Statue of Liberty trying to be the real thing. Kitsch is like a deodorant next to good perfume.[6]

Art that has no other purpose than popular appeal, as Kenneth Myers has shown, will seek to gratify its audience's desires but in doing so will offer them nothing of real value. By pandering to the lowest common denominator and appealing to the simplest emotions, the art of popular culture—whether television dramas, romance novels, or kitsch—restricts rather than enlarges its audience's experience.[7]

There is probably nothing wrong with occasionally indulging in sentimentality or buying a tacky souvenir of one's trip to the Grand Canyon to preserve the experience. There is probably nothing wrong with even "liking" a piece of kitsch—because it has nostalgic associations or because it is funny or because it is so outrageously bad. Seerveld suggests, however, that an unrestrained and uncritical pursuit of kitsch can be harmful:

> The harm to human sensibility is this: kitsch canonizes immaturity; it panders to introverting experience—like the satin sheets advertisements in the *National Observer*—because kitsch thrives only on sentimentality. And while it is healthy to be sentimental for a period during one's adolescence, one needs to firm up gradually his or her sentiment so it can be outgoing rather than ingrown. But kitsch wallows in self-congratulatory longings, superficially fulfilled, and therefore encourages one to be babyish. Whenever you meet those mock ducks and swans or elfin, semi-pastoral figures of colored plaster on someone's lawn, as you pause on the sidewalk before the front door, it's a little bit as if someone is greeting you with baby talk and a goochie, goochie tickle under the chin. But baby talk can be utterly sincere, we must never forget it.[8]

Christians with a more sophisticated taste should not look down upon those whose taste is relatively undeveloped. A taste for kitsch is a taste for art, a taste which simply needs to be nourished and educated so that it can grow up.

Many Christian bookstores stock—and sell—more kitsch than books. Although such work and those who buy it may certainly be sincere, Christians should try to grow in their tastes as well as in the other areas of their lives. The problem with religious kitsch is that its cuteness and self-gratifying nature can domesticate and thereby distort the Biblical faith. Christianity is not a sickly sweet religion, contrary to the saccharine plaques and greeting cards that clutter up the bookstores. The anemic figurines of Jesus Christ are poor testimonies to His deity and His Lordship. The self-congratulatory moralism and sentimental self-indulgence of many Christian books and wall hangings encourage complacency rather than true holiness. In evaluating religious art, we must keep in mind the solemn warnings of the Ten Commandments, not only the admonition against graven images, but also the admonition against taking the Lord's name in vain.

The fine art of the museums must also be judged by aesthetic standards. Although much abstract art is skillfully designed, balancing colors and lines for complex aesthetic effects, the framed black canvas or the brick on the floor must be seen as aesthetic nonentities. Minimalism—finding the least possible gesture to constitute a work of art—has been fashionable in modern art, but such a movement is negligible aesthetically. The more the form is pared down, the less there is to evaluate.

Many artistic experiments today are consciously subverting traditional concepts of form. Jackson Pollock surrenders artistic control by allowing paint to drip randomly onto a canvas. The artist who offers a silver cube and photographs it as it corrodes is not only surrendering artistic control but, in manufacturing a "self-consuming" work of art, is playing ideas of impermanence against traditional ideas of static, eternal form.[9] The Mapplethorpes and Serranos are trying to replace conventional responses of aesthetic enjoyment with the more extreme emotions triggered by the violation of taboos. These artists may create work that fulfills their intentions and may raise provocative or interesting issues. This does not mean, however, that their works are aesthetically successful. Indeed, they are often *purposeful* violations of aesthetic principles.

Part of the problem is that twentieth-century art, for all its pretensions towards abstractionism, is actually very conceptual. That is, artists are often trying to make a conceptual statement by means of their art—about the limits of art, the meaninglessness of life, the possibilities of human expression. Thus, the concept claims precedence over artfulness. Technical execution and the crafting of an object become less important than having a clever idea. The urinal installed on a museum wall, Warhol's Brillo boxes, the signed bicycle wheel—such pieces show no artistic qualities, nor do they intend to. They may be humorous, or clever, or suggestive of the nature of contemporary culture, but they can hardly be considered good art. To judge them so, ironically, is to miss the artist's point and to fail to see the joke.

The kitsch of popular art and the inanities of fine art can, with confidence, be judged as aesthetically bad. There is no reason to shrink from making a critical judgment or to be intimidated by fine art. Valid criticism, of course, should be fair, based on knowledge and understanding rather than a snap judgment based on a gut-level response. Good art similarly demands knowledge and understanding. Good art, such as that by Rembrandt, rewards close attention, whereas bad art dissolves under the scrutiny.

A WALK THROUGH
THE MUSEUM

*A*rt is continually changing. Because the thought forms of an age are uniquely reflected in its art, as the culture changes, art too must change. To walk through an art museum is therefore to walk through the history of Western culture, with both its high points and its low points. The blind spots of each era are glaringly evident in its art—the exaggerated rationalism of the Enlightenment, the exaggerated emotionalism of the Romantic movement, the anarchy of the twentieth century. The achievements of each age are also in high relief—the Enlightenment's ordered harmony, Romanticism's sensitivity to natural beauty, the twentieth century's introspective searching. In order to understand a culture—its assumptions, values, and nuances—one can do no better than to study its art.

Aesthetically, though, there are some constants. Works of excellence can leap the gap of time and startle us with their beauty and their relevance. Aesthetically successful styles (and not all styles *are* aesthetically successful) may prove valuable to Christians despite their origins. Impressionism, for example, grew out of a late Romantic subjective view of nature, which a Biblical worldview would reject. And yet, there is no denying the beauty of a good impressionistic painting. The inadequate beliefs of the artist do not negate the beauty of the work. Artists sometimes do more than they know. Since artists *must* work with the raw materials that God made available in His original creation—light, color, shapes, natural objects—they will often succeed in creating worthy objects of art. The credit, though, goes not to the artist's personal philosophy of life or of art, but to the overarching sovereignty of God.

This chapter will survey the course of Western art in an imaginary walk through a museum. The different styles and periods discussed here will be represented at most good-sized art museums. I offer therefore a sort of generic guidebook. My concern is to show how each period reflects its age and to point out the aesthetic dimension of each style. I will sometimes be criticizing the intellectual contexts that gave birth to the various styles, but I also want to salvage what is valuable, to suggest a Christian approach to the arts that is both critical and appreciative.

Of course, this brief survey will not do justice to the subject, any more than an afternoon's stroll through a museum is a substitute for in-depth scholarly study. Still, this chapter should help promote what has been called "artistic literacy," the ability to "read" works of art, to understand their significance and to respond to them with judgment and taste.

We will hurry through the galleries of ancient art this time, though this odd assortment of pottery, idols, tools, Egyptian sarcophagi, and Greek statuary, is in many ways the most intriguing, mysterious, and time-encrusted part of the museum. In those days as in other societies less sophisticated and less fragmented than our own, there were no museums. Rather, art of the most cunning craftsmanship was part of the everyday texture of life, adorning cooking implements and weapons, employed in worship and in the burial of the dead. We will discuss the art of the ancient world—that of the Hebrews, their neighbors, and the Greeks—later in this book. For now, pause long enough to soak up the Biblical associations. Then continue into the next gallery.

THE MIDDLE AGES

As we gaze about the room, we notice that except for the suits of armor and the tapestries symbolizing courtly love, this art deals almost exclusively with Christianity. There are paintings of Christ as a child with His mother; images of Christ dying on the cross; icons of Christ *pantokrator*, the risen, glorified, all-powerful Lord. At that time, the church was the major patron of the arts, which were employed to express the mysteries of the Incarnation, Atonement, and Resurrection in a tangible way.

At its best, the Middle Ages produced great Christian art, reconciling form and content, integrating artistry and faith. This is more difficult than it might seem. For example, Christianity teaches that Jesus Christ is both true God and true man. How can such a truth be portrayed in art? In the history of religious art, some depictions exalt Jesus in a way that stresses His divinity, but makes Him seem remote and nonhuman. Other depictions portray His humanity in such a way that His divinity is obscured. Much medieval art falls into the first category, depicting Him as the divine judge rather than the personal Savior (just as nineteenth-century art tends to depict His human gentleness rather than His sovereignty as judge). Medieval art, however, often achieves the theological balance that characterizes Christian orthodoxy.

We see on the walls of the museum a rendition of a baby held by his mother. She holds her child with striking human affection; he reaches back, like any baby, to hold on to his mother's dress. He is playing with a ball or a pet bird. This is a human child, but there is a difference. His face shows a striking maturity; he is signing a blessing. The baby and his mother are dressed in simple clothing, the dress of the ordinary people of the time, yet around them is the glory and lavishness of beaten gold. This is a child, yet more than a child. Or consider the crucifixes. The pain they show is often gruesome, with distended rib cages and blood splashed everywhere—yet there is the gold, the singing angels, the cross flowering into a tree of life. What these works depict are the paradoxes of the gospel: Christ is true man and true God, sacrificed in a grisly death which means life and glory to us.

Medieval art is symbolic rather than realistic. The bird the Christ-child is playing with, for example, would be a goldfinch, which had the reputation for eating thorns. The goldfinch would thus call to mind a rich succession of truths: This baby will grow up to wear a crown of thorns; Adam's curse—the thorns of Genesis 2:18—will be undone; Christ's thorny suffering will be swallowed up by the victory of the Resurrection. Medieval art is crowded with such symbols—the pelican wounding herself to feed her nestlings with her own blood, the double-natured griffin, the phoenix rising from the ashes.

This art is interested not so much in appearances as in meaning. The figures in a painting will not be rendered according to their actual size or spatial perspective. Rather, the most important figures will be drawn the largest, with the less important people arrayed around and taking up less space. A good example is Duccio's *Temptation of Christ on the Mountain* (Fig. 4.1).

In this depiction of Jesus being tempted by the devil (Matthew 4:1-11), the painter knew full well that the historical Jesus was not actually taller than the buildings. Showing Jesus and the devil looming over the cities and the castles, however, dramatizes the spiritual

FIG 4.1   DUCCIO, *Temptation of Christ on the Mountain*

warfare for us weak mortals who face such an adversary and who
have such an advocate.

Satan is shown as formidable and repulsive, but he is no match
for Christ. Satan's opposite is not Jesus but the unfallen angels. The
painter refutes the Manichean heresy (which taught that there are
two gods, one good and one evil, locked in cosmic combat) by the
very composition of the painting. The dark-winged figure of Satan
on the left is balanced by the bright-winged figures of the angels on
the right. Satan is no evil god, as the heretics taught, on a par with
the Lord; rather Satan is nothing more than a fallen angel. Between
the good and the evil angelic beings, in absolute control, is the compelling figure of Christ. His countenance, no less than His size,
expresses His strength and authority. At the same time, He is
depicted as fully human. Christ is painted with rounded features and

a sense of solidity that is in marked contrast to the relatively flat, spiritualized angels.

Because medieval artists tried to convey meanings rather than appearances, they were relatively uninterested in the canons of "realism." Instead they preferred rich symbolism, golden backgrounds, two-dimensional perspectives, and stylized figures, all of which give medieval art an "other-worldly" flavor. Medieval artists were attempting to portray eternity.

Some art tried to balance time and eternity. "Narrative paintings" depicted Biblical stories by means of a series of simultaneous images. A painting of the Christmas story might show in one corner Mary and Joseph riding a donkey; then in another corner we see them turned away at the inn; in the center is a manger scene; in another corner we see the wise men; in the last corner we see the Holy Family on the donkey again, fleeing to Egypt. The painting consists of five little paintings, five moments, which together convey a single story of eternal significance. Rather than choosing one historical moment to capture, in the manner of later art, medieval art presents the entire narrative in a single view. The painting by Duccio is one of fifty panels in a vast altarpiece that depicts the entire life of Christ at a single glance. Historical moments constitute eternal truth.

Pure, nonrepresentational design also flourished in the Middle Ages, as in the tapestries and illuminated manuscripts. The illuminated manuscripts, besides the ornate calligraphy, included pictures of Bible stories, scenes from everyday life, symbolic tableaux, and, surprisingly, creatures of sheer fancy—half-human and half-animal figures, fabulous beasts, comical-looking creatures, gargoyles that gape across the sacred page. Such grotesque and humorous figures form the waterspouts of the great cathedrals, and they pop up in other unlikely places.

What place do these creatures of sheer fantasy have in the art of Christendom? It has been suggested that they symbolized vices or other philosophical truths, but this explains their meaning rather than their form. I would suggest that they represent a tradition that is both Biblically grounded and aesthetically important. As we shall see, the Ten Commandments warn against making "any likeness of anything that is in heaven above, or that is in the earth beneath, or that is in the water under the earth" (Exodus 20:4 RSV). If this restricts imitation, the depiction of forms that already exist, it encourages creativity, the imagining of forms that do not exist. The commandment may temper the "realistic" impulse, but in doing so it makes room for "likenesses" of things that are not in heaven or earth or water. Making up a monster, rearranging physical details and structures of nature into new and terrifying or amusing combinations, is the equivalent of abstract art, rearranging geometrical forms and colors into aesthetically pleasing combinations.

The Biblical tradition seems uniquely hospitable to radical fiction, to purely fantastical works that make no pretense of being real, but that exist as what Tolkien describes as subcreations of the human imagination.[1] Authors who have tried to be explicitly Christian in their works have often favored the genre of fantasy. Consider Edmund Spenser, John Bunyan, George MacDonald, J. R. R. Tolkien, C. S. Lewis, Madeleine L'Engle, and others. This literary tradition began in the Middle Ages with the tales of knights, allegorical fantasies, and fairy tales.

If the Middle Ages represent a high point of Christian artistry, its fusion of faith and aesthetics was not without its problems. Theoretically, the use of art in prayer was simply to help the worshiper focus on the person of Christ. In practice, however, the icons themselves became adored. Some were seen as more sacred than others, with miracles being ascribed to particular images. They were honored, adored, and addressed in prayer.

Nor was the religious use of art restricted to depictions of Christ and scenes from the Bible. Many people lived in a state of semi-paganism. They had replaced their statues of Diana with statues of the Virgin Mary, but they used them in exactly the same way. People venerated the saints by giving homage to their portraits. Images of Mary were often more evident than images of her Son.

Whereas Scripture teaches that "there is one God and one mediator between God and men, the man Christ Jesus" (1 Timothy 2:5), in practice there came to be many mediators, which obscured the sufficiency of Christ's sacrifice and the essence of the Christian gospel. The transcendent focus of medieval art furthermore split nature and grace, segregating the spiritual realm from the physical world of everyday life.[2] The implication was that God is remote and impassive, a mystical other-worldly being rather than the loving and active sovereign of all existence who is to be served in this world as well as the next. The medieval fusion of aesthetics and faith was a great achievement, but, ironically, it lent itself to idolatry.

THE REFORMATION

Walking from the medieval section to the Renaissance collection, we see a sudden drop off of religious paintings. The paintings from northern Europe instead depict people at their work—farmers, shopkeepers, soldiers, politicians; we see family groups and individual portraits. In the paintings from Italy, we see scenes from classical mythology. There are still some religious pictures—madonnas, nativities, and crucifixions—but they are strikingly different from those of the Middle Ages; the gold leaf is gone. Instead, they are set in natural landscapes; the figures are rounded and individualized. All of the paintings have the illusion of three-dimensional perspective. All of these paintings seem realistic, this-worldly. Secularism seems to be running rampant.

Ironically, the secularization of art was one of the great legacies of the Reformation. In seeking to restore the gospel and to place the Bible at the center of the Christian life, the Reformers attacked what they saw as the idolatry of the medieval church. The devotion to images, the use of art to promote false doctrines, and the spirit of self-gratifying aestheticism even in the papal court were real obstacles to Biblical faith and did violate the commandment against idolatry. Reformation iconoclasm was not, however, anti-art. Rather, the rejection of graven images resulted in a major rechanneling of art.

The Reformed churches of Calvin and Zwingli objected to the religious use of art, but not to art as such. "I am not gripped by the superstition of thinking absolutely no images permissible," writes Calvin, "but because sculpture and paintings are gifts of God, I seek a pure and legitimate use of each."[3] Zwingli, an extreme iconoclast, even permitted paintings of Christ as long as they were not in churches or offered reverence. According to Zwingli, "Where anyone has a portrait of His humanity, that is just as fitting to have as to have other portraits."[4]

This acceptance of portraiture led to a flowering of the art form in the Reformed countries. Leo Jud, a colleague of Zwingli and a fellow iconoclast, distinguished between artificial images of God made by human beings and the true image of God made by God Himself. In other words, those interested in seeing the image of God need only look at a human being, whom God Himself made in His own image. Portraits depict "living images made by God and not by the hands of men."[5] This profound concept underlies the work of those painters known as the Dutch masters, including perhaps the greatest Protestant painter, Rembrandt.[6]

In the face of his subjects—children, merchants, ordinary families—the depths of their personalities are suggested. One can discern their dignity and value as having been created in the image of God (Fig. 4.2).

This portrait by Rembrandt depicts an ordinary Dutch family with affection and depth. The three little girls are impish and lively

FIG 4.2   REMBRANDT, *Family Group*

(clearly not paying attention or sitting still for the artist). The parents are strong and authoritative, yet kind and loving towards their children (holding them in line, slightly amused, though imminently serious in their parental roles). Each of the five members of the family is a distinct individual, and each face suggests a complex and unique personality. Moreover, it is clear that the artist feels love for his subjects (look at the face of the little girl in the middle). Rembrandt has drawn a Christian family, not only in its appearance but in its meaning.

The subject of this painting, while apparently secular, goes to the heart of the Reformation controversies. Medieval Catholicism taught that a fully spiritual life requires celibacy. The Reformers insisted that marriage and family life are of inestimable value, part of God's divine order and a sphere of Christian love.

Furthermore, the Reformers taught that one need not be a priest or a nun to lead a godly life, but that all vocations—those of farmers, merchants, magistrates, artisans, painters—can be means of serving God and one's neighbor. This blurring of the distinction between sacred and secular vocations is also evident in the Dutch paintings of this time. Many depict people at work: a butcher in his shop, soldiers marching by, businessmen in a meeting, servants at their chores. The new religious status of the laity led to an emphasis upon literacy (so that each Christian should be taught to read the Scriptures) and thus to an explosion in education. The Biblical worldview, which taught that God made the world and that He acts

FIG 4.3   CRANACH, *The Repose in Egypt*

in history, led to a new appreciation of the natural order, manifesting itself in scientific investigations and in a new realism in the arts.

The new religiously inspired secularism of the arts did not mean that religious art was completely abandoned. Not all of the Reformers were iconoclasts. After his condemnation by the Emperor, Luther came out of hiding at the risk of his life precisely to put down the riots of image-burning and stained-glass-window-smashing that had broken out in Wittenberg. Luther rejected only art that interfered with the message of Christ. Images of Mary and the legendary saints were removed, with all of the attendant devotions and "works" associated with them. Crucifixes, depicting the all-sufficient atonement for sin, and other Biblical paintings and church decorations were retained.

One of Luther's good friends and the godfather of his children was the artist Lucas Cranach. His religious paintings, in marked contrast to the transcendent mysticism of the Middle Ages, are "down to earth," locating Biblical and spiritual events squarely in the ordinary, natural world (Fig. 4.3).

This painting, *The Repose in Egypt,* is a rendition of the Holy Family resting during their escape from Herod's campaign of infanticide. The Biblical figures here look like real people, not stylized symbols. Joseph is a doughty German carpenter, his hat in his hand. Mary is a peasant woman. Jesus is an actual baby, squirming in His mother's arms. They are located, not in a transcendent realm signified by beaten gold, but in a startlingly realistic and detailed natural landscape. Such is Cranach's reconciliation of nature and grace that even the angels are rendered as naturalistic children, crowding around the adults' knees so they can play with the Baby Jesus.

The painter's approach is different from medieval art, yet it maintains a continuity with the work of the past. On the left, the perspective becomes unworldly again, with the angel getting water from a mysteriously hovering rock. This detail is an allusion to the Israelites' similar sojourn in the wilderness between Egypt and Palestine. Not only did God provide His people with water in the desert, but the miracle, according to Paul, was an emblem of a deeper spiritual truth: "For they drank from the spiritual rock that accompanied them, and that rock was Christ" (1 Corinthians 10:4b). Just as Christ sustained the Israelites wandering in the desert, the Incarnate Christ-child in Cranach's painting is giving a moment of spiritual refreshment to His parents in the midst of their dangerous journey. The implication is that He can do the same for us.

The great nonrepresentational art form of the Reformation

was music. The Reformers from Luther to Zwingli reveled in it. Music, praised throughout Scripture, is art without images. It conveys no "likenesses" whatsoever, yet it is art of the highest craftsmanship and aesthetic impact. The Reformation created an outpouring of music, not only in hymns (music with the content of the Word), but also in instrumental music.

The Reformation's musical legacy finds its culmination somewhat later in the piety and artistry of perhaps the greatest of composers, Johann Sebastian Bach. His manuscripts, whether for church music or music for the secular court, often begin with the Latin abbreviation for "Jesus Help." They end with the Reformation slogan *Sola Deo Gloria:* "to God alone be the glory." Bach's music was born in prayer and praise. In Bach's fugues, each instrument plays a separate melody, yet together the diverse voices merge into a unified order of dazzling beauty. His music is both intricate and patterned, passionate and intellectual, attaining the perfect balance of form and freedom.

THE RENAISSANCE

The sixteenth century marked the rediscovery of the Bible and with it the Hebraic tradition; it also marked the rediscovery of ancient Greece and with it the classical tradition. This movement, known as the Renaissance, accompanied and gave impetus to the Reformation (especially in the Greek scholarship which made possible vernacular translations of the New Testament). In other ways, it was in tension with the Reformation. Since the Renaissance at first was mainly an Italian phenomenon, the great Renaissance thinkers and artists, although often critical of the medieval church, were Roman Catholics. They thus lacked the iconoclasm and the Biblicism that characterized the Reformation countries. There is no denying, however, the astonishing accomplishments of the Renaissance on almost every level of culture. The wide-ranging genius of artists such as Leonardo da Vinci and Michelangelo and the new knowledge spurred by the Renaissance were high points of Western civilization.

Like the Greeks, the artists and thinkers of the Renaissance stressed ideal forms, spatial organization, rationalistic analysis, and a human-centered perspective. Renaissance statues, such as Michelangelo's *David*, portray ideal forms, not individuals. Scenes from classical mythology often take precedence over natural and human scenes. The figures in the paintings are handsome, beautiful, and mathematically perfect; but they lack the grit and the realistic

FIG 4.4   RAPHAEL, *The School of Athens*

imperfections that make the art of northern Europe seem so "down to earth."

Perhaps the most obvious technical contribution of Renaissance art was the discovery of perspective, the ability to create the illusion of three-dimensional space on the flat surface of the painting. By careful mathematical calculation, these painters developed techniques of foreshortening in accordance with the principles of human perception. As a result, pictures acquired depth and a heightened sense of realism (Fig. 4.4).

Raphael's *The School of Athens* shows the Renaissance fascination with Greek philosophy. The painting depicts a meeting of Plato (pointing up, an allusion to his focus on transcendent ideals) and Aristotle (pointing out, to the concrete world that was his philosophical focus). Visually, the painting is a masterpiece in the depiction of perspective. Closer figures are larger and those farther away are smaller, in perfect proportion. The arches within arches and the convergence of the painting's lines to a vanishing point create the illusion of vast space and depth within the painting.

Time itself is rendered spatially, suspended in the Greek manner into a never-changing ideal instead of a continuous narrative. The subjects of the painting are frozen in mid-motion. The painting captures a single moment, suspending it forever, lifting it out of history. Such techniques mark a true advance in realistic art and were adopted by the Reformation artists as well. They signal, though, a profound conceptual shift in our civilization in the direction of humanism and subjectivity.

Renaissance perspective is achieved by presenting reality *from the point of view* of an individual human being. Medieval artists violated "realistic" perspective, not out of incompetence (notice that Duccio's individual castles in Fig. 4.1 are rather skillful in their foreshortened perspective), but because they were attempting to present the point of view of God. Renaissance paintings, on the other hand, present a subjective, human-centered point of view. The perspective lines extend outside of the plane of the painting to the eyes of the viewer, who becomes the center of the painting's universe.

Reason tells me that all of the human figures depicted in the painting would be actually about the same size; some only appear to be smaller because that is how our eyes render distance. Looking down a highway, we see the road diminishing until the two sides come together on the horizon. We know the sides of the road are parallel and do not really touch—we know better than to trust our subjective sense impressions uncritically. Appearances, apprehended by the senses, and the reality, apprehended by the mind, are not always the same. We are in need of objective absolutes to fully comprehend reality, whether we are looking down a highway, making a moral decision, or coming to terms with God. Since the Renaissance, reality has often been interpreted according to "what I see" and "how I see it," rather than what I know is true by reason or by faith. The self becomes the center of the universe.

The Renaissance, with its Greek rationalism, was far more objective than subsequent periods. Nevertheless, the Renaissance marks the beginning of modern subjectivism. The human perspective came to replace God's perspective. To be sure, the present-centeredness of the Renaissance may be closer to a Biblical historicity than the static eternity conveyed in medieval art. The Renaissance exaltation of the human point of view dovetails with the Reformation's insistence on a *personal* relationship with God and the *individual's* right to the Bible. Renaissance humanism was by no means incompatible with Christianity. And yet, secular humanism begins here. Making human beings the measure of all things, reducing moral and religious issues to a subjective preference rather than objective truth, minimizing the spiritual to concentrate solely on the realm of the senses—such habits of mind were literally unthinkable before the Renaissance.

FIG 4.5   EL GRECO, *The Agony in the Garden*

MANNERISM

As we walk on through the gallery, we notice that Renaissance humanism, for all its initial confidence, begins to change, to question itself. The paintings grow darker, with odd effects of color and light. The human forms are sometimes elongated or distorted. A sense of movement replaces the static composition of the earlier paintings. This new style of the late Renaissance is known as Mannerism. It reflects a healthy disillusionment and introversion after the surge of humanistic optimism, an inwardness that is sometimes deeply questioning and sometimes deeply religious.

Manifestations of Mannerism would include Michelangelo's late statues of human beings tearing themselves out of the rock, Shakespeare's inexhaustible tragedies, and El Greco's eerily contorted but passionate religious paintings such as his depiction of Christ's agony in the garden (Fig. 4.5).

El Greco's painting swirls and flickers like fire. Even the stone behind Christ is caught up in the energy and seems somehow impalpable. The sleeping disciples below the angel purposefully violate the perspective—they are shut out of the experience, appearing as if they are enclosed inside the rock. El Greco's landscapes are dreamlike, reflecting his inward-looking mystical vision.

THE BAROQUE

By now we have moved into the seventeenth-century galleries. The oddly unsettling Mannerist paintings give way to still another style. These paintings are ornate, "busy," and, to many tastes, overdone. The statues are huge, posed in grandiose gestures, with every fold of clothing intricately detailed. The art combines vast scale with intricately detailed ornamentation, charged with emotion and energy. Everywhere we see crowds of massive forms seemingly set into motion. This is the style known as Baroque.

Although this style is evident among Protestant artists, scholars have traced it to the Counter-Reformation, to the Council of Trent, which corrected some of the abuses of the medieval church. The Council of Trent began a revival of Catholic spirituality by a double emphasis upon both the very spiritual and the very material, upon transcendent mystical experience combined with devotion to the Incarnation and to the sacraments in all of their tangibility. Baroque art has this same quality of being both transcendent and fleshly.

At its best, Baroque art approximates a fully Christian balance of the spiritual and the physical, the emotional and the rational. It resulted in splendidly ornate architecture and in painters such as Rubens, known for his corpulent angels and fleshly saints. In his painting *The Last Judgment*, heaps of massive bodies tumble over themselves as they spiral upwards to Christ or cascade down into Hell (Fig. 4.6).

The effect is that of a double tornado, swirling in two opposite directions. The damned souls maul each other and are tormented by palpable demons, while the saved souls (in back, farther away from the viewer) ascend to Christ. The figures are so *heavy*, a mountain of flesh and bone, defying their own gravity by their spiritual destinies.

Such spiritualization of the flesh, which characterizes both Rubens and the Baroque in general, is not unbiblical. Christianity does speak of the material order—Christ came in the flesh; there will be a bodily resurrection; we will be given spiritual *bodies*. The tangibility of Baroque art, combined with its emotional intensity and

FIG 4.6   RUBENS, *The Last Judgment*

its visual energy, can leave one breathless. The harmony of opposites such as Baroque art attempts is difficult to achieve, however. This style easily veers into the absurd or the tastelessly overdone. Ironically, its vast scale, dynamic motion, and intricate detail were perhaps most consistently achieved in the nonvisual arts and by Protestants—in Milton's poetry and Bach's music.[7]

THE ENLIGHTENMENT

In the next gallery, the exuberance of the Baroque suddenly gives way to subdued portraits of aristocrats in wigs and orderly, well-kept landscapes. The eighteenth century was the age of neoclassicism, a time in which the humanism and the classicism of the Renaissance developed into a genuinely secular movement known as the Enlightenment.

This was the age of reason, scientific discovery, and human autonomy. Many intellectuals dismissed Christianity and devised a religion of their own based on reason instead of revelation. The result was Deism, which taught that the orderliness of nature does prove the existence of a rational creator (Enlightenment thinkers were big on order). Once this deity created the universe, like any other mechanic, he left it to run on its own. The deity, according to this view, does not interfere or intervene in his creation—miracles, revelation, and the Incarnation are excluded as superstitious primitivism. Human beings are autonomous. Nature and society comprise a vast, complex machine. The Biblical system of ethics based upon transcendent absolutes is replaced by utilitarianism—something is good if it works, if it makes the system run more smoothly. This is the view that could justify slavery and the exploitation of child labor in the name of economic efficiency. Today, it is the view that favors abortion because it reduces the welfare rolls and sanctions euthanasia because it reduces hospital bills.

What one notices first in the gallery is that the men are all dressed like George Washington, in powdered wigs, tricorn hats, and tight hosiery. The women are wearing elaborate hairstyles and capaciously elaborate gowns. The earlier paintings, oddly enough, do not create such a sensation of datedness. Their people are clearly of their time, but their clothing is relatively simple, and it does not call attention to itself. The people in earlier paintings seem more universal. The Enlightenment, on the other hand, was very conscious of its modernity. Those who present themselves as fashionably up-to-date always end up dating themselves, appearing old-fashioned as soon as the fashions change.

FIG 4.7   GAINSBOROUGH, *Robert Andrews and His Wife, Mary*
            Reproduced by courtesy of the Trustees, The National Gallery, London

Consider Gainsborough's *Robert Andrews and His Wife, Mary*
(Fig. 4.7).

The Enlightenment distrusted emotion, but admired achievement. The husband and wife are both smug, arrogant, and in control. Nature has been conquered—the hay field has been planted and
cut in neat rows; the sheep in the background are securely fenced
away; the dog is fawning on its master; and Mr. Andrews, a hunter,
is cradling his gun. Mrs. Andrews is sitting on an imminently civi-
lized piece of furniture which has been brought outside to further
domesticate nature. The couple dominate the painting, but they are
set to one side so that we can admire how much they own. The
painting proclaims human self-sufficiency, pride, rationalism, and
dominance over nature.

Yet if we compare this portrait to Rembrandt's (Fig. 4.2), we
see what has been lost. The faces here lack depth, passion, and complexity. Mr. and Mrs. Andrews seem relatively shallow; they seem
unloving and, worse, unlovable. Ironically, we see that humanism
has resulted in a loss of the human.

The Enlightenment was a time of authentic achievement. Not
everyone rejected Christianity—this was the time of the Wesleys as
well as the Deists. Many superstitions of the past did need to be challenged, especially in the social and political spheres. The Declaration
of Independence and the United States Constitution grew out of this
period. Neoclassical architecture and literature were often models of
simplicity, grandeur, and good taste. However, the illusion of self-

sufficiency and the narrow rationalism of the time were distortions of human nature, and human beings could not live under those terms for long.

ROMANTICISM

The galleries of nineteenth-century art show another change. Instead of nature scenes that depict neatly cultivated farms, we start to see storms, chasms, and craggy mountains. Instead of contemporary ladies and gentlemen, we see violent battles, exotic vignettes of alien cultures, and emotion-charged portraits. We have passed into Romanticism.

If artistry consists of both imitation and creation, we could say that the imitative mode dominates Renaissance and Enlightenment art. The artists were reflecting the rational, and thus idealized, order of the external universe. They were not trying to "express their feelings," which became a concern of Romanticism. The Romantics recovered the creative mode of art. Although the art of Romanticism was still representational, it became charged with the artist's personal vision, a means of personal expression. Whereas the Enlightenment preferred the typical and the familiar, the Romantics were fascinated by the unusual and the exotic. Scenes from remote history, ruined castles, foreign cultures, and ancient legends returned to art as both creations of the imagination and as stimulants to the imagination of their viewers.

Whereas the Enlightenment stressed the order of nature, Romanticism stressed its wildness. Romantics saw nature not as a complex machine but as a living organism, charged with beauty, sublimity, and mysterious significance. Albert Bierstadt of the American "Hudson River School" was a master of the panoramic, sublime landscape (Fig. 4.8).

A tribe of Indians is in the foreground, setting up one plane of perspective. Behind them is a waterfall, the relatively small size of such a huge cataract creating the illusion of vast distance. Looming still farther in the background and dwarfing the waterfall is a range of mountains. Behind the range is a peak more colossal still. Farther still in the background, indistinctly, are more and more mountains, until everything is lost in light. The effect is one of vastness, of infinity. The viewer is struck breathless at the grandeur of nature.

Whereas the Deists stressed God's utter transcendence, to the point of saying that the deity is uninvolved in his creation, the Romantics stressed God's immanence, finding the divine in and

FIG 4.8   BIERSTADT, *The Rocky Mountains, Lander's Peak*

through nature. This was sometimes exaggerated into pantheism, a more sophisticated version of the old pagan nature worship. Indeed, there is something of the Gothic cathedral in Bierstadt's nature paintings, a use of light and infinite space to induce reverence as well as awe. The orthodox Christian view, of course, is that God is both transcendent and immanent. Nature is an ordered creation, but it also testifies to God's glory. Christians can draw on both movements as long as they see each as partial—acknowledging the order of nature with the Enlightenment artists while enjoying the sublimity of the Romantic landscapes.

Whereas the Enlightenment stressed reason, Romanticism stressed feeling. The Romantic paintings such as the landscapes try to evoke emotion in their viewers. The pictures of human beings often depict emotion—Romantic art is full of deathbed scenes, people at graveyards, young couples in love, soldiers on battlefields, and people in pensive contemplation. Such art, with its theatrical poses, is often ludicrously sentimental and self-indulgent.

Romanticism glorified nature, and it also glorified the self. It was good to recover individual uniqueness, inwardness, and the expression of feelings after years of Enlightenment idealism, rationalism, and suppression. And yet as always human beings go too far. The Romantics replaced a utilitarian ethic with an ethic of self-fulfillment—what is good is what fulfills the self, what expresses my emotions and contributes to my personal growth. This view, which enshrines selfishness as a moral principle, is still being advocated in the pop psychology of our current culture and has utterly eroded Biblical morality. For artists, particularly concerned with their individualism and their self-expression, bohemianism, the deliberate flouting of conventional standards, became the fashion.

As we walk on through the nineteenth-century gallery, we notice some reactions against Romanticism. Paintings of stark realism—scenes of animals eating other animals, scenes of labor and poverty—reflect the naturalism of Darwin and Marx. The meticulous objective detail of many of these paintings reflects the new ideology of scientific materialism. On the other hand, painters such as Courbet and Daumier could combine social realism with a Romantic celebration of ordinary life, resulting in affectionate and life-affirming paintings of peasant farmers, washerwomen, and others usually looked down upon in a class-conscious society.

Now, stopping before *The Blessed Damozel* by Rossetti, we come across a new strain of Romanticism. The Pre-Raphaelites were fascinated with all things medieval. As their name implies, they wished to return to the time before the Renaissance master Raphael.

FIG 4.9   ROSSETTI, *The Blessed Damozel*

They painted scenes of fantasy that somehow combine spirituality with sensuality (Fig. 4.9).

This painting by Dante Gabriel Rossetti illustrates his poem, "The Blessed Damozel." (Pre-Raphaelite art was self-consciously "literary," telling stories and illustrating works of literature, an emphasis that modern art would react against strongly.) It depicts a woman in Heaven pining after her lover who is still on earth and pining for her. They are separated by an uncrossable horizontal line, which divides the painting into two utterly different realms. Rossetti's painting depicts a "blessed soul," but her thoughts are filled with images of earthly love, flitting above her starry crown.

The damsel is in Heaven, but instead of contemplating God, she is contemplating her boyfriend; instead of experiencing the ultimate bliss, she is melancholy. The incongruity of the subject is ludicrous in the extreme. Rossetti is not being satiric; he is clearly affected by the pathos he has conceived. He evidently does not understand the concepts with which he deals. Usually, the living mourn the dead; here, the dead person is grief-stricken because her lover is alive. The Blessed Damozel is so focused on the world, one wonders what she is doing in Heaven in the first place. The effect of the poem and the painting is to exalt adolescent puppy love *ad absurdem*, as if the pangs of lost love could outweigh the infinite joy of eternal life. This is a classic case of bathos, of an elevated concept deflated by the intrusion of the commonplace, the sublime collapsing into the ridiculous.

Visually, the painting is not without interest. The damsel is both ethereal and sensuous. The expression on her face is haunting. The angels, although they look more like depressed teenagers than seraphim, are unsettling. Rossetti's device of visually portraying the damsel's thoughts is ingenious and effective. He is good at what he does.

The large-eyed maidens, the lush natural backgrounds, and the eerie atmosphere of Pre-Raphaelite art is sometimes compelling and sometimes repellent. The fantasy, the balance of flesh and spirit, and the unashamed emotionalism can be intriguing and even refreshing, despite its tendency to excess. Some Pre-Raphaelites described themselves as pagans, who self-consciously turned the pursuit of beauty into a religion, pioneering the modern faith of secular aestheticism. Others were devout Christians. In fact, some of our cherished but overly sentimental pictures of Christ derive from this school of nineteenth-century art.

FIG 4.10   MONET, *Water-Lily Pond*
                Reproduced by courtesy of the Trustees, The National Gallery, London

IMPRESSIONISM

As we come to the end to the art of the nineteenth century, we find
a gallery of shimmering color. When we stand close to one of these
paintings, it seems to consist only of daubs of paint. When we stand
back, however, the colors coalesce to form images of water, boats,
clouds, trees, or crowds of people. We are looking at the work of
the Impressionists. Here is Monet's *Water-Lily Pond* (Fig. 4.10).

It might seem strange to classify Impressionism as realistic.
There are no hard edges; everything is strangely out of focus. And
yet at its best an impressionistic painting creates the illusion of a
bright summer day, the sun dazzling the eye, or a serene evening, the
growing darkness erasing details but leaving shapes still discernible.
Monet is not painting water lilies as they are in themselves; rather
he is painting the optical *impression* of water lilies.

The Impressionists painted according to how the human eye actually perceives objects. When we look out into space, we are not able to focus upon everything at once. Blurs, indistinct shapes, tricks of light and shadow are all part of our perception. Our minds sort them out and allow us to focus sharply upon certain objects and to filter out the rest. Just as a television image consists of tiny dots of light that the mind assembles into realistic-appearing shapes, human perception is based on the mind's ability to assemble and interpret optical information as light makes faint *impressions* upon the retina. The Impressionists studied optics and the physiology of perception and tried to capture the play of light in daubs of color that fuse into effervescent images of reality.

What the Impressionists offer is not objective reality, but reality as it appears to a human observer. In other words, they present nature from a purposefully subjective point of view. The Renaissance painters' experiments with perspective began this process, but their Greek idealism ensured a firm distinction between the appearance of things and what they are objectively. The Impressionists were not interested in what nature is in itself, its hard-edged objectivity; rather they focused upon appearances alone.

EXPRESSIONISM

The growing inwardness that characterizes modern art entered its next phase when various artists reacted in different ways to the mere surface orientation of Impressionism. The next gallery will be characterized by bold colors, anguished figures, and violent brush strokes. Here we find the haunting South Sea images of Gauguin and the hallucinatory but lyrical masterpieces of Van Gogh. We also find nightmare images and fantasies born of fevered imagination. All these are the work of the Expressionists.[8]

Rather than imitating the external world, these artists *express* what is inside themselves. Color, shapes, and realistic figures may be used, but only to convey a state of mind. Standing before a painting by Van Gogh, one notices not only the subject but the brush strokes, thrown on to the canvas with such passion that the artist's mental turbulence seems to take visible shape, as in his famous *The Starry Night* (Fig. 4.11).

Van Gogh is truly great. At his best he achieves that balance of form and freedom that is the hallmark of Biblical creativity. He renders nature in a spirit of affirmation while expressing his tumultuous inner life. Van Gogh was deeply religious; tragically, he was tor-

FIG 4.11   VAN GOGH, *The Starry Night*

mented by acute mental illness. He makes an important case study for the church's relationship to its artists.

Growing up in a Dutch Reformed church where his father was pastor, young Van Gogh was a zealous Christian obsessed with Bible study. He preached and taught the Bible at a Methodist chapel. His desire to become a pastor, however, was thwarted when he flunked out of seminary. He then became a missionary to Belgian coal miners—preaching, teaching the Bible, and sharing in their poverty. Because of his obvious emotional instability, however, his mission society stopped supporting him. Thwarted yet again in his desire to serve the church and deeply hurt by the continued rejection, Van Gogh bitterly repudiated the institutional church.

He threw himself instead into his art. For Van Gogh, art was never a product of his madness; rather art was relief from it, a way to fight it off. Periods of lucidity, in which his creativity was joined with a luminous sense of compassion and serenity, would alternate with periods of utter derangement. He cut off his ear; he assaulted his friend Gauguin; he was plagued with bouts of despair and horrifying hallucinations. Finally he was committed to the mental hospital of Saint-Remy where he received the enlightened care he needed. Here he painted some of his greatest works. Despite progress in his mental condition, he had moments of relapse. In one of them, he killed himself.[9]

However much we sympathize with him, the seminary faculty and the mission board were surely right in blackballing him from the ministry. Van Gogh would have been a terrible pastor. There can be no doubt that his true God-given vocation was to be an artist. Tragically, his church did not understand his gifts and refused to tolerate his admittedly quirky personality. If the church had taught him that painting can be as legitimate a calling from God as preaching, he would have been saved much frustration. If the church had affirmed him *as an artist* and had the patience to offer him the love, the healing, and the discipleship he so desperately needed, his story might have had a happier ending. Van Gogh is an object lesson for the church and its ministry to artists, who often require special sensitivity and pastoral care. At any rate, Van Gogh's troubled faith, dismissed by secular critics as merely part of his madness, is essential to his art. Unlike most other Expressionists, his paintings of human beings and of nature, for all of their hallucinatory intensity, are suffused with love.

Perhaps more representative of Expressionism is Edvard Munch. His lithograph *The Cry* offers a generic image of sheer horror (Fig. 4.12).

The wavy lines suggest the piercing sound waves of a loud scream, but they also suggest the disorientation of panic, the sense that the person's world is coming apart. An Expressionist may express a wide range of feelings, but most Expressionistic paintings are cries of anguish, reflecting with piercing honesty the spiritual void that characterizes post-Christian culture.

MODERN ART

In the early years of the twentieth century, it seemed as if Romanticism had fractured, with its emphasis on nature developing into Impressionism and its emphasis on the self developing into Expressionism. A new anti-Romantic classicism developed with Paul Cézanne. He was concerned with objective form. In his still lifes (paintings of common objects—bowls of fruit, bottles, dishes) and in his landscapes, Cézanne sought to analyze the ideal forms that constitute physical objects (Fig. 4.13).

In Cézanne's art, mountains are broken up into their constituent squares and triangles; houses become architectural blocks;

Fig 4.12   Munch, *The Scream*

FIG 4.13   CÉZANNE, *Mont Sainte-Victoire Seen from Bibemure Quarry*

apples become massive little spheres. Cézanne even challenged the subjectivism of Renaissance perspective by setting up an illusion of depth, then purposefully violating it in the name of a higher objective order.

Cézanne's approach was the starting point for Picasso. His style, known as Cubism, was another attempt to pin down objective form. Picasso would present a subject from many different angles at the same time, as he does in *Girl Before a Mirror* (Fig. 4.14).

Picasso shows his subject from all sides at once. Here we see a woman's profile (her nose pointed to the right), superimposed on a frontal view (her two eyes and her mouth facing the viewer). Her body is broken into a pattern of circles, curves, and other geometric patterns. The multiple perspectives are compounded by having her form reflected in yet other permutations in the mirror.

Picasso would break down the volume and space occupied by an object into a grid of cubes or other geometrical analogues. He would observe the object's formal characteristics, then exaggerate and recombine them. Such experiments are often intriguing. Picasso's approach was perhaps a healthy antidote to Romantic sub-

FIG 4.14   PICASSO, *Girl Before a Mirror*

jectivism and humanistic perspective. His brand of classical formalism, however, was excruciatingly ironic. Picasso was zealously intent
upon rendering objects as they are, instead of as they appear to be;
as a result, the objects in his paintings became unrecognizable. He
was so uncompromisingly realistic that he became abstract. The
actual figure would dissolve under Picasso's analysis, leaving only
grotesque caricatures or mathematical patterns.

    In terms of our form and freedom dichotomy, we might say

that nature itself has more freedom than such modern formalists as Cézanne, Picasso, and their followers allow. The nuances of existence, the free-flowing variety in the natural order, and the intractable uniqueness of every entity resist formalistic generalization. Human reason has validity, but when it is made the sole arbiter of truth, apart from God's revelation, it is too clumsy to accurately grasp the human condition—like trying to perform surgery while wearing boxing gloves. Rationalistic attempts to systematize light, space, and unity into a rigid analytical grid will oversimplify. The fullness, the range, the plenitude of creation (Psalm 104) will be neglected, and the life will be taken right out of the subject. As Wordsworth said, "We murder to dissect."[10] Picasso's scintillating dissections of the human form call to mind a coroner's table.

Picasso was a great artist, his career actually spanning a wide range of styles from the whimsically realistic to the nearly (but never completely) abstract. His work is often obscure, but never meaningless. Picasso, however, represents a turning point in art history. Art becomes cut off from ordinary perception and dependent upon theory. The work of art no longer can stand alone; it needs an explanation. It makes no concessions to the uninitiated, and thus becomes increasingly elitist. Objective forms are not simply received but broken down and manipulated, put into new configurations according to the artist's will.

This reflects twentieth-century humanism, as opposed to Renaissance humanism. Renaissance paintings exalt humanity, positing a rational, ideal order. Picasso undercuts this order and makes his own. It is true that when he paints someone he loves or expresses the anguish of human suffering, a deeper humanness resurfaces, proving that he could not be consistent with his presuppositions. Still, Picasso's art, like modern humanism, tends to reduce human beings to objects, no different from a guitar or wine bottle. Both Renaissance optimism and twentieth-century despair fall short of the Christian synthesis, in which human beings are both valuable and depraved, and existence is ordered by God though beyond purely human control.

Fragmentation was a method for Picasso, but in his wake the arts themselves became fragmented, as the subsequent galleries of modern art make clear. From this point on, trends and movements and manifestoes attempt to reinvent art, as if nothing had gone before. The Futurists devised a sort of dynamic Cubism that glorified energy, motion, and the machine. They combined this artistic platform with militant Fascism. The surrealists rejected external order altogether for the subconscious world of dreams and nightmares.

Salvador Dali's surreal paintings of melting clocks and hard-edged
but unintelligible landscapes recreate the uncanny disorientation of
dreams. The Dadaists rejected even the psychological meaning of
surrealism. The name Dada was chosen as an example of meaningless babble. They were nihilists and artistic anarchists, trying to violate every artistic norm. Ironically, their "anti-art"—bicycle wheels
and urinals that were merely signed, then put up on the wall—were
designed to outrage the artistic establishment, yet the establishment
embraced it in all seriousness. It is not clear whether the joke was
on the Dadaists or the art critics.

    In the meantime, abstract art blossoms. Some consists of geo-
metric shapes and fields of color; this school of abstractionism is
concerned with pure, nonrepresentational forms, a sort of quasi-
classical objectivism. This style is countered by Abstract
Expressionism, characterized by paint flung randomly onto the canvas, purporting to express the artist's initial creative energy. Thus
both the imitative and the creative modes of art, the formalistic and
the expressive, manifest themselves in abstract styles.

    Dominated by existentialist assumptions which dismiss the
objective world as meaningless, the arts turn away from the external realm in favor of purely human constructions. Many of the pioneering abstract artists were also involved with theosophy, the
synthesis of occultism and Eastern religion that was a major pro-
genitor of the New Age movement. Theosophy rejects the idea of an
objective creation as an illusion; rather reality is seen as a projection
of the self. Such a worldview corresponds well with the practices of
modern abstract artists. Kandinsky, the first to abandon all references to the external world, was a theosophist, as was Jackson
Pollock.[11]

    This is not to say that all abstract art is philosophically tainted
or worthless. Much abstract art is pleasant to the eye. The gallery
walls are filled with bright colors and curious optical effects. The
whimsical dancing shapes of Klee or Miró are aesthetically pleasing.
We might be intrigued by the optical illusions created by the "op
art" of the 1960s despite its psychedelic origins. The problem is not
with abstractionism as such, which, as we shall see, has a Biblical
heritage. The problem is that the art world suffers under a certain
legacy of Gnosticism, that ancient heresy that denied the Incarnation
of Christ, rejected the value of the material world, and interpreted
salvation as *knowledge* given to an elite few. The self-absorption, the
nebulousness, the triviality, and the elitism that inhibit modern art
are related to its philosophical bankruptcy.

    As we go through the last galleries, we notice heralds of a new realism. Paintings of Campbell Soup cans are banal, but at least they are recognizable. Politically charged paintings of suffering humanity may also be evident. Photo-realism is a style in which paint imitates the camera. Such realism, though, is often as nihilistic as the abstractionism. Do you see the janitor standing in the corner with his broom next to the bag lady? Look closer. They are both sculptures. Every pore is in place, but they are lifeless, both literally and in their meaning. It is as if the artist is saying to the befuddled gallery walkers, "You want realism? OK, I'll give you realism." The artist then condescends to the viewer and to the subject by presenting a stereotyped caricature, the artist's smirking vision of the common man and the common woman. The photo-realistic paintings will usually be of a drive-in or a decaying city street. The pop art will depict commercials or movie stars—whether such subjects are real or not is highly debatable, and that is the point. Reality tends to be presented as shallow, meaningless, or cruelly absurd. The creation is drained.

Many modern artists have produced wonderful and moving work. The Jewish painter Marc Chagall draws on figures from folk tales, the Bible, and Jewish history—combining them with fantasy and symbolism all rendered in bright colors and boldly original designs. His art, true to his Hebraic heritage, partakes of pure design, yet conveys powerful human emotions. Henri Matisse plays with color and form in a delightful, stimulating way. There is good modern art and bad modern art. The problem is, many in the art world today, as the next chapter will show, refuse to make the distinction.

As our tour through the art museum draws to a close, we find artists who are furiously attempting to extend the bounds of art. Some artists are replacing paint with the camera—both in conventional photography, which is a worthy art form in itself, and in new art forms that employ video technology, neon lights, and interactive computers. We might come across multimedia presentations complete with music and light shows. Today artists want to break down the barriers between the artist and the viewer. This can mean sculptures designed to be touched, interactive computer art in which the viewer manipulates the image, or efforts to tease a response out of their viewers by offending them. As we come to the end of our trek through the museum, we should therefore monitor our responses. Maybe we will be shocked by something. Maybe we will have our minds opened.

So much of this sort of thing tries to be experimental but does not even manage to be original. Boxes of kitty litter? More urinals?

The Dadaists already did that sort of thing in 1916. Weird and shocking nightmare images? They probably are not more weird, shocking, and nightmare-like than Dali's were in the 1930s. Art consisting of chance patterns from a computer? Jackson Pollock exhausted the possibilities of random art (which did not take long to do) in the 1940s. When contemporary artists cannot even manage to be contemporary, there is not much left.

The impression one receives from the course of contemporary art is one of exhaustion, as if everything has been tried already. This desperate groping for something new helps explain the uncritical experimentalism of contemporary art. If art has reached a dead end, however, it is not because there is nowhere else to go, but because it has taken a wrong turn. Everything has not been tried; more can be done. Art can find new life when the artists find a new life.

Artistic expansion has always depended upon a philosophical expansion. Today the art world is becoming a victim of its own narrowness of vision and shallowness of spirit. What art most needs today is inspiration, something to ignite creativity, to awaken art from its despairing cynicism, its jaded role-playing, and its spiritual paralysis. Christianity is more than a passing style; it is a view of the world that is larger than its competitors, whole and complex, capable of being rendered in many styles, yet transcending and energizing them all.

THE ABDICATION
OF THE ARTS

A problem in defending the arts is that many works of art today are indefensible. I can spend hours explaining to my students how to appreciate the beauty and significance of art, exhorting them to pay attention to human creativity and waxing eloquent on the richness of aesthetic experience. Then they go to a museum. They tell me about the featured sculptures: a brick on the floor, two basketballs floating in water, a box of cat litter. They tell me about the painting that consists of three wavy lines. Another painting is a black canvas without a frame; hanging next to it is a frame without a canvas. Then they ask me to explain the beauty and significance of these works of art.

The average person's indifference or contempt for this kind of art is understandable. He thinks, *People get excited about this sort of thing and pay a lot of money for it, and yet it all seems sort of . . . stupid. Or maybe I'm stupid for not understanding it.* Public bewilderment tends to meet with amused condescension from the artists. In fact, bewildering or outraging the middle class has become a game for those who consider themselves avant-garde. Their status as an inner circle of sophisticates is defined by the people they exclude. The masses are deprived of art not simply by their lack of cultivation but by the elitism of the art world.

Ironically, the true enemies of art today include much of the artistic establishment. This should not be surprising, since artistic establishments have often squelched genuine creativity. Styles have come and gone, some successful and some not. The explicit rejection of beauty, creativity, and meaning *on principle*, however, is unprecedented.

Statements that once came from those who know nothing about art are now taken seriously by artists and critics and assumed to be unanswerable: "Who is to say what is art?" "How do we know what later generations will consider to be significant?" "What might be garbage [or pornography, or kitsch] to one person might be art to someone else." As a result, we have critics who are unable to criticize, accepting the most vulgar trivialities on a par with works by Rembrandt and Van Gogh. This is why museums are exhibiting empty frames, bricks on the floor, photographs of urine, and sado-masochistic pornography.

Secularists today are genuinely unable to tell the difference between works with aesthetic merit and those with none. In this aesthetic vacuum, fashion statements, celebrity-mongering, and political grantsmanship have come to dominate the art world. Art is lost. Those who would defend the arts must do so, ironically, against much of the contemporary artistic establishment, which seems bent on trivializing and vandalizing the rich legacy of human artistry. That this is done in the name of art only makes its hostility to aesthetic merit more perverse.

Christians, who have a conceptual basis for truth, also have a conceptual basis for beauty. This chapter is an indictment of what Leland Ryken has termed "the anti-art movement."[1] I am by no means opposing modern art as such, nor am I opposing abstract art. Rather my target is a set of assumptions and poses that hinder the true flowering of modern art. Nor is the basis of my criticism primarily the moral or theological failings of contemporary art. I will focus instead on its aesthetic failings (although many of them are due to the moral and theological emptiness of contemporary culture).

None of this should be construed as another narrow-minded conservative attack on modern art. I will be *defending* art against what I see as the narrow-minded conservatism of the artistic establishment (which only *thinks* it is being revolutionary when it is actually the plaything of the rich and powerful). My purpose is not to denigrate the arts and certainly not to denigrate artists, who are simply being victimized. Rather I hope to clear the ground for something better—a view of the arts grounded in Scripture which, unlike the emptiness of modern thought, can promote works of complexity and beauty.

We will examine three diseases that, in various manifestations, are proving fatal to the arts: the rejection of humanness; the cult of the artist; and the elitism of the art world.

ANTI-HUMAN ART

The elimination of the human element in art has been a major project of much modern artistic theory. Concepts such as creativity and beauty have been subjected to a radical critique. The image of an artist laboriously creating an aesthetic object of complexity and depth, perhaps creating the illusion of reality, has been challenged. A painting is nothing more than colors on a flat surface. The traditional claims about art's value—the talk of beauty and meaning—are repudiated. Art is whatever an artist does. In a kind of crazed secular puritanism, contemporary theorists have been seeking to "purify" art, to strip it of its human content and to reduce it to its barest minimum. The consequence has been the dehumanization of art.

Jackson Pollock, for example, devised ingenious methods of achieving randomness in painting. He would put a huge canvas on the floor, suspend cans of paint from the ceiling, and make them drip onto the canvas. Instead of giving the paintings titles, he would number them in order to divorce them from human language and meaning. Pollock considered himself an expressive, even psychological painter (he was an Abstract Expressionist), and yet by surrendering his artistic control to random, nonhuman processes, he was in effect abdicating his own creativity.

Pollock's experiments were matched in the field of music by John Cage, whose compositions were based on random sounds, sometimes determined by casting lots. Artists who exhibit the paintings of gorillas or who program a computer with a video terminal to make art based on random images or who exhibit a "found object" they did not create (Duchamp's bicycle wheel and the urinal) are continuing in this tradition. In each case, the artist is rejecting creativity on principle.

Such work may be visually intriguing or conceptually provocative. Still, it can hardly be aesthetically successful. To be random, by definition, means to be without order; hence, random art lacks not only content but, even more ruinously for any kind of art, it lacks form.

Worse yet, such art is profoundly dehumanizing. Art was once seen as evidence of human greatness, the supreme example of the human capacity to imagine with the mind and to work with the hands. Art manufactured by a machine or determined by subhuman natural processes is nothing more than another symptom of the mass, technical, impersonal culture.

Accompanying this rejection of creativity is the rejection of beauty. Today, works are often purposefully ugly. Their aim is not to give pleasure but to affront the sensibilities of their audience, thereby "waking them up" to the meaninglessness of reality. While it is true that aesthetics can encompass negative or unpleasant experiences, as seen in the great tragedies, contemporary art often pursues repulsiveness with zestful glee.

This emphasis derives largely from existentialism, perhaps the dominant philosophy of the twentieth century. Existentialism teaches that life is meaningless, considered objectively, but that, once this is realized, individuals can impose their own meanings upon reality. This is the root of situation ethics, that "there are no absolutes," but that instead people must choose their own values. It is also the root of intellectual relativism, that "what is true for you may not be true for me."

In art, existentialism manifests itself both in abstract art and in realistic art. Certainly, if the external world is meaningless, a web of absurdities, there is little reason to paint it. If meaning must instead be created from the individual's private choices, artists may "create their own realities" apart from any reference to the external world. Those who accept these philosophical assumptions will naturally turn to abstract art.

Although modern art has become almost a synonym for abstractionism, realistic art has never faded away and today enjoys a new vogue. The realistic images of modern art, however, tend also to reflect the existentialist idea that reality is absurd. Their purpose is to rub the viewer's nose into the brutality and emptiness of life, "decentering" the viewer in hopes of raising consciousness and provoking new personal choices. Modern landscape paintings tend to be bleak, gray, and ominously threatening; portraits tend to be anguished distortions or grotesque caricatures.

An important tenet of existentialism is that people who refuse to face the absurdity of life are "inauthentic." Such people, constituting the masses of humanity, complacently accept the status quo imposed on them by others. They are afraid of confronting the horror of their condition and instead conform to a comfortable security wherein one's peers or society or the church makes all of their decisions for them. They refuse the "burden of freedom" and the challenge of choosing their own meaning. They need to wake up to the reality of their condition, take control of their own lives, and live in "openness," wherein there are no certainties and no absolutes.

Art, therefore, should challenge the viewer's complacency about the "real world." Rather than displaying its beauties, as in the landscapes and portraiture of traditional art, realistic work should disclose the absurdity of the external world. Alternatively, artists can demonstrate how what we perceive as order in existence is actually the arbitrary construction of human beings, meaningless fragments assembled into a personal order. The collage, for example, assembles objects and images from the external world into a pattern of the artist's own devising, thus constituting almost a paradigm of existential practice. Collections of abandoned objects (that is to say, garbage), bleak landscapes that are almost suffocatingly depressing, condescending caricatures of ordinary people, violent images that proclaim the horrors of living—all are realistic, but they reflect specific assumptions about what is real.

Beauty is rejected on principle. The idea that nature is beautiful, its details and effects worthy of being reproduced in art, flies in the face of existentialist assumptions. Existentialists would admit that nature can be beautiful and is highly ordered, but that beauty and order only heightens its absurdity; that is, its indifference to human beings. The birds sing, and the water reflects the sunny sky while a person drowns. The constant operation of natural laws is like the compulsions of a mental patient who monotonously repeats the same words over and over. The order of nature is seen as "meaningless repetitions" that signify nothing; its alluring beauty is a monstrous hoax because there is nothing behind it. Artists, therefore, should either ignore the beauty of nature in order to create their own, or they should draw nature in such a way as to reveal its futility. They must call attention not to beauty, as in traditional art, but to ugliness.

Christians have been criticized for their "puritanical" suspicions of pleasure and beauty. And yet the most flesh-denying ascetic, flagellating himself in a desert cave, and the most furious, tight-lipped Puritan, smashing stained glass windows and pillorying the playwrights, would be hedonistic voluptuaries compared to the existentialists. No Christian dare go so far in denigrating the physical world. Although Christians must sometimes deny themselves pleasures, they are not allowed to utterly reject what God has made (1 Timothy 4:4). The Bible's teaching that the universe was created by God and that He proclaimed the physical order to be "very good" (Genesis 1:31) implies that the universe, contrary to existentialism and as confirmed by ordinary experience, is a good place to be. Although it partakes in the fall and thus comes short of perfection, the creation is not meaningless. Behind the physical universe looms an infinite but personal God, the source of its meaning, its goodness, and its beauty. Secularists are trapped in a suffocatingly narrow and oppressive worldview, perversely rejecting beauty while still trying to make art.

Another manifestation of this puritanical dismantling of art is the curious trend towards minimalism, the efforts to systematically tear away from art all of its complexity, richness, and illusion-making power. This was done, to complete the analogy with Puritanism, in the name of "purity." Tom Wolfe sums up the development of postwar art as a series of reductions, with each new movement getting rid of something else:

How far we've come! How religiously we've cut away the fat! In the beginning we got rid of nineteenth-century storybook realism. Then we got rid of representational objects. Then we got rid of the third dimension altogether and got really flat (Abstract Expressionism). Then we got rid of airiness, brush strokes, most of the paint, and the last viruses of drawing and complicated designs (Hard Edge, Color Field, Washington School).

Enough? Hardly, said the Minimalists, who began to come into their own about 1965. Bourgeois connotations, they argued, still hung on to Modern art like a necktie. What about all those nice "lovely" colors that the Hard Edgers and the Color Fielders used? . . .

And how about the painting frame? . . . So Frank Stella turned the canvas itself into a frame and hung it on the wall with nothing in the middle. That got rid of the frames, and the era of "shaped canvases" began.

Sure, but what about this nice sweet bourgeois idea of *hanging up pictures* in the first place . . . all in their nice orderly solid-burgher little rows? . . . So artists like Robert Hunter and Sol Lewitt began painting directly on the gallery walls or on walls outside the gallery window. . . .

But what about the wall itself? What about the very idea of a work of art as something "on a wall" at all? How very pre-Modern! . . . .

But what about the very idea of the gallery or museum? . . . So began Earth Art, such as Michael Heizer's excavations in the dry lakes of the Mojave Desert and Robert Smithson's *Spiral Jetty* in the Great Salt Lake.

What about the idea of a permanent work of art at all, or even a visible one? Wasn't that the most basic of all assumptions of the Old Order—that art was eternal and composed of objects that could be passed from generation to generation, like Columbus's bones? Out of that objection came Conceptual Art.[2]

According to the tenets of conceptual art, only the artist's genius and the *process* of creation are essential. Conceptual artists planned works of art that exist for awhile but then consume themselves.

Wolfe cites Peter Hutchinson's *Arc*, which consisted of a rope with a weight at either end. Attached to the rope were plastic bags filled with gas and rotten vegetables, which would create more gas as they decayed. This was all thrown into the ocean. The gas bags would lift the rope into an arc. An underwater photographer then took pictures of the "installation." The photographer would come back at regular intervals to record the bursting of the gas bags as the vegetables decayed, the arc collapsed, and the work of art disappeared. The photographs and the "documentation," the written account of the idea, were sold to the Museum of Modern Art.[3]

Conceptual art can be taken even farther, to the point that *there is no art*. Only the idea—the documentation—is exhibited as art. What iconoclasts, Puritans, and the uncultured masses could never accomplish (and in fact would probably never want to) becomes a project of artists themselves—the utter annihilation of art.

THE CULT OF THE ARTIST

How could empty canvases and decaying vegetables ever be considered art? Part of the reason is a conceptual shift of focus away from the object of art to the person of the artist. In other words, art becomes defined as whatever an artist does.

Tom Wolfe ends his brilliant dissection of recent artistic trends with conceptual art, which one might think is the ultimate *reductio ad absurdem*. Since his book was written in the 1970s, "performance art" has come into fashion. Whereas conceptual art reduced art to genius and process, the next reduction eliminated process, leaving only genius.

A few years ago one might have gone into a gallery and seen, not a painting, but an artist hanging on the wall. The artist took the place of the work of art. This sort of thing soon developed into performance art. Artists would simply present themselves to their audience. Sometimes they would "dialogue" with those who came to see them; other times they would deride them. The public ate it up. Making use of the new technology, these self-displays were integrated with electronic music, light shows, and multiplied video images. The artist might improvise a baffling surrealistic monologue. Today the performances have become more structured. The artist puts together a routine, which may have affinities to stand-up com-

edy, music videos, or old-fashioned storytelling. Performance art
sometimes becomes indistinguishable from drama or from dance.

A performance artist in Milwaukee entertained his patrons by
screaming abuse at them. Then, dramatizing his point that wealthy
art consumers feed on the suffering of artists, he stuck fishhooks
under his skin and cut himself with razor blades. The art critic
reviewing the exhibition for the local newspaper reported that the
audience was very uncomfortable throughout the performance,
especially when the artist started bleeding. Some people cried out for
him to stop and others walked out. Patrons of the arts have become
so "sophisticated" that making them squirm and provoking them to
a negative reaction is no easy task.

Performance artists have discovered ways to use sex to simultaneously titillate and outrage the public, drawing big crowds while
infuriating the bourgeoisie. Annie Sprinkle describes herself as a
"post-porn Modernist." Her performance art consists of masturbating, and then inviting the patrons to come up and inspect her gen-
italia with a flashlight. Karen Finley expresses a more feminist
theme. She takes off her dress, pours gelatin into her bra, slathers
her body with chocolate, and sticks bean sprouts over her body (calling them sperm).[4] Robert Mapplethorpe's photographs of his sado-
masochistic sexual practices and Andrés Serrano's photographs of
his urine are part of this fashion in which art consists of *anything*
done by an artist.

Oddly enough, such veneration has not necessarily improved
the plight of most artists, who are laboring away in poverty and
obscurity. Artists, like Roman Catholic saints, must be officially canonized before they may be venerated. When Duchamp submitted his
notorious urinal, entitled "Fountain," to a prestigious exhibition in
1917, he did so under the name "R. Mutt." The work was refused.
Only when it became known that the urinal was actually submitted
by the famous Marcel Duchamp was it accepted and acclaimed as a
revolutionary statement.

Conversely, works that were once rapturously praised as
expressing the genius of the great masters (such as several works
attributed to Rembrandt) plummet in value and esteem once scholars determine that they were actually painted by someone else. If the
work is beautiful and profound, does it matter if it was executed by
one of Rembrandt's apprentices or imitators rather than the master
himself? It does when art is defined in terms of the artist rather than
the work. Today artists are under pressure to become celebrities. If
they cannot be Rembrandts, they can be Andy Warhols, charming

the wealthy elite with their eccentric personalities and becoming prized guests and status symbols at cocktail parties.

This cult of the artist is profoundly anti-art. When attention shifts away from what good artists can actually do—that is, create objects of beauty and significance—art is trivialized. Critics and patrons are reduced to fashion-mongering dilettantes, requiring no intellectual understanding nor aesthetic perception. Uncritically accepting the dictates of the artistic establishment, they take part in one-upmanship games and, like adolescents, chase after the latest fad. When artists are turned into "objects of art," they themselves are trivialized. Artistic skill, craft, and production are assigned little value. Artists must display themselves and demean themselves, becoming little more than social climbers and objects of titillation. Negating their true personhood and artistic potential, they prostitute themselves and their art insofar as they sell out their integrity for success with the art establishment.

THE ART WORLD

According to Tom Wolfe, the art world—that is, the network of patrons, curators, and critics that sets the fashions for artists, corporations, and museums—consists of 10,000 people. (This does not include artists, who, oddly enough, must seek the approval of the people who matter but are not included in their number.) Wolfe's figures embrace all of the movers and shakers in the entire *world*: about 1250 people in Italy, 1750 in Paris, 1250 in London, 2000 in Germany, 3000 in New York, and perhaps 1000 scattered throughout the rest of the globe.[5] In other words, the "art world" is about the size of a very small town.

Everyone else follows. "The notion that the public accepts or rejects anything in Modern Art," Wolfe writes, "the notion that the public scorns, ignores, fails to comprehend, allows to wither, crushes the spirit of, or commits any other crime against Art or any individual artist is merely a romantic fiction, a bittersweet Trilby sentiment. The game is completed and the trophies distributed long before the public knows what has happened."

The public that buys books in hard-cover and paperback by the millions, the public that buys records by the billions and fills stadiums for concerts, the public that spends $100 million on a single movie—this public affects taste, theory, and artistic outlook in literature, music, and drama, even though courtly elites hang on somewhat desperately in each field. The same has never been true in art. The public whose glorious numbers are recorded in the annual reports of the museums, all those students and bus tours and moms and dads and random intellectuals . . . are merely tourists, autograph seekers, gawkers, parade watchers, so far as the game of Success in Art is concerned. . . . Not even the most powerful organs of the press, including *Time, Newsweek,* and *The New York Times,* can discover a new artist or certify his worth and make it stick. They can only bring you the news, tell you which artists the *beau* hamlet, Cultureburg, has discovered and certified.[6]

Wolfe may be exaggerating—regional and special interest artists have their own enclaves. Nevertheless, in places where the arts are flourishing with genuine home-grown creativity, the local art reviewers and museum curators will still make regular pilgrimages to New York City to find out what is happening in the "art world."

Unfortunately, art has become inextricably tied up with wealth and status, concerns which Christians have long seen as "worldly" temptations. Just as the temptations of the world are corrupting spiritually, they are corrupting aesthetically. The decadence of the arts is partially due to the peculiar social dynamics of the arts community, specifically, to artists' bohemianism and to the way the upper classes have appropriated the arts as a fashion statement. The result is an elitism that has removed the arts from ordinary people, impoverishing both the people and art.

Many artists since the nineteenth century have affected the pose of bohemianism. According to this view, artists are a breed apart from the masses of humanity. Because of their sensitivity and creativity, they cannot be expected to conform to conventional social standards. Eccentric behavior, defiance of society's expectations, and the uninhibited pursuit of experience become hallmarks of the creative personality. In practice this has meant lifestyles of purposeful squalor and immorality. And yet bohemianism is also characterized by high ideals, by rejection of society's materialism to devote oneself exclusively and in the face of all suffering to Art. Another corollary is that true artists will strive to be avant-garde, ahead of their times, on the cutting edge.

Bohemianism means a certain self-image for the artist, but it also means a way of looking at others. The vulgar masses, oblivious to the arts and caught up in their narrow little lives, are held in contempt. Borrowing the terminology and the class reductionism from Marxism, bohemian artists scorn the bourgeoisie, the middle class. Flouting "middle class values" and outraging "middle class conventions" becomes a self-righteous mark of identity, an inside joke, setting off the inner circle from the uncomprehending crowd.

Bohemianism has proven disastrous for the personal lives of artists and for the art to which they dedicate themselves. The idea that someone who can draw pictures, make music, or put words together in an interesting way is morally or spiritually superior to those who cannot is absurd. Christians know that "God does not show favoritism" (Romans 2:11), that all human beings stand under God's law and are objects of God's love. To exalt oneself and to denigrate others is a sign of the rankest hypocrisy and pride, which, tragically, can lead to complete moral dissolution.

The aesthetic problem of bohemianism is that in looking down their noses at ordinary folk, artists cut themselves off from the rich texture of common life that has always inspired the greatest art. If ordinary life—the process of birth, growing up, getting married, working, raising a family, growing old, dying—is unworthy of their attention, what is left? Their art becomes inhuman, an academic exercise in abstract theories, an increasingly esoteric self-indulgence that has nothing to do with the human condition.

The bohemian contempt of the middle class is almost comically off target. When artists combine Marxist proletarian poses with upper class social snobbery, the contradiction is farcical. Actually, one is hard pressed to think of a good artist who was *not* middle class. Among poets, Shakespeare was a small businessman; T. S. Eliot, though impeccably avant-garde, was a bank teller; Wallace Stevens was an insurance executive. The great modern painter Matisse was almost stereotypically bourgeois, with his conservative suits and intense work ethic. Even many artists who struggled with poverty had a middle class background. What class do the bohemians aspire to? They wear blue work shirts and labor in "low-rent" studios, but do they think that working class people would appreciate their experimentations with minimalism or conceptual art?

The answer, of course, is that artistic success places them with another class who likewise despises the bourgeoisie—the upper class. The wealthy elite, in turn, patronize the avant-garde artist because in doing so they can pose as bohemians themselves. Just as their social status is marked by wearing the latest fashions, people of wealth and influence collect the latest art and the latest artist. They employ the arts to proclaim their prestige and to enhance their self-image. In the words of Tom Wolfe, who fully explores this strange and mutually hypocritical alliance between bohemianism and enormous wealth:

Today there is a peculiarly modern reward that the avant-garde artist can give his benefactor: namely, the feeling that he, like his mate the artist, is separate from and aloof from the bourgeoisie, the middle classes . . . the feeling that he may be *from* the middle class but he is no longer *in* it . . . the feeling that he is a fellow soldier, or at least an aide-de-camp or an honorary cong guerrilla in the vanguard march through the land of the philistines. This is a peculiarly modern need and a peculiarly modern kind of salvation (from the sin of Too Much Money). . . . That is why collecting contemporary art, the leading edge, the latest thing, warm and wet from the Loft, appeals specifically to those who feel most uneasy about their own commercial wealth . . . See? I'm not like *them*—those Jaycees, those United Fund chairmen, those Young Presidents.[7]

None of this, neither the posing of the artist nor the posing of their patrons, can have anything to do with genuine art.

PATRONAGE

The handful of influential critics who mold opinion, the "name" artists who supply the cutting edge, and the upper class patrons who pick up the bills constitute a closed, self-contained circle. Although genuine artists can still make works of authentic merit that find appreciative audiences, the established "art world" artificially skews public tastes and markets. A regional museum, instead of buying the work of a skillful local artist, may increase its prestige by buying a minimalist or conceptualist work by someone with a "name." New artists seeking recognition will be tempted to ape the latest fad rather than to pursue their own vision.

The phenomenon of grants further illustrates this inbred elitism. Art projects can find funding by applying to corporate or governmental agencies such as the National Endowment for the Arts or its equivalents on the state or local level. Charitable foundations and private businesses also provide funds. These grants are usually awarded by a process known as "peer review." Proposals are submitted to panels of experts—in other words, to recognized critics and artists. As a result, artists seeking grants must satisfy, not the viewing public, but once again the "art world."

Similarly, corporations investing in art or satisfying the requirement that a certain percentage of the building cost be set aside for decorative art hire "consultants" drawn of course from the "art world." This is why so much public sculpture that clutters up city parks and building lobbies is so loathed by the people who must live with it. They were never consulted; such decisions about what works of art they should buy must be left to their betters.

That the National Endowment of the Arts has funded Robert Mapplethorpe's sado-masochistic photographs, Andrés Serrano's urine, and Karen Finley's nude performance art with taxpayers' money has provoked virulent controversy. Some lawmakers want to shut down the endowment completely; others at least want guidelines to prevent grants from going to such blatantly offensive works. Others are more concerned about the dangers of censorship, worrying that restrictions and tampering with peer review will interfere with free speech and suppress artistic freedom.

The real issue, as one defender of the NEA has acutely observed, is not censorship but patronage.[8] To refuse to buy something is not the same as outlawing it. To force taxpayers to pay for works that offend them is the real coercion. Artists have always had to please their patrons if they expected the money to keep flowing. The tradition of governmental support for the arts may go back to the Italian Renaissance, but if Michelangelo had mocked the values of Lorenzo de Medici, he would have lost more than a challenge grant—he would have lost his head. In the midst of the unprecedented freedom artists enjoy in this society, to brand patronage guidelines as censorship is grotesquely off target. As the much-censored cartoonist Garry Trudeau has observed in "Doonesbury," a government-supported avant-garde is a contradiction in terms. The spectacle of supposedly bohemian, anti-establishment artists quivering with indignation and ranting with hysterical rhetoric at the prospect of not receiving money from the bourgeois establishment they attack in their art is glaringly hypocritical (also deliciously ironic).

It may well be that the public interest is served by a governmental agency promoting the arts. Subsidizing a local orchestra or supporting an inner-city drama group is a worthy purpose, which can provide both tangible and intangible benefits to a community. Whether taxpayers as a whole should bear this burden, or whether private sources and those who would immediately benefit from these ventures should pay for them is debatable, with art lovers on both sides.

A deeper question is whether or not the present system of grants has helped the cause of the arts. Has the NEA fulfilled its purpose of promoting a rich cultural life among the populace? Are Americans more appreciative and more knowledgeable about the arts as a result of the NEA, or have the grants further separated the arts from the people? Has the NEA enabled poor or working class people to afford to go to the symphony or otherwise enrich their lives with the arts, or have NEA funds been a subsidy for the wealthy? My concern is that America has become less aesthetically conscious, that grantsmanship, with its politics and its inbreeding, has further insulated the arts from the public, to the detriment of both.

The recovery of the arts in this country and in the church will take place when ordinary people develop a taste for the arts and for aesthetic excellence. The flowering of the arts in northern Europe during the Renaissance and the seventeenth century was largely financed by the middle class. The unrivaled Dutch painting of the seventeenth century—the landscapes, portraits, family scenes, and paintings of people working—was nothing if not "bourgeois."

This does not mean that the arts should capitulate to the mediocrity of mass culture. Works that people "like" for superficial reasons may be aesthetically and intellectually worthless. Candy bars and soap operas are immensely popular, but they are not particularly beneficial. The knickknacks, the black velvet paintings, and the tacky ugliness of much popular art and architecture demonstrate our culture's aesthetic impoverishment. Ironically, the high art establishment shares that impoverishment. Aesthetically, there is little difference between the painting of Elvis on black velvet and Andy Warhol's painting of a Brillo box. Both, in a way, can be funny, but ultimately they are trivial, signs of a deeper cultural and spiritual poverty.

What is needed on every level is a recovery of the arts. In *King Lear*, the king rejects his own daughter Cordelia, whereupon her fiancé, seeing that there will be no dowry, does the same. The visiting king of France, appalled at her ill treatment, is moved to love her and to claim her as his bride:

> Thee and thy virtues here I seize upon,
> Be it lawful I take up what's cast away.
> Gods, gods! 'tis strange that from their cold'st neglect
> My love should kindle to inflam'd respect.[9]

In the same way, the rejection of aesthetic excellence by both the popular culture and the high culture of today should inflame our respect for the rich legacy of the artistic traditions. Christians are in a position to "take up what's cast away." In doing so, they will find themselves rescuing the arts, discovering their true value, and recovering an influence in our culture, which, whether it realizes it or not, is starved for what the arts can give.

"And now I will show you the most excellent way," said St. Paul, turning from the squabbles of the Corinthian church to the great exposition of love (1 Corinthians 12:31b). From the scorched earth of contemporary aesthetic theory, we will start rebuilding. We will begin by exploring the Biblical foundations—the sanctions, warnings, and examples that testify to God's purpose for the arts.

PART TWO

THE BIBLICAL FOUNDATIONS

THE VOCATION
OF BEZALEL

Not only does the Bible have a great deal to say about the arts, but it gives a rather detailed description of a particular artist and his ministry. Bezalel is not so well known as Moses, Daniel, or Paul, but his significance as a Biblical model for the arts is recognized within the Jewish tradition. (The major art museum in Israel is named after him.) Bezalel was the grandson of Hur, who, with Aaron, held up Moses' arms during the battle with the Amalekites (Exodus 17:8-13) and was one of Moses' trusted aides (24:14). According to Jewish tradition, Hur was the husband of Miriam, Moses' sister, which would make Moses Bezalel's great-uncle. In order to make the works of art God planned for the Tabernacle, Bezalel was given a special calling and special gifts.

When the children of Israel had been redeemed from slavery in Egypt, the Lord led them to Mount Sinai. Here God gave them the moral law in the Ten Commandments. Nearly every aspect of life came under God's sovereignty, as Moses received the social law for the theocratic community and the ceremonial law detailing the worship acceptable to God. In this context, Moses was told of the calling and empowering of artists (Exodus 31:1-11). Later, Moses recounted to the people what God had said:

> And Moses said to the people of Israel, "See, the Lord has called by name Bezalel the son of Uri, son of Hur, of the tribe of Judah; and he has filled him with the Spirit of God, with ability, with intelligence, with knowledge, and with all craftsmanship, to devise artistic designs, to work in gold and silver and bronze, in

cutting stones for setting, and in carving wood, for work in every skilled craft. And he has inspired him to teach, both him and Oholiab the son of Ahisamach of the tribe of Dan. He has filled them with ability to do every sort of work done by a craftsman or by a designer or by an embroiderer in blue and purple and scarlet stuff and fine twined linen, or by a weaver—by any sort of workman or skilled designer. Bezalel and Oholiab and every able man in whom the Lord has put ability and intelligence to know how to do any work in the construction of the sanctuary shall work in accordance with all that the Lord has commanded."

And Moses called Bezalel and Oholiab and every able man in whose mind the Lord had put ability, every one whose heart stirred him up to come to do the work. (Exodus 35:30–36:2 RSV)

BIBLICAL PRINCIPLES FOR THE ARTS

This passage suggests several principles about art. First, *art is within God's will*. The Tabernacle, designed to glorify God and to instruct His people, was to involve "artistic designs." God did not want to be worshiped outdoors or, as we say, in nature. Worship in the woods or on the mountains, as in the pagan nature religions, was specifically forbidden (Deuteronomy 12:2-5). Nor was the true God to be worshiped in a bare, unfurnished tent. Rather the Israelites were to "make the Tabernacle with ten curtains of finely twisted linen and blue, purple and scarlet yarn, with cherubim worked into them by a skilled craftsman" (Exodus 26:1). The furnishings were to be of pure gold, delicately carved wood, and precious stones (Exodus 25).

The Lord's specifications for the Tabernacle and later for the Temple take up a good part of the Old Testament, as those who resolve to read through the entire Bible find out to their dismay. The details of how many hooks to place in the curtains, how many cubits the frames must be, what to cover with beaten gold, and what to make from bronze are tedious to modern readers and have caused the abandoning of many a well-intentioned Scripture-reading project. But it pleased God to include such details in His holy Word, not only for Bezalel but for us. God, the designer and maker of the universe, clearly places great value on details of design, construction, and artifice.

Why was everything to be so lavish? The Lord tells Moses that "you shall make holy garments for Aaron your brother, for glory and for beauty" (Exodus 28:2 RSV). The priestly vestments—the gold filigree, the twisted golden chains, the emeralds and sapphires and diamonds, the golden pomegranates and bells, the woven coat, the embroidered sash (28:39)—all were to be made "for glory and for beauty."

God was to be glorified. Only the finest, the best that human beings have to offer, is appropriate to glorify the Lord. The glory of the Tabernacle seems to have been intended as a reminder, a faint copy, of heavenly glory (Hebrews 8:5). Those dazzled by the sublimity of the Tabernacle were perhaps experiencing a glimpse of the much more dazzling grandeur of the infinite God enthroned on "as it were a pavement of sapphire stone, like the very heaven for clearness" (Exodus 24:10 RSV).

Besides manifesting glory, Aaron's garments were to be made *for beauty.* Beauty is thereby an appropriate end in itself. The inventor of colors, of form, of textures, the author of all natural beauty, clearly values the aesthetic dimension *for its own sake.* According to the clear statements of Scripture, art has its place within the will of God.

The Bezalel passage also indicates that *being an artist can be a vocation from God.* "See, the Lord has called by name Bezalel, the son of Uri, son of Hur, of the tribe of Judah" (Exodus 35:30 RSV). The term *vocation* means "calling." We think of people being called to the ministry or to the mission field, but the Reformation stressed that even secular occupations can be true, God-given callings, suitable for the service of God and our neighbor. The Bible here clearly states that God "called" Bezalel for the work of constructing and adorning the Tabernacle. This calling was not generalized, addressed to everyone. It was personal, a special calling—the Lord called Bezalel by name. This suggests that a person may be called by God to be an artist.

The passage further indicates that *artistic ability is God's gift.* "And Moses called Bezalel and Oholiab and every able man in whose mind the Lord had put ability, every one whose heart stirred him up to come to do the work" (Exodus 36:2 RSV). All who wanted to help make the Tabernacle, "whose heart stirred him up to do the work," did so because the Lord had "put ability" in their minds. Artistic talent is not to be thought of as some innate human ability, nor as the accomplishment of an individual genius, but as a gift of God.

THE GIFTS FOR THE ARTIST

The passage not only states that artistic talent is from God, but it goes on to detail the specific gifts needed by an artist. The analysis of what artistry involves is so incisive that it deserves our close attention.

These gifts should not be thought of as some miraculous zap from Mt. Sinai which changed a bumbler with ten thumbs into an artistic genius. Bezalel was probably already a skilled craftsman in the normal course of things before he received this divine commission. Moses' task, as the bearer of God's Word, was simply to tell Bezalel what he was to do. Ancient Egypt is renowned for its magnificent art, and although it glorified the Pharaohs, much of the actual labor was done by slaves. Perhaps Bezalel had been forced to adorn a pyramid. The Lord speaking to Moses indicated that He had given these gifts to Bezalel prior to the Sinai revelation. Furthermore, He states that He gave similar ability to others who would be helping Bezalel. ("I *have* called . . . I *have* filled . . . I *have* given to *all able men* ability.") The implication is that these gifts apply not only to one miraculous commission, but that they apply to all artists.

"He has filled him with the Spirit of God" (Exodus 35:31). This is the first gift given to Bezalel, and the most important for the Christian artist. Bezalel is the first person described in the Scriptures as being filled with the Holy Spirit.

According to the New Testament, the Holy Spirit is given to all Christians and bears fruit in many areas of life (Galatians 5:22-23; Ephesians 5:9). In the Old Testament, before the Resurrection and before Pentecost, the Holy Spirit seems to have come not as a permanent presence in the lives of the faithful, but as a temporary empowerment. The Spirit of God came upon someone who thereby became a prophet (Judges 6:34; 11:29; 13:25; 1 Samuel 10:5-6). In other words, the Holy Spirit enabled the prophet to proclaim the Word of God. The Spirit of God here empowers Bezalel "to devise artistic designs." The implication is that the works of Bezalel will express, in the medium and in the language of art, the Word of God. Bezalel's conception of the Tabernacle came not from any inner vision, but from the external Word of God—the detailed instructions given to Moses, who relayed them to Bezalel, who then followed them to the letter (Exodus 39:42-43).

Bezalel's possession of the Holy Spirit means that he was a man of faith. A Christian artist must, above all, be a Christian. The first priority must be a relationship to God through Christ, a work of the

Holy Spirit in the heart. In all of these senses, the Spirit of God filled Bezalel and inspired him in the making of the Tabernacle.

"He has filled him . . . with ability" (35:31). The second gift given to Bezalel was talent. Not everyone is able to paint or carve or weave. Not everyone can write great poetry or act or sing or play the violin. The potential to do so, the aptitude, the "ability" is God-given.

One of the greatest pleasures I find in the arts is to be astonished at human ability. When I look at a painting, I like to peer closely at the brush strokes. These dabs of color, with the lines of the paintbrush bristles still visible, were controlled so carefully that when seen from a greater distance, they can create the illusion of reality itself. From the almost microscopic precision of the miniscule illustrations in an illuminated manuscript to Van Gogh's thick slabs of paint that seem ripped out of his soul, I am dumbstruck at what human beings can do.

I studied piano only enough to learn how hard it is. I will laboriously plunk out a tune, my eyes looking up and down from my music to my hands on the keyboard, losing my place, hitting the wrong keys, and trying again in a herky-jerky rhythm that sends people out of the room. A real pianist, though, can play smoothly through a score that is black with chords and thirty-second notes. Every finger is called upon to do something different; the mind must keep track of flats and sharps and nuances of tempo. Then, as if the technical demands were not enough, the musician's heartfelt expression can animate every note. It all seems so effortless, so fluent and graceful. Such a spectacle of gratuitous talent incites me, not only to praise the artist, but to praise God for giving such ability to human beings.

"He has filled him . . . with intelligence" (35:31). The third gift is intelligence. A person may have talent, but that alone is not enough for great or God-pleasing art. God gave Bezalel a measure of understanding, of reason, of common sense.

The popular image of an artist today is of someone completely intuitive, passionate, and even irrational. We assume that beauty and reason are opposed to each other (which would surprise the ancient Greeks). We take a simple (and not fully proven) physiological hypothesis about the different functions of the "right brain" and the "left brain" and use it to classify people and drive yet another wedge between our minds and our emotions. Art, at least the best art by the best artists, addresses the entire mind, thereby engaging the faculty of intelligence.

To build the Tabernacle, Bezalel needed not only inspiration and talent but also intelligence. Solving the practical problems of making art requires a clear mind and a rational temperament. Designing a sculpture that will not tip over, managing the laws of perspective and geometry in painting, deciding how to choreograph a play, planning the logistics of an exhibition or a performance—being a successful artist requires a pragmatic and almost mathematical way of thinking.

Intelligence implies a way of looking at life. Great art is always incisive, the work of a mind that sees through false perceptions and stereotypes. The popular image of the creative person notwithstanding, the great artists that come to mind—da Vinci, Cervantes, Shakespeare, Bach—all display this keen, analytical frame of mind. When we were studying *The Divine Comedy*, one of my students, an agnostic, wrote how impressed he was by Dante's "intelligence." Such a tribute is appropriate for one of the most passionate of all poets.

"He has filled him . . . with knowledge" (35:31). The fourth gift is knowledge. Whereas intelligence involves the faculties of the mind, knowledge refers to what is in the mind. Bezalel, in addition to talent and mental acuity, needed to *know* certain things. He needed to recognize and know how to prepare acacia wood. He needed to know how to cast bronze and how gold can be beaten to microscopic thinness without tearing. Besides knowing his materials, he had to know his subjects—both the natural (the structure of almonds, flowers, and pomegranates) and the supernatural (the appearance of the cherubim and the meaning and function of the mercy seat on the Ark of the Covenant).

Some artists scorn education. Their gifts are "natural," they think, a function of their inner creativity that they need only express without inhibition, without tradition, without knowledge of anything outside of themselves. The Scriptures, however, say that knowledge of things beyond the self is critical for an artist.

All good artists do, in fact, tend to be open to knowledge. They are interested in learning about their art, its history and traditions. They are interested not only in their own work but in that of others, especially the great masters of their craft. The best artists want to know things besides art—physics, geography, anthropology, history, politics. They read books. They tend to agree with Samuel Johnson that they would rather know something about a subject, no matter how trivial, than to remain ignorant about it. They seek knowledge not only to find subjects for their art, although wide reading certainly increases the scope and depth of their work, but because openness to the outside world is a hallmark of genuine sensitivity, the prerequisite of an artist.

A common modern assumption about artists is that they must experience all of life in order to know it fully and render it in their work. Many would-be artists experiment with drugs, expose themselves to physical danger, and play with moral degradation so that their art will have scope and depth, and so that it will reflect "real life." Stephen Crane advocated this principle in his writings and practiced it in his short life. His greatest work, however, was *The Red Badge of Courage,* a vivid evocation of combat during the Civil War. Veterans of the war praised its accuracy, its re-creation of what war felt like. Actually, the twenty-four-year-old author had never seen a battle. He simply imagined what it would be like. Great art is a matter of imagination more than experience.

To be sure, a wide range of experiences can be valuable for an artist—working in a steel mill, traveling, firsthand research. If the pursuit of experience leads to sin, however, the result is not knowledge. Scripture says that sin has a way of "suppressing the truth" (Romans 1:18). Sin hardens the heart, making us less—rather than more—sensitive to the truth. I have known of would-be artists who think they are exquisitely creative, and yet an alcoholic haze keeps them from being productive. Illicit love affairs, hedonistic indulgence, and vicious infighting can turn a promising artist into a vain, cynical, unfeeling caricature of a human being. Real knowledge, in contrast, is God's gift for art.

"He has filled him with . . . all craftsmanship" (35:31). In addition to talent, intelligence, and knowledge, an artist needs craftsmanship, the mastery of technique. Craftsmanship involves skill at working with one's medium, whether words or paint or stone, causing that medium to do one's bidding. In artistic craftsmanship, the human dominion over nature, bestowed at the creation, is at its highest.

The artist's dominion over matter involves intimacy and commitment, not tyranny or exploitation, as the object through infinite care and effort begins to conform to the artist's will. Scripture goes so far as to portray artistic craftsmanship in the recurring figure of the potter and the clay as an analogy of the relationship between God and His people (Isaiah 64:8; Jeremiah 18:6; Romans 9:21).

"And he has inspired him to teach" (Exodus 35:34). Not only was Bezalel given the gifts necessary to build and adorn the Tabernacle, but he was further empowered to transmit these gifts to others. (The RSV translation of the Bible uses a wonderfully appropriate term for the teaching vocation: He was "inspired" to teach.)

Since art depends upon such intangible and inherent qualities as talent and craftsmanship, many question whether artistry can really be taught at all. While agreeing that art involves extraordinary gifts, Scripture indicates that it can. God's gifts, including the gift of salvation, are given and brought to fruition through human instruments. An aspiring artist may have many innate talents, but those talents normally come to fruition only through the efforts of a teacher.

Conversely, artists who are teachers can pass their gifts on to their students. This does not mean that the students' abilities are any less dependent on God's gifts or that a good teacher can automatically teach anyone to be an artist. It simply means that teaching and learning are the normal means by which God develops His gifts— ability, intelligence, knowledge, craftsmanship—in those He has chosen for the artistic vocation, to "every one whose heart stirred him up to come to do the work" (Exodus 36:2). This Scripture, by the way, suggests that the desire to be an artist may be a sign of one's potential. Those who want to take art lessons may have potential that a good teacher can draw out.

Many, if not most, artists find themselves teaching. Aspiring novelists or poets end up teaching in a university writing program. Musicians give piano lessons. Painters teach art classes in a public school. Many artists are disappointed that they cannot support themselves solely by their work, that they must teach to make a living. Scripture, however, suggests that teaching is as much related to art as craftsmanship or any of the other gifts. Whether one teaches in a college, a public school, an arts and crafts shop, or in the time-honored relationship of master and apprentice, teaching is by God's design part of the artistic vocation.

THE BIBLICAL ARTIST

Ability, intelligence, knowledge, craftsmanship, and teaching were all necessary for Bezalel and his colleagues "to devise artistic designs" (Exodus 35:32). Some secular theories about artistry emphasize innate talent; others emphasize training; others emphasize technique. Some think artistic ability is hereditary, part of one's genetic code. Others think artistic ability is a "learned behavior." Secular theories tend to be narrow and partial, reducing human complexities to a simplistic formula. It is characteristic of Scripture (and of truth in general) to be comprehensive and complex.[1] The Bible says that ability *and* intelligence *and* knowledge *and* craftsmanship *and* teaching all work together to make an artist.

Bezalel's gifts provide simple criteria for evaluating a work of art: Does this work show ability? intelligence? knowledge? craftsmanship? Recognizing such qualities is not the same as agreeing with the implicit message in a work of art or even understanding what it is all about; it simply means recognizing its artfulness. By these standards, a sculpture by Michelangelo or a painting by one of the Dutch masters clearly measures up. Picasso too, although his works may seem baffling, exhibits extraordinary talent, intelligence, and technical skill.

Duchamp's *Bicycle Wheel,* which is simply a bicycle wheel displayed as a sculpture, shows no particular talent on the part of the artist (although other of his works do). Its craftsmanship is that of the factory worker who made it, not the artist. Andrés Serrano's photograph of a crucifix immersed in his urine shows no ability or craft. All the artist did was to urinate and photograph the results. Other examples, such as Andy Warhol's prints of Brillo boxes and Campbell Soup cans and Jackson Pollock's experiments in the random patterns made by paint flung onto a canvas, might exhibit some cleverness, I suppose—as in, whoever would think to do such a thing?—but no real intelligence or knowledge. Some artists may demonstrate knowledge but no craft, or ability but no intelligence. The best artists will exhibit all of Bezalel's gifts.

We should perhaps not draw too much from the example of Bezalel. The Tabernacle with its animal sacrifices has been fulfilled and superseded by Christ, through whom God "tabernacled" with us (the literal translation of John 1:14). Elaborate and gorgeously ornamented church buildings are not necessary for New Testament Christians, who worship "in spirit and in truth" (see John 4:20-24). Bezalel was called for a specific purpose; artists sometimes have other purposes that may be more problematic. Nor was Bezalel, the desert craftsman, in the "high art" tradition. He was not creating for art museums, nor did he have the same consciousness about art that we have in our culture. As we shall see, Scripture has other things to say about art, including the danger of idolatry.

Nevertheless, there can be no doubt that "artistic design" and the purposes of "glory and beauty" are sanctioned by the Word of God. Anyone who rejects the aesthetic dimension in principle or who denies that art can be an appropriate vocation for a Christian does so against the clear statements of Scripture.

The account of the calling of Bezalel gives an authoritative model of the artistic vocation, describing in surprisingly comprehensive detail the gifts that God makes possible for artists. Now we should examine what Bezalel made.

SEVEN

THE WORKS OF BEZALEL

*H*aving called and empowered Bezalel with artistic gifts, the Lord went on to specify what sorts of art He desired for the Tabernacle and later for the Temple. In chapter after chapter, the Bible describes God-ordained works of art.

Francis Schaeffer has observed that the making of the Tabernacle involved "almost every form of representational art that men have ever known."[1] Here we can see specific positive examples of how various types of art—abstract, representational, and symbolic—can function to the glory of God and the benefit of His people.

ABSTRACT ART

When we read the Scriptural accounts of the Tabernacle, the Temple, and their furnishings, the imagination soon fails. The details of wooden forms inlaid with gold and bronze, the "ten curtains of finely twisted linen and blue, purple and scarlet yarn" (Exodus 26:1), the gold filigree and twisted chains become difficult to picture in our minds. The colors and forms called for are dazzlingly various, the textures and shapes extraordinarily complex. Much of what Bezalel made can perhaps best be appreciated in terms of abstract art, that is, of pure design, which most essentially represents the "artfulness" of art.

By abstract art I mean art that represents nothing outside of itself. Forms and colors are arranged in designs that are not representations of anything; rather they are beautiful in themselves. As we have seen, much contemporary abstract art consists of studies in randomness, experiments in "minimalism," and arid conceptual statements drawn from impoverished worldviews (although some modern abstract art does shows concern for pure design in the older sense).

When I refer to "abstract" art, think not so much of Jackson Pollock, but of a Persian tapestry or the margins of a medieval illuminated manuscript. The designs are beautiful—highly ordered, incredibly intricate—reflecting the lush, intertwined complexity of existence as orchestrated by a sovereign God. The problem with so much contemporary abstractionism is that it is so simplistic, void of complexity and of design. Monotheistic abstractionism, on the other hand, fosters images that represent nothing outside themselves but are beautiful, just as a tree or a flower represents nothing outside itself and is beautiful.

Consider "Jakin" and "Boaz," the two freestanding columns that were to stand just outside of the Temple:

> He [Huram] cast two bronze pillars, each eighteen cubits high [twenty-seven feet] and twelve cubits around [eighteen feet]. . . . A network of interwoven chains festooned the capitals on top of the pillars, seven for each capital. He made pomegranates in two rows encircling each network to decorate the capitals on top of the pillars. He did the same for each capital. . . . The capitals of both pillars, above the bowl-shaped part next to the network, were the two hundred pomegranates in rows all around. He erected the pillars at the portico of the temple. The pillar to the south he named Jakin and the one to the north Boaz. The capitals on top were in the shape of lilies. And so the work on the pillars was completed. (1 Kings 7:15-22)

These gigantic bronzes, standing about thirty-three and a half feet high (counting the capitals) with a diameter of about five and a half feet, are examples of abstract art. As Schaeffer has observed, "they supported no architectural weight and had no utilitarian engineering significance. They were there only because God said they should be there as a thing of beauty."[2]

This is not the sort of sculpture many of us prefer. It was not a statue of Moses with the Ten Commandments or Joshua riding a horse. Representational sculptures were very prominent in pagan temples and in pagan art. Occasionally, realistic statues would be placed in the Temple by blaspheming kings (2 Kings 21:7; see also, in the Apocrypha, 1 Maccabees 1:54 for a Greek statue being placed in the Temple). Such images were condemned as the most monstrous abominations. These sculptured pillars, on the other hand, were not idolatrous. Imposing in size, yet intricate in their fine detail, their only purpose was glory and beauty.

This is not to say that such abstract art is totally without meaning. Abstract art can present abstractions—power, order, beauty, glory—without representing a creature found in the world. In the case of the pillars, they were given names. Captions or titles of works of art are ways of attaching words, and thereby meaning, to visual images. Jakin means "he establishes." Boaz means "he comes in strength."[3] The qualities of the bronze monoliths, their stability and their imposing presence as they stand in empty space, strong but supporting nothing that can be seen, recall the establishing work of God and His strength. Jakin and Boaz do not represent God, but they do call to mind and illustrate the work of God. The present tense of the Hebrew names testifies to God's continuing action, that God is still establishing and still coming in strength. These truths would come to mind every time the people saw the monuments.

REPRESENTATIONAL ART

The pillars Jakin and Boaz bore carvings of pomegranates and lilies. The sacred lampstands were to feature almond blossoms (Exodus 25:31-35). The Temple's ten stands of bronze were engraved with lions, oxen, and palm trees (1 Kings 7:2-37). The debacle of the golden calf notwithstanding, the bronze laver for ceremonial cleansing was to be supported by twelve metal bulls (7:25). Not only were representations of nature prominent in the Tabernacle and Temple, but representations of supernatural beings, the cherubim, were everywhere—carved on the furnishings, woven into the veil of the Holy of Holies (Exodus 26:31), and sculpted on the central shrine of the invisible God, the Ark of the Covenant itself (1 Kings 7:29, 36; Exodus 25:18-20). Clearly, representational art is also acceptable to God.

Archaeologists in Jerusalem have recently discovered an art object that they believe was actually used in Solomon's Temple. It is a likeness of a pomegranate, a luscious many-celled fruit, which for some reason was especially favored in Hebraic art. Scholars have determined that this tiny artifact, only 1.68 inches high, was fastened to a staff held by a priest. On it is the inscription, "Belonging to the Temple of the Lord Yahweh, holy to the priests." This graceful, delicate figure, according to scholars, "is the only sacred object . . . that survives from the Temple built by Solomon" (Fig. 7.1).[4] The piece is simple, yet intricately crafted, especially for such a tiny object. The Bible says that the hem of Aaron's garment was adorned with pomegranates (Exodus 28:33-34), as were the pillars Jakin and

FIG 7.1   *Ivory pomegranate from priest's staff, Solomon's Temple*

Boaz (1 Kings 7:42). Gazing at this exquisite piece of ivory, we see an object that was actually *there*, present when the glory of the Lord dwelt in His house, when the sacrificial blood was poured on the Ark of the Covenant, when Nebuchadnezzar finally razed the Temple to the ground—a staggeringly tangible witness to the factuality of the Bible.

The art of the Temple specifically avoids representing God Himself, in marked contrast to the art of the pagan temples. Rather the emphasis is on the works of God, the designs that He made in creating the universe. This is why the Temple was so filled with representations from the natural world—lions, palm trees, floral designs, and pomegranates. Adorning God's house with images of His own works was a way to offer praise.

REPRESENTATIONS OF THE SPIRITUAL

Not only is nature, particularly plants and animals, featured in the art of the Tabernacle and Temple, but the supernatural is also represented. In the figures of the cherubim, spiritual beings are represented by means of tangible, material images. A cherub is not the cute winged baby of conventional religious art. The cherubim are angelic beings whose spiritual form, when manifested to the senses, overloads our finite imaginations. Ezekiel, granted a more-or-less direct vision of angels, records that "this was their appearance":

> . . . they had the form of men, but each had four faces, and each of them had four wings. Their legs were straight, and the soles of their feet were like the soles of a calf's foot; and they sparkled like burnished bronze. Under their wings on their four sides they had human hands. And the four had their faces and their wings thus: their wings touched one another; they went every one straight forward, without turning as they went. As for the likeness of their faces, each had the face of a man in front; the four had the face of a lion on the right side, the four had the face of an ox on the left side, and the four had the face of an eagle at the back. Such were their faces. And their wings were spread out above; each creature had two wings, each of which touched the wing of another, while two covered their bodies. And each went straight forward; wherever the spirit would go, they went, without turning as they went. . . . And the living creatures darted to and fro, like a flash of lightning. (Ezekiel 1:5-12, 14 RSV)

Ezekiel's vision of such beings is unimaginable. In a sort of divine Cubism, they are apparently revealed to him from all dimensions, from four sides at once, and they are simultaneously covered by their wings and disclosed to him in detail. Such a spiritual encounter, which should help keep us from anthropomorphizing the heavenly realm, is impossible to visualize fully or to represent pictorially.

Later, Ezekiel describes how representations of these living creatures were carved into the wall of the Temple:

> . . . And on all the walls round about in the inner room and the nave were carved likenesses of cherubim and palm trees, a palm tree between cherub and cherub. Every cherub had two faces: the face of a man toward the palm tree on the one side, and the face of a young lion toward the palm tree on the other side. They were carved on the whole temple round about; from the floor to above the door cherubim and palm trees were carved on the wall. (Ezekiel 41:17-20 RSV)[5]

What we have here is a simplified and stylized depiction of the beings Ezekiel saw, a two-dimensional bas-relief. The concept of "accommodation" is helpful here. Ezekiel's vision defies static pictorial depiction. The artistic images are schematic diagrams, accommodated to the limited capacities of human beings, who can perceive only in terms of the senses. In fact, Ezekiel's vision was also an accommodation whereby spiritual, nonmaterial beings were manifested to a human being, limited and bound by merely physical senses.

Images of cherubim were everywhere in the Tabernacle and the Temple. Bezalel was commanded to adorn the tapestries of the Tabernacle "with cherubim skilfully worked" (Exodus 26:1 RSV). Solomon's Temple included two colossal statues of cherubim, each with a fifteen-foot wingspan, in the Holy of Holies (2 Chronicles 3:10-13). Cherubim also figured in the construction of the most important and significant work of art in the Old Testament—the Ark of the Covenant.

> And you shall make two cherubim of gold; of hammered work shall you make them, on the two ends of the mercy seat. . . . The cherubim shall spread out their wings above, overshadowing the mercy seat with their wings, their faces one to another; toward the mercy seat shall the faces of the cherubim be. And you shall put the mercy seat on the top of the ark; and in the ark you shall put the testimony that I shall give you. There I will meet with

you, and from above the mercy seat, from between the two
cherubim that are upon the ark of the testimony, I will speak
with you of all that I will give you in commandment for the people of Israel. (Exodus 25:18-22 RSV)

The significance of these details is heightened again by Ezekiel's
vision. Above the real cherubim, he glimpsed something even more
staggering:

And above the firmament over [the cherubim's] heads there was
the likeness of a throne, in appearance like sapphire; and seated
above the likeness of a throne was a likeness as it were of a
human form. And upward from what had the appearance of his
loins I saw as it were gleaming bronze, like the appearance of fire
enclosed round about; and downward from what had the
appearance of his loins I saw as it were the appearance of fire,
and there was brightness round about him. Like the appearance
of the bow that is in the cloud on the day of rain, so was the
appearance of the brightness round about. Such was the appearance of the likeness of the glory of the Lord. And when I saw it,
I fell upon my face. (Ezekiel 1:26-28 RSV)

Ezekiel's vision is necessarily full of similes and comparisons to
earthly analogues. In the theophany that he experienced, Ezekiel
dared not say that he was looking on God; rather he was seeing "the
appearance of the likeness of the glory of the Lord" (1:28). What he
sees is four levels removed, established by concentric prepositional
phrases, from the Godhead. Throughout his description he sees not
a throne but "the likeness of a throne"; the phrase "as it were" is
repeated over and over again. Gazing upon "the glory of the Lord,"
he perceives "a likeness as it were of a human form." What he is perceiving is the image and likeness that God shares with human beings
from the creation (Genesis 1:26) and, more profoundly, the Second
Person of the Trinity, Jesus Christ, whose human nature is ever sub-
sumed into the Godhead.

Ezekiel was seeing something real but accommodated to his
limited human faculties. No mortal can look on God and live
(Exodus 33:20). The merest glimpse is enough to make Ezekiel fall
on his face. Yet the infinite God deigns to reveal Himself to mortal
flesh, making Himself known in tangible form fully and completely
in Jesus Christ, but also in copies and shadows (Colossians 2:17)
fitted to the different capacities of human beings, "expressing spiritual truths in spiritual words" (1 Corinthians 2:13).

A vision of God such as Ezekiel's was not rendered artistically on the Ark, of course. Above the cherubim and the mercy seat, Bezalel made nothing, although from that empty space God's presence and God's word were present in a special way (Exodus 25:22). The Tabernacle is revealed to have been "a copy and shadow of what is in heaven" (Hebrews 8:5). The Ark represented in an artistic image the actual court of God, which through grace He was establishing on earth with His chosen people, dwelling in their midst in a desert tent. The Ark as imaging the very presence of God speaks to us also of Christ, the incarnate God, who "became flesh and dwelt among us," who, translated literally, "tabernacled" with us (John 1:14).

The point is, art can portray spiritual realities. The highest and most ineffable, the very presence of the Deity with His heavenly hosts, God commissioned Bezalel to represent in the Ark of the Covenant. Art can represent spiritual reality, expressing the invisible in terms of the visible (Romans 1:20). Such representations are never exhaustive of their subject matter; rather they accommodate themselves to the human imagination.

The difference between the images made by Bezalel and those forbidden by the commandment against graven images is that the former communicate what God reveals. They do not receive worship, but point beyond themselves to the true object of worship. They do not pretend to contain the infinite God, only to praise Him and communicate His reality to others (1 Kings 8:27-30).

Notice that representational art does not necessarily mean "photographic realism," itself largely a product of scientific materialism. To paint the cherubim as described by Ezekiel in hard-edged visual detail in a style of naturalistic realism would be aesthetically ludicrous and theologically misleading. The cherubim would seem more like science fiction monsters rather than spiritual entities, whose shifting appearances point to their unfathomable trans-sensory dimensions. (This is a mistake of many contemporary illustrations of the book of Revelation.) A schematic or expressionistic style would be more appropriate, conveying a sense of mystery and sublimity.

Even paintings of the natural world need not be photographic. Francis Schaeffer has observed that some of the pomegranates that adorned the garments of the priest were blue, a color that never occurs in natural pomegranates.[6] This is the sort of thing one associates with Chagall or Matisse. Painting an apple blue instead of red, depicting nature in new ways by experimenting with color and form, helps us to see the object in a new way, not as inevitable and ordinary, but as the creative handiwork of God.

Artists have always enjoyed painting still lifes and landscapes; depictions of flowers, fruits, trees, and animals seem universal in both Western and Eastern art. There is also the impulse to go beyond nature, whether to create blue pomegranates or to represent the most sublime spiritual truths in visible form. Both kinds of art, as well as art that represents nothing at all, had their place in the Holy of Holies, commanded by the very Word of God.

SYMBOLIC ART

Art can adorn by its beauty of design; it can represent entities in the world. It can also teach by embodying and communicating ideas. In other words, art can be symbolic. Such art was prominent in the Tabernacle and the Temple, where its purpose was not only to glorify God but to build the faith of the worshipers.

Consider again the design of the central object in Israelite worship, the Ark of the Covenant. A gilded wooden chest about four feet long, two feet wide, and two feet deep, it contained the tablets of the Law, an urn of manna, and Aaron's rod (Hebrews 9:4). On its lid of pure gold (the name of which is variously translated as "the mercy seat" or "the atonement cover"), the two cherubim faced each other, looking down. Once a year on the Day of Atonement (Yom Kippur), in a solemn drama, the high priest would enter the Holy of Holies, the ark obscured by a cloud of incense, and sprinkle the blood of the scapegoat on the mercy seat as atonement for the sins of the people (Leviticus 16).

What is symbolized here is the very gospel itself, the central mystery of salvation through which the Old Testament saints and we ourselves are reconciled to God. Coming between the presence of God, in His terrifying holiness, and the tables of the Law, broken by human sin, is the blood of atonement. The heavenly cherubim look down and see not the Law but the sacrificial blood, which covers all sins. These symbols look ahead to and have their fulfillment in Jesus Christ, the Lamb of God who takes away the sin of the world (John 1:29):

> When Christ came as high priest of the good things that are already here, he went through the greater and more perfect Tabernacle that is not man-made, that is to say, not a part of this creation. He did not enter by means of the blood of goats and calves; but he entered the Most Holy Place once for all by his

own blood, having obtained eternal redemption. . . . How much
more, then, will the blood of Christ, who through the eternal
Spirit offered himself unblemished to God, cleanse our con-
sciences from acts that lead to death, so that we may serve the
living God! (Hebrews 9:11-12, 14)

On the Day of Atonement it was not the blood of the goat that took
away sins (Hebrews 10:4); rather the symbolism of the ark, the ritual, and the sacrifices were designed to provoke faith. As "copies of
the heavenly things" (Hebrews 9:23), they were to instruct and prepare God's people for the fulfillment of the promise that was to come
in Christ. The Old Testament saints were saved, never by works, but
by grace through faith (Ephesians 2:8). For us, Christ's death is in
the past; for them, Christ's death was in the future. But Christ's
atonement spans eternity, covering the people of the Old Testament
also, although they knew it only by glimpses, prophecies, and symbols.

    Many other artifacts described in the Old Testament were also
symbolic. Consider the bronze "sea" supported by the twelve bulls
(1 Kings 7:23-26). The bulls were symbolic of the twelve tribes of
Israel. The huge laver they supported was used for the ceremonial
cleansing necessary for Temple worship. This practice looks forward
to Christian baptism and the cleansing power of the Word of God,
which rests upon the foundation of the apostles (twelve disciples;
twelve tribes; twelve oxen) and the entire history of Israel (Ephesians
2:20). A wooden table was to be covered with gold and adorned
with complex moldings (Exodus 25:23-30). On it was to be kept at
all times the "bread of the Presence" (Exodus 25:30), calling to mind
the truths of God's nourishment and intimate presence with His people that finds its Christian expression in Holy Communion. The
golden lampstand, the lavers, the altars, all have a teaching purpose
besides being beautiful and ritually functional.

    The holy garments of the priest, for example, were to be
adorned with twelve different jewels—ruby, topaz, beryl, turquoise,
sapphire, emerald, jacinth, agate, amethyst, chrysolite, onyx, and
jasper—all set in gold filigree, each carved with the name of one of
the tribes of Israel (Exodus 28:15-21). "Whenever Aaron enters the
Holy Place, he will bear the names of the sons of Israel over his heart
on the breastplate of decision as a continuing memorial before the
Lord" (Exodus 28:29). Thus, whenever Aaron or the high priest
brought the sacrificial blood into the Holy of Holies and poured it
upon the Ark of the Covenant, he did so on behalf of all of God's
people. The jewels symbolize more than the tribes being brought

before God. They also suggest God's love for His people. To Him, each tribe is a precious stone, different from each other, but each full of value and light as with the redeemed in Heaven (Revelation 21:9-21).

Dorothy L. Sayers makes a useful distinction between "conventional symbols" and "natural symbols."[7] A conventional symbol has only an arbitrary connection to the idea it symbolizes. Language is based on conventional symbols. The word *lion* in English stands for a particular animal that has other names in other languages. As long as everyone in the language group agrees that a certain sound will refer to a particular concept, communication can take place. It does not matter whether the golden-maned creature is called *ari* (Hebrew) or *Löwe* (German) or *lion*. When the word is written down by means of squiggles on paper, which symbolize sounds, language again makes use of conventional symbols.[8] A lion can also be used as a symbol for Great Britain—this would be another conventional symbol, deriving from ancient heraldry rather than any actual association between England and jungle cats.

A lion, though, can also be used as a symbol for strength. The connection here is not arbitrary. A lion actually is strong, and in contemplating a lion, one can make discoveries about the qualities it exemplifies. The lion's strength can be terrifying and dangerous, yet at the same time compelling, even beautiful. The lion can teach us about strength in general, its sublimity as well as its danger. Contemplating the symbol is a way to explore the idea. Symbolism in which the sign has a real connection to the idea is called "natural symbolism."

Whereas conventional symbols have the virtue of clarity, since they can be defined with the utmost precision, natural symbols are richly evocative and can bear many levels of meaning. They appeal to the imagination as well as to the intellect. Interpreting a natural symbol demands more than finding a one-to-one literal correspondence; it demands and offers a meditative process.

Scripture uses the lion as a symbol for both the devil and Christ. This is by no means a contradiction. Different aspects of the natural symbol are used to illustrate different ideas.[9] The Bible describes the devil as a "roaring lion looking for someone to devour" (1 Peter 5:8). Here the passage focuses upon the ferocity and cruel hunger of a ravening lion, qualities that reveal the nature of our spiritual enemy. Elsewhere, the Bible describes Christ as "the Lion of the tribe of Judah" (Revelation 5:5). Here we are to think of the sublimity of a lion, its power and regal splendor. An artist can take a natural symbol and delve into its depths. In *The Chronicles of Narnia,* Lewis symbolizes and thereby explores the person of Christ by means of the lion Aslan.

Two intersecting lines perpendicular to each other make up a cross. This sign can serve as a conventional symbol for the mathematical process of addition or for the twentieth sound in the alphabet. The cross as a natural symbol can stand for death (as in an obituary) and for health (as in the Red Cross); for suffering (as in "bearing one's cross") and for faith (as in the crosses of a church). These wide-ranging meanings and their emotional implications are held together because there is a real connection between the symbol and its meanings. The cross of the historical Jesus was a means of execution and the basis for salvation. It exemplifies death, health, suffering, faith, and more—defeat and victory, judgment and love, the eternal intersecting time, God intervening into human history. In Christianity's most potent symbol inheres the inexhaustible mysteries of the faith.

ART AND CULTURE

The Metropolitan Museum of Art in New York City has excavated and restored on its grounds an ancient Egyptian temple. While walking through it and thinking about Moses and the children of Israel, I noticed with a thrill of recognition that this temple built to a pagan god consists of three inner chambers, exactly like the plan of the Tabernacle and the Jerusalem Temple. In fact, the threefold structure of the Temple was common throughout the ancient world, as were portable "arks," tents of worship, certain details of ritual, and even what seem to be figures of cherubim. Archaeological research and Old Testament scholarship have uncovered many parallels in Hebrew life and worship to various Egyptian, Syrian, and Canaanite practices.

Liberal theologians make much of these connections, using them to minimize the uniqueness of God's special revelation and relationship to the Jews. However, the connections have nothing to do with theological truth but with the relationship between art, culture, and religion. Art is, by its very nature, open to and a function of human culture, so that sacred truths can be expressed through a wide variety of culturally conditioned art forms.

The Hebrews, schooled in the commandment against graven images, knew that art is not sacred. Its meaning or use may be sacred, but art in itself is not, nor can it contain or limit the infinite God. Solomon understood this point. He distanced himself from his pagan neighbors when he dedicated the Temple: "The heavens, even the highest heaven, cannot contain you. How much less this temple I have built!" (1 Kings 8:27). In fact, when the people began to use the Temple and the Ark of the Covenant in an idolatrous, faithless way—trusting in holy objects while neglecting what God desired, namely, holiness in their lives—God ordained their destruction (Micah 3:11-12).

The artifacts, while instituted by God's command, were made by and for human beings. Therefore, by God's gracious accommodation, these would agree with the assumptions and the imagination of the people who used them. When the Hebrews thought of a temple, they thought of a three-part division, as in all the other temples they had seen. That is fine. God's Word can be heard in a building with that sort of architecture. The Hebrews could not build a Gothic cathedral. They had neither the technology nor the culture for it; they would not have understood it. But Gothic cathedrals are not sacred either, although again God can use them to make Himself known.

The Canaanites, on the other hand, did believe in sacred places and sacred images.[10] The Philistines identified the Ark as the Hebrew God (1 Samuel 4:7); for them, what was happening to the image of Dagon was happening to Dagon himself (5:1-7). However, the Biblical view holds that since God alone is sacred, the special places and the particular styles of art do not really matter.

When the Temple was to be built, Solomon simply turned to the best artists he knew, the Phoenicians: "You know there is no one among us who knows how to cut timber like the Sidonians" (1 Kings 5:6 RSV). So Solomon sent to Hiram, the king of Tyre, asking him for material and workmen. Notice that Solomon, wishing to glorify God, was concerned first with excellence, not doctrinal purity in the artists. Although complimentary to Israel's God in his correspondence with Solomon, Hiram was not one of God's chosen people and almost certainly was not a believer. (The Sidonians worshiped the goddess Ashtoreth, according to 1 Kings 11:5.)

The actual craftsman sent by King Hiram to supervise the construction of the Temple was Huram (in some translations rendered Hiram like the name of his king). In the words of King Hiram's letter to Solomon,

I am sending you Huram-Abi, a man of great skill, whose mother was from Dan and whose father was from Tyre. He is trained to work in gold and silver, bronze and iron, stone and wood, and with purple and blue and crimson yarn and fine linen. He is experienced in all kinds of engraving and can execute any design given to him. He will work with your craftsmen and with those of my Lord, David your father. (2 Chronicles 2:13-14)

Huram, the craftsman of the Temple, was thus the counterpart to Bezalel, the craftsman of the Tabernacle.

Huram's mother was a Hebrew and his father was a Phoenician. He would have been considered a Jew, since he was the child of a Jewish mother (assuming the Jews then followed their present definition), although his mixed parentage would have scandalized orthodox Israelites. Surely his mother, the widow of an Israelite before her marriage to a Phoenician, had taught him about the true God of Israel despite his thoroughly pagan environment. His father was also a "craftsman in bronze," from whom, no doubt, Huram learned his trade (1 Kings 7:14). The art of the Temple, therefore, must have been Phoenician, in accordance with the training that he had received.

The Bible makes clear that unbelievers were also employed in the construction of the Temple. Solomon set the "aliens" in the land to work on the Temple, both as laborers and overseers (2 Chronicles 2:17-18); these were remnants of the Canaanites, who continually tempted the Israelites towards idolatry (Joshua 23:7; Judges 2:2-3). Nevertheless, the Temple and its art pleased God and was made an instrument of His purpose (2 Chronicles 7:12-16).

The implication is important for a Christian perspective on the arts. Because a painter is not a Christian, that does not mean that his paintings cannot be enjoyed or even imitated by Christians. To be sure, any thematic content must be scrutinized very critically through the lens of Scripture, but aesthetic design is essentially neutral.

Was the person who made my shoes or cooked for me in a restaurant a Christian? Or the scientist who discovered penicillin? Or Beethoven? I may never know. I should pray so for the sake of the person, but even if he or she was not a Christian, I am not harmed spiritually by my clothing or my meal, by taking medicine or listening to a symphony. Art is a part of human life, on the same order as food, clothing, scientific knowledge, and social customs. All of these are valuable gifts of God in His creation, essential parts of our humanity created by sinners in need of Christ's redemption but who may or may not know Him. For aesthetics, although not for theology, a Christian may "go to the Sidonians."

Always a function of human culture rather than divine revelation, no particular style or type of art ought to be sacralized or made into an absolute.[11] The history of art shows continuous change. This is partially because cultures change through technology, the facing of new problems, and the accumulation of different kinds of ideas and experiences. Art also has an inherent tendency to change for aesthetic reasons. If art exists to heighten experience, to help us notice and appreciate what we are so used to that we ignore, an artistic style itself will tend to become so familiar that it no longer startles us with fresh perceptions. It fades into the background, into the decor. We no longer pay any attention to it. Art must be in a continuous process of change to remain alive and effective. Unlike human culture, however, Jesus Christ does not change (Psalm 90; Hebrews 13:8). The infinite God, who is never limited by finite forms or human works, can bear His testimony through a multitude of forms, as the history of religious art makes strikingly clear.

It follows that Christians need not be overly scrupulous in regard to types of art. Abstract, representational, and symbolic art all have prominence in the Scriptures. Certainly the content of art, the underlying assumptions and messages conveyed, must be examined with wariness and Scriptural discernment. Anti-scriptural content is not always merely an intellectual idea that can be analyzed and dismissed. Scorn for "ordinary people," moral permissiveness, the habit of mockery, self-pity, voyeurism, the sense of how terrible life is—all these attitudes and feelings can be more poisonous spiritually than any propositional statement, and they can be absorbed easily through art. Aesthetic excellence in itself is good, but as Augustine has pointed out, it can be a seductive lure to falsehood.

Pure questions of form, though, are basically indifferent spiritually. Christian freedom enables believers to pursue or to enjoy any formal mode of art they find congenial. It is the secular aesthetes who take artistic movements and manifestoes with such dogmatic seriousness. Christian artists have worked with classical, Romantic, realistic, and Modernist styles. Christian painters or art patrons can create or enjoy abstract art if they want to (actually, it is probably the safest for those who fear the commandment against graven images), or photographic realism or Expressionism or whatever style they please, as long as it is congenial to a Christian worldview.

Since art is a function of history and culture, Christian art may also be contemporary. To be deliberately old-fashioned in our tastes, returning to earlier styles that seem "more Christian," may be an empty gesture. One style is not "more Christian" than any other. Christianity is not merely a nineteenth- or sixteenth-century religion, a faith that has nothing to say to the contemporary imagination. Throughout the psalms it is a *new* song that is to be offered to the Lord.[12]

MANIFOLD WORKS

The Tabernacle and the Temple offer concrete examples of artistry commanded and employed by God. Not only are abstract, representational, and symbolic art given prominence, but also music in all of its forms—instrumental (1 Chronicles 23:5; Psalm 150:3-5), vocal (1 Chronicles 9:33; 15:16, 27), and dance (2 Samuel 6:14; Psalm 149:3; 150:4).

When the Temple was completed, "the priests stood at their posts; the Levites also, with the instruments for music to the Lord which King David had made for giving thanks to the Lord—for his steadfast love endures for ever—whenever David offered praises by their ministry" (2 Chronicles 7:6 RSV). Here the purpose of the instruments is to give thanks to God for His steadfast love. That musical instruments are a means of nonverbally "giving thanks" is a profound statement of the religious value of art. Here art is described as a human response to God's blessings, an offering of beauty to the Designer and Creator of existence, the ultimate source of all blessing and all beauty.

This Scripture indicates moreover how the audience is involved. When the trumpets, psalteries, harps, and cymbals were playing, David "by their ministry" could also "offer praises." The picture is of a person praising God by means of the music performed by others. Music is described as a ministry. What is true here of music is true of all the arts. They can be a response to God and a ministry to other human beings, valuable both as an expression of the artist and as a catalyst for the audience.

There are many types of aesthetic forms. What Bezalel made for the Tabernacle and his counterpart Huram the Sidonian made for the Temple were not, of course, museum pieces. The practice of isolating beautiful objects away from their contexts in ordinary life is a modern invention and would have been incomprehensible to someone like Bezalel. Still there is a connection between the works of Bezalel and those of artists in the high art tradition of our modern culture. In both cases great skill is expended in making aesthetic designs. Whether these designs are made to function in worship or to be contemplated in a museum, whether they are part of the texture of ordinary life or assigned a special status, the same gifts are involved in their making.

In the Old Testament, God commanded that certain designs be created for glory and beauty, but they were also to express in a compelling way His nature and love for His people. The aesthetic and expressive dimensions of art are thus sanctioned by Scripture.

Moreover, nearly the whole range of the arts can be found in God's Word. This is true not only of the visual arts and of music; in literary art, poetry is exemplified in the psalms, fiction in the parables, drama in the street theater of the prophets (2 Kings 13:14-19; Jeremiah 19; Ezekiel 4:1-3). Just as God's works are "manifold" (Psalm 104:24 RSV), that is, incredibly diverse, so are the works of human beings made in His image.

EIGHT

THE IDOLATRY OF AARON

*E*xodus 31 describes the calling of Bezalel, establishing a precedent for the Biblical artist. The very next chapter, Exodus 32, describes God's purposes for art gone completely awry. Another gifted artist, Aaron, creates an object that gives rise to sin and apostasy.

The Bible sanctions art, but it also describes how it can go wrong. The Bible's austere warnings against idolatry must not be dismissed or interpreted away. Works of art can glorify God, but they can also be instrumental in leading people away from Him. Idolatry, the deifying of created objects rather than the Creator, is a temptation for modern sophisticated cultures, no less than for primitive tribes. Not only is idolatry deadly for the faith; ironically, it is also deadly for art.

GOLDEN CALVES

While Moses was on Mount Sinai, receiving the Law and the commission of Bezalel, the people turned to an artist and to another god:

> When the people saw that Moses delayed to come down from the mountain, the people gathered themselves together to Aaron, and said to him, "Up, make us gods, who shall go before us; as for this Moses, the man who brought us up out of the land of Egypt, we do not know what has become of him."
>
> And Aaron said to them, "Take off the rings of gold which are in the ears of your wives, your sons, and your daughters, and bring them to me." So all the people took off the rings of gold which were in their ears, and brought them to Aaron. And he

received the gold at their hand, and fashioned it with a graving tool, and made a molten calf; and they said, "These are your gods, O Israel, who brought you up out of the land of Egypt!" When Aaron saw this, he built an altar before it; and Aaron made proclamation and said, "Tomorrow shall be a feast to the Lord." And they rose up early on the morrow, and offered burnt offerings and brought peace offerings; and the people sat down to eat and drink, and rose up to play. . . .

When Joshua heard the noise of the people as they shouted, he said to Moses, "There is a noise of war in the camp." But he said, "It is not the sound of shouting for victory, or the sound of the cry of defeat, but the sound of singing that I hear." And as soon as he came near the camp and saw the calf and the dancing, Moses' anger burned hot, and he threw the tables out of his hands and broke them at the foot of the mountain. And he took the calf which they had made, and burnt it with fire, and ground it to powder, and scattered it upon the water, and made the people of Israel drink it.

And Moses said to Aaron, "What did this people do to you that you have brought a great sin upon them?" And Aaron said, "Let not the anger of my Lord burn hot; you know the people, that they are set on evil. For they said to me, 'Make us gods, who shall go before us; as for this Moses, the man who brought us up out of the land of Egypt, we do not know what has become of him.' And I said to them, 'Let any who have gold take it off'; so they gave it to me, and I threw it into the fire, and there came out this calf." (Exodus 32:1-6, 17-24 RSV)

The people who would so generously bring their valuable possessions to adorn the Tabernacle (Exodus 35:4-9; 36:3-7) here bring them for the casting of an idol. Aaron, the master of language and the high priest of the true God, uses his gifts and his office to proclaim the worship of a god that he himself manufactured. The picture is of offerings, sacrifices, celebrations, and art—all of which had earlier been described as appropriate in service to the true God— misdirected and thus turned into an abomination.

At the focus of the apostasy is an object of art—a golden calf. A piece of sculpture is honored as the god "who brought you up out of the land of Egypt." Just as the Bible elsewhere sanctions nearly every art form, here we see nearly every art form perverted. Visual art replaces God. Aaron's talent with language (the writer's gift) is used to make eloquent proclamations urging worship of the calf. Music, the supreme nonrepresentational art form, is used sinfully to praise the calf with singing and dancing. When art supplants God, its Creator, the nature of art itself is distorted. Aaron was sinning against God; he was also sinning against the arts.

IDOLATRY

The essence of idolatry is explained in Romans 1:25: "They exchanged the truth of God for a lie, and worshiped and served created things rather than the Creator." Our sinful nature is such that we tend to desire not the Creator but the things He created. We love what He has made, but rebel against its Maker, even though He is the source of everything we find so attractive in the created order.

Some idolators worship what God has created. God's creations are by all means good (Genesis 1:31), but they are not to be worshiped. No mere creature is to be treated as the source of life or allowed to usurp the Creator's place in our affection. Those who explicitly worship nature, whether primitive animists or more sophisticated pantheists, are guilty of idolatry. So are materialists who ascribe attributes of deity such as infinity and eternity to the physical universe.

Other idolators worship what human beings have created (see Psalm 115). Any religious system dreamed up by human beings apart from God's self-revelation given in His Word is idolatrous, even though it may be abstract and highly conceptualized. Our self-made personal religions, in which we put together various beliefs that we "like" rather than what is true, are idolatrous. Trusting in our own works for salvation rather than in the work of Christ can be another manifestation of idolatry, insofar as we put our faith in what we do rather than in what God through Christ has done.

Idolatry is more than simply having a false religion. This passion for created things rather than the Person who created them manifests itself on nearly every level of our lives. Colossians 3:5 states that greed, the unlawful desire for material possessions, is idolatry. Those who devote their lives to accumulating more and more wealth are in danger of idolatry, of being so oriented to "this world" that in affections, time, and service the Lord is displaced by "created things."

Anything, even if it is good in itself, can be the occasion for idolatry. Whether it is a once-useful and soul-winning artifact such as the bronze serpent (2 Kings 18:4) or even a member of one's own family (Matthew 10:37), it can take the Creator's place. No wonder Scripture spends so much time warning against idolatry. It is not merely the practice of primitive nature religions that no one believes in anymore anyway. It is a sin that inheres in the very core of our being, an inclination that is always present in us, from which we are saved only by the blood of Christ.

GRAVEN IMAGES

The Old Testament clearly relates idolatry, this worship of created objects at the expense of the Creator, to art. A statue of Baal or Ashtoreth is a "created thing" which, as an object of devotion and an emblem of a false religion, can lead people away from the true God. The scope of the warnings against "graven images," however, goes far beyond the religious practices of ancient Canaan.

The Ten Commandments, meant to encode the moral law for all time, include an explicit prohibition against worshiping art:

> You shall not make for yourself a graven image, or any likeness
> of anything that is in heaven above, or that is in the earth
> beneath, or that is in the water under the earth; you shall not
> bow down to them or serve them; for I the Lord your God am
> a jealous God. (Exodus 20:4-5 RSV)

The essence of the commandment is the jealousy of God, a startling but beautiful expression of God's love for us. His love is not mere abstract good will but, like all love, a passionate and exclusive longing for another person. When the beloved rejects the lover for someone or something else, the lover feels pain and fury. When one of His beloved commits idolatry, God feels it like a loving husband whose wife commits adultery, a figure consistently and powerfully employed in Scripture (Jeremiah 3; Hosea 1—3). God's jealousy is the other side of His steadfast love.

The commandment specifically forbids making a "graven image, or any likeness of anything," whether in the heavens, the earth, or the water. Some have taken these words to forbid art altogether. This is to misread the commandment and to neglect the rest of Scripture which, as we have shown, sanctions the arts. Bowing down and serving the images constitutes the idolatry. The forbidden "likenesses" refer, on one level at least, to the specific pagan religions that were always competing for the Israelites' faith—the worship of the stars, planets, and sky gods (Deuteronomy 4:19); the worship of animals, animistic gods, and earth goddesses (the golden calf, Baal, Ashtoreth); the worship of water deities such as the fish gods, the leviathans, and others common among the Egyptians and Canaanites.

To assume that the commandment forbids all representational art would contradict the orders given for the construction of the Tabernacle and the Temple. Even when taken in its narrowest sense, the prohibition of likenesses does not rule out all art. As we have seen, it makes room for the vast range of nonrepresentational art. Yet we must be careful not to deny the full force of the commandment as it applies to art. Not only may we not worship idols; we may not *make* any object for worship. Worshiping works of art arouses the jealousy of God.

What does it mean to worship art? Rather than taking the anthropological approach and criticizing the ancient Canaanites, consider some commonplaces that are heard over and over again in academic and artistic circles: "Art is the means of giving order to the chaos of experience." "Art represents the source of human values." "Art gives meaning to life." These statements, of course, reflect the modern existentialist assumption that meaning is something bestowed or imposed by the individual on a meaningless world. These critical clichés place art and the artist squarely in the position of God—as creator ("giving order to chaos"), as lawgiver ("the source of values"), as redeemer ("giving meaning to life").

Matthew Arnold predicted that, as human beings continued to progress, religion would be replaced by poetry.[1] Among the well-educated this has happened, if we substitute the arts in general for poetry. The vocabulary of aesthetic criticism is now replete with language borrowed from religion: "inspiration," "vision," "transcendence," "myth," "epiphany," "revelation." Artists are described as special people, above the humdrum limits of ordinary society, endowed with mystical powers, a sacred aura, and authority. The artist, in effect, is treated as a seer, a prophet, or, more precisely, a shaman.

The work of art is treated as an oracular utterance of inexhaustible depth, an authoritative guide to life. Often the arts are presented as esoteric mysteries. The "art world" becomes a privileged inner circle, possessing secret knowledge from which the nonelect are excluded. As in the mystery religions of old, membership in the inner circle requires initiation. The priests of the art world would be the teachers and critics who introduce their congregations to the arcane language and secret knowledge of the elect. These clergy also preserve the relics of the departed saints and construct elaborate theologies of the arts, which they defend with sectarian zeal and enforce with inquisitorial rigor.

In addition to the professional clergy are the laity who, sometimes motivated less by understanding than by guilt and a vague

sense of obligation, give substantial offerings to the "arts." Dressed
up in their best clothes, they make up the congregation of the concert hall or the theater and find the key to a richer, more meaningful life in pursuing aesthetic pleasure.

For many people, especially in academia and among the well-
educated and wealthy elite, religion has been displaced completely
by the quasi-religious "high culture." This secular aestheticism,
ironically, assumes the form of the most primitive, credulous, and
unsophisticated religions, replete with priestcraft (intellectual elitism
and hermetic theories), superstitious veneration of objects (devotion
to the most trivial works by canonized artists), irrationalism (an
experiential emotionalism and the rejection of rational discourse),
and lack of rigorous moral teachings (the permissive lifestyles cultivated in artistic circles). The religion of modern secular aestheticism
is, in fact, structurally similar to that of the ancient Canaanites.

THE AESTHETIC AND THE RELIGIOUS

The problem comes when aesthetic values are confused with spiritual values. Indeed, because art does possess great intrinsic value and
because it can create a profound impression on its viewers, it is little wonder that art is easily confused with religion. The calf of solid
gold must have been splendid to see. It must have been breathtak-
ing as it caught the firelight. It is little wonder that the people who
experienced its beauty and mystery would confuse those feelings
with the beauty and mystery of the Lord. Certainly, its beauty must
have been more immediate and accessible than that claimed for the
God who veiled Himself in the pillar of fire and the pillar of smoke.
Aesthetic experiences can be very close and are perhaps related to
religious experiences, but they are not the same.

I tend to agree with the neo-Platonists who see in earthly
beauty—the grandeur of nature, a sublime poem, a glorious symphony—a participation in the divine beauty which is its ultimate
source. This does not mean, however, that the aesthetically pleasing
objects or the human beings who made them are themselves the
source of greatness. To think so is again to confuse "created things"
with the Creator. Art can be awe-inspiring, mysterious, comforting,
or edifying, but these very strengths can cause art to be confused
with religious truth.

This confusion is heightened by the fact that art exists to give
pleasure. Aesthetic experience, by definition, involves pleasing its
audience in some way.[2] Pleasure is part of the gift of art and should
never be ascetically rejected on principle. The point is simply that

art's purpose is to be pleasurable, while true religion frequently is not. The splendor of the golden calf was very different from the splendor that was breaking out on Mount Sinai, which filled the people with terror (Exodus 20:18).

The living God does not exist to gratify people. Art, of course, does. Moreover, art can gratify people by giving them quasi-religious experiences—a sampling of wisdom, a taste of transcendence, a flash of moral insight. These experiences, when mediated solely through art, appeal to a deep human yearning. Yet they require no commitment and are safely under human control. God, on the other hand, is never under human control and demands everything.

Idolatry, whether it be a homemade religion of positive thinking or a comfortable aestheticism, can thus offer a sort of domesticated spirituality. Our human need for transcendence, for meaning, for value, can be met to a degree in, for example, a majestic symphony without the pain of repentance and the cost of discipleship, without what Flannery O'Connor has called "the sweat and stink of the cross."[3] Properly, the sense of transcendence in a symphony, the sensation of being swept out of ourselves into something high and beautiful, can and should make us mindful of the transcendent realm of the infinite Lord. Yet it need not. Many people are satisfied with the "richness of life" offered by aesthetic stimulation, which by its nature can make few self-consuming demands.

The Danish philosopher Søren Kierkegaard has usefully explained the difference between the aesthetic and the religious realms. In speaking of the ways by which people can orient their lives, he distinguishes between three spheres or stages of existence—the aesthetic, the ethical, and the religious.[4] One need not accept Kierkegaard's "Christian existentialism" to appreciate these distinctions. In witnessing to those whose religion is secular aestheticism, I find that they will recognize and respect the name of Kierkegaard and agree to his analysis. A crucial Biblical twist, however, must be added to Kierkegaard's religious phase to complete the point.

According to Kierkegaard, living in the aesthetic sphere means to live for oneself, to live one's life solely for personal pleasure. For some, this quest for pleasure may manifest itself in sensuality and hedonism. For others, the quest for pleasure may be more refined, manifesting itself in the connoisseur's exquisite taste for food and wine or in the sophisticated cultivation of the arts. Others, to shift to non-Kierkegaardian examples, may live for the instant gratification of television and the mass culture. This ego-centered

quest for personal pleasure, according to Kierkegaard, must ultimately prove unsatisfying. The aesthetic stage ends in despair.

A person disillusioned by the quest for pleasure may advance
to the next stage—the ethical. Here one lives no longer for the self
but for others. This is more than simple moralism, which may be
motivated by nothing more than the pleasure of self-righteousness.
Ethical acts involve self-sacrifice, putting another's pleasure,
another's good, ahead of one's own. Life in the ethical sphere is
noble. Yet, according to Kierkegaard, this too, followed honestly,
ends in despair. Living for the other person involves contradictions,
impossibilities, and failures. That is to say, human beings cannot perfectly fulfill the moral law.

At this impasse, a person may move on to the third sphere—
the religious. In this stage, the pleasures of the world are no longer
ultimate, nor are the demands of moral perfectionism. Even suffering can be embraced as the inner life blossoms. Kierkegaard's
Christian existentialism tends to minimize the objective content of
faith, stressing a subjective openness and uncertainty instead of the
solid assurance provided by Biblical doctrine. An evangelical appro-
priation of Kierkegaard completes his paradigm better than
Kierkegaard did himself. In Biblical terms, to live in the religious
sphere means to exist in conscious dependence upon the grace of
God. As in the aesthetic realm, one only receives. As in the ethical
realm, one lives for others. Faith in Jesus Christ transfigures everything.

In other words, we cannot find salvation through the pursuit
of sensations (the aesthetic), nor by good works (the ethical), but
only by grace through faith (the religious). Cultivated and well-educated people often vacillate between the aesthetic and the ethical,
indulging in every kind of physical stimulation from sex to drugs to
music, then shifting to fanatical exercises in self-denial, from vege-
tarianism to physical fitness to political activism. In their search for
a purposeful life, they too seldom hear the gospel of Jesus Christ, in
whom both their desires and their aspirations can find fulfillment.

The religious sphere does not deny the aesthetic any more than
it denies the ethical. Just as religion affirms moral values, so it can
affirm aesthetic values, although neither can be the absolute basis for
life. Each has its place in God's will—personal pleasure as well as
moral action—but apart from God's will they can result in the tyran-
nies of egoism, sensuality, or legalism. The religious sphere gives
each its place, as long as the three are not confused with each other.

THE LIBERATION OF THE ARTS

Art, unfortunately, is often the means by which human beings worship themselves. When art is turned into a religion, the worshiper ultimately will be profoundly disappointed. Art will refuse to betray its Master.[5] When it is twisted to purposes alien to those of God, the art, as well as its devotee, suffers.

When art becomes a religion, it becomes stuffy, dogmatic, and sterile. It exacts ascetic devotion rather than pleasure and inspires righteous zeal rather than aesthetic contemplation. Pagan religions that employ images of their gods do not make their images to be enjoyed. Aesthetic considerations are irrelevant to the efficacy of the sacred image. As we have seen, the same is true of the objects now favored by the secular aesthetes. Nor may the sacred image be tampered with by aesthetic experimentation or innovations of craft. Pagan societies are ultra-conservative. Change is not permitted. Everything is taken too seriously. The Bible's warnings against idolatry, although they seem to condemn art, actually are liberating. When art is freed from the burden of having to "give meaning to life," it is free to fulfill its own nature.

The golden calf must have looked very similar to the bronze oxen used to support the cleansing "sea" of the Temple. Why was one condemned as an abomination while the other was commanded by God? The difference is not in their form but in their content. What made the golden calf an idol was its meaning and the way it was used by its worshipers, not its aesthetic design.[6] The golden calf gave the children of Israel the same kind of religion all the other nations of the time followed, a made-up mythological religion, worshiping a god under human control. In practice this means a god that is impersonal and subhuman; that is, an animal. The meaning of the oxen in the Temple had to do, no doubt, with the twelve tribes of Israel, expressing the foundations of God's revelation in the history of the Jews (Ephesians 2:20).

The figurative designs of plants and animals featured in the Temple—the floral patterns, palm trees, and cherubim carved on the wall panels (1 Kings 6:29), the lions and bulls engraved on the Temple furnishings (7:29)—are not, however, interpreted or given an explicit meaning by Scripture. This suggests that their major function was decorative. Although the meaning of art and its status as a religious object are often problematic, according to Scripture, the sheer aesthetic qualities of art, its capacity to adorn and to enhance with beauty, are affirmed.

Archaeologists have seen similarities between the Bible's

descriptions of religious artifacts and those used in pagan religions of the time. A horned altar (Exodus 27:2) evidently could be used for the worship of Baal or for the worship of the Lord.[7] This does not mean that there was no substantial difference between the faith of the Jews and the faith of their neighbors. Rather it suggests that aesthetic forms as such are not restricted by the Biblical faith.

When art goes wrong theologically, it is usually because of its content rather than its form. Artfulness as such, the formal aesthetic design that gives a work its beauty, falls under the universal sovereignty of the Creator. Whether a work is "Christian" or "non-Christian" has to do with its meaning, not its form. The implication is that Christians may in principle use any style, any set of techniques, any type of artistic expression.[8] If they are zealous of Biblical truth, they may employ practically any artistic form without fear of committing Aaron's sin.

THE RESPONSIBILITY OF THE ARTIST

In some ways it may be easier for artists to resist idolatry than for their audiences. Matthew Arnold's proposal that poetry be made the new religion has received the most scathing denunciation from poets.[9] Artists generally know their work too well to make false claims for it. And yet artists sometimes find themselves pressured by their audience to create works that will be misused, testifying to a worldview or a way of life that from the Christian perspective is false, sinful, or idolatrous. This pressure may come from artistic peers, teachers, publishers, or exhibitors, or, what is worse, the "paying public" who will only buy or support what they find congenial. In a non-Christian world, there is not always a market for art that does not conform to the prevailing intellectual trends, as Christianity, indeed, must not.

If Bezalel is a positive model for the Christian artist, Aaron stands as a negative example. Aaron was a man of faith, chosen and called by God (Psalm 105:26; Hebrews 5:4). He was the witness, spokesman, and instrument of God's power through Moses (Exodus 4:15-16), entrusted with the ministry of the priesthood. Why did he make the golden calf? How did such a hero of the faith become party to apostasy?[10] The answer is simple. He pandered to his audience. He gave in to the pressure. The people insisted on an idol, so he took their gold and made them one.

Today artistic integrity, let alone spiritual integrity, is often compromised by the marketplace and by the dictates of "the art world." One creates not necessarily what one wants to create but what sells, what is being published, what is fashionable. The concern is to present something that will gain peer approval rather than what one really believes. Now that nihilism, ironically, has become the established religion, those who seek to convey some other values, some other worldview, often feel either that they must remain unknown or that they must compromise and give the audience what it wants. By the same token, if Christians would patronize the arts more than they do, the marketplace could be influenced to work the other way.

Aaron acquiesced. And when explaining it to Moses, he blamed the people for what happened. The craftsman disclaimed all responsibility: "Let not the anger of my Lord burn hot; you know the people, that they are set on evil. For they said to me, 'Make us gods. . . .' And I said to them, 'Let any who have gold take it off'; so they gave it to me, and I threw it into the fire, and there came out this calf" (Exodus 32:22-24 RSV). It just "came out"; he had nothing to do with it.

Aaron's sin, though, was not simply making a statue. His sin was caring too little for his audience, having insufficient love for the people. "And Moses said to Aaron, 'What did this people do to you that you have brought a great sin upon them?'" (Exodus 32:21). Even at the expense of popular success, artists must care for their audience enough to avoid corrupting them, causing them to sin through false or salacious content. Christian artists and Christian audiences can avoid idolatry by testing the message and effect of art by the Word of God.

NINE

CREATION AND IMITATION

*T*he Biblical legacy for the arts goes deeper than a checklist of permissible artifacts or warnings against inappropriate uses of art. Unlike the succession of manifestoes that characterize art history, the Bible does not offer a theory about the arts. Rather, it offers a theory about theories, a broad conceptual framework upon which the whole range of human artistry can build. Moreover, the Bible is itself a major source of Western culture. The most basic achievements of our civilization, including the arts, have been shaped by the Bible's profound influence.

The ancient Hebrews, the people of the Bible, contributed one strain of our civilization's lineage; the ancient Greeks contributed the other. Both had different assumptions about the arts. The Hebrews saw art in terms of creation; the Greeks saw art in terms of imitation. Christianity, in which "there is neither Jew nor Greek" (Galatians 3:28), brought the two cultures and their two views of art together. The result was a fruitful tension that has energized the arts in the past and that has the potential to do so today.

THE CREATION

The primal Biblical text for the arts is the first three chapters of Genesis. God's act of creation is the ultimate model and enabler of human artistry. That God created the universe out of nothing, according to His own free and sovereign will, is a radical concept. Other world religions and mythological systems posit a preexisting matter, which was merely given shape by some organizing power. The Bible makes clear that the universe was not merely shaped but created from nothing. This means that God's power and design underlie its every detail. The universe is God's work of art. God's creation established the foundational necessities—the physical, aesthetic, and human realities—that make subsequent art possible.

As Elizabeth Douglas has observed, the first chapter of Genesis describes God establishing at the very onset of creation the prerequisites for art—light, space, and unity.[1] God's initial act in creation was to call forth *light* (Genesis 1:3-4). All of the visual arts involve working with light: separating light from darkness (thereby emulating what God did); copying the properties of light as it illuminates a surface; playing with the colors that light makes possible.

God next established *space*, separating the waters from the sky, so that there is now an "above" and "below" (Genesis 1:6-7). The universe became three-dimensional. Ever since, sculptors, architects, and visual artists rendering perspective and balance have been organizing space.

God then created the details, calling forth earth, vegetation, stars, "living creatures" for the water, earth, and sky, and finally human beings. Such diverse creatures were to replicate themselves in an orderly way, "according to their kinds," and were to exist in harmony with each other in obedience to their Maker. Thus, *unity*, the third prerequisite for art, is built into creation. God's creation is teeming with variety, with each facet contributing to the whole. He continues to orchestrate the seemingly random details of life into His providential design. This, on a far lesser scale, is what an artist does in making the parts coalesce into a whole, arranging details so that they take their place in a larger unifying design. Such unity in diversity has always been a key principle of aesthetics and the goal of a good artist.[2]

God's creativity culminated in the forming of human beings, who themselves were empowered to create. God thereby multiplied His creativity exponentially. God built creativity into the universe, just as He enabled all living things to replicate themselves, giving them a part in the ongoing creation of new life.

God, like an artist painting a self-portrait, expressed Himself by creating Adam and Eve in His own image (Genesis 1:27). The concept of human beings having been created in God's image is unutterably profound, the basis for the preciousness of all human life (Genesis 9:6) and the foundation of all human greatness. This is not to say that even the unfallen Adam was in any measure equivalent to God, any more than a self-portrait, daubs of paint on canvas, is in any way equal to its human artist. The artist's life, actions, and personality go far beyond what is portrayed in the flat, static image in the frame—a metaphor that helps explain how God is far above our comprehension.

The doctrine that human beings were created in God's image is central to a Biblical view of humanity. It means, among other things, that since God is personal, human beings are personal. Those qualities that go into being a person—consciousness, the capacity to think and to feel, to will, act, respond, communicate, and enter into relationships—are inherent in human beings as in no other part of creation. Personhood is grounded in the person of God. Part of God's personality is His ability to make things, a capacity inherent also in those who share His image.[3]

Genesis next describes how these human beings were given dominion over what God had made (Genesis 1:28). This too has implications for the arts. Artists' capacity to mold raw materials until they do their bidding is a manifestation of that dominion. The ability to capture the beauty of creation in art must be part of that loving stewardship assigned to Adam and his descendants.

God also gave Adam autonomy of language. "Now the Lord God had formed out of the ground all the beasts of the field and all the birds of the air. He brought them to the man to see what he would name them; and whatever the man called each living creature, that was its name" (Genesis 2:19). Although the creation itself was brought about by God's Word and although the capacity for language is intrinsic to the divine image, God allowed Adam to devise his own language. Adam was given his own sphere of linguistic creativity, a chance to exercise his dominion and to take an active part in laying the foundations of human culture.

The Christian author Walter Wangerin, Jr., has seen in the act of "naming" the essence of what he does as an artist.[4] A writer "names" by rendering experiences or ideas in language, thereby making them comprehensible and enabling others to recognize them. Other kinds of artists use visual or musical language, of a sort, to call aspects of the world to our attention and to comment on them with a distinctly human voice. The Scripture about Adam being allowed to devise names for the animals prevents us from assuming that there is one holy language or one holy culture, since such things are devised by human beings and not by God. Expression can be purely human.

Adam's sphere of autonomy, of course, was not absolute; he had to exercise it in obedience to God. When he fell, rejecting God's purposes, everything was ruined. Even nature was brought down by the rebellion of its master. Unity gave way to strife. Sin shattered the divine image. God's artistry in making the physical universe and human beings was not totally effaced, only vandalized.

Nevertheless, artistic creativity after the fall remains as a sign of God's original creation. Those who argue that human beings are merely animals have a difficult time accounting for art. Our popular image of "cavemen" as apelike beasts derives from Darwin's theory of evolution. Actually, what little we do know about the ancient dwellers in caves, as Chesterton has pointed out, is that they decorated their caves with exquisite paintings.[5] The universe is not merely functional; it is also beautiful. Human beings do more than survive; they can perceive the beauty of the universe and go on to make new objects of beauty. This human impulse to create is an inescapable mark of the divine image.

MONOTHEISTIC ABSTRACTIONISM

Ever since the fall, however, human beings have been in revolt against God, turning their gifts against the Giver. Nature and the self have been twisted by being turned into objects of worship. Art, along with nearly every other human faculty, has been tainted by the fall. Indeed, one of the first phases of the disintegration brought by sin was the usurpation of art for the purpose of idolatry. Fallen humanity, writes Paul, "exchanged the glory of the immortal God for images made to look like mortal man and birds and animals and reptiles" (Romans 1:23).

The seriousness of idolatry is evident in that God specifically condemns this misuse of art in the Ten Commandments: "You shall not make for yourself a graven image, or any likeness of anything that is in heaven above, or that is in the earth beneath, or that is in the water under the earth" (Exodus 20:4 RSV). The commandment forbids idolatry, both that practiced by the Hebrews' Canaanite neighbors and, as we have seen, its more sophisticated forms. It does not forbid all representational art, as the instructions for the Tabernacle and the Temple make clear. And yet, the warnings against making "likenesses of anything" strike at the essence of representational art.

To the Hebrews, statues that imitated the forms of animals or human beings were associated with idolatry. As a result, they were very cautious when it came to realistic art. This hesitancy to make "likenesses" did not mean that the people of the Old Testament rejected art. Rather, their artistry was channeled in a different direction. The ancient Hebrews found a way of making art without making likenesses.

FIG 9.1   *Jerusalem painted pottery*

Whereas the other ancient civilizations of the Egyptians, the Greeks, and the Assyrians were making artifacts covered with images of animals, human beings, and their gods, the Hebrews were making artifacts such as these (Fig. 9.1).

On this pottery are patterns, shapes, and colors arranged in aesthetically pleasing designs. The art is not "of" something in the external world, which could be construed as a "likeness" forbidden by the commandment. This art is nonrepresentational.

Nonrepresentational art is nothing unusual or radical. The colors and patterns of clothing, the design on the wallpaper, the pattern of a quilt, the Washington Monument, and most decorative schemes are designed solely for their aesthetic impact, not as any sort of likeness. Abstract art in this sense can be thought of as form without content. The problem with much modern abstract art is not that it refuses to portray the outside world, but that its form as well as its content is minimal or nonexistent. The Hebrew pottery with its artistic control and aesthetic attractiveness is a far cry from modern abstract minimalism, with its lack of order, its ugliness, and its triviality.

Monotheistic abstractionism has continued throughout the Jewish tradition, which has generally rejected representational art while remaining extremely creative. Josephus records how the Jews rioted when Pontius Pilate brought into Jerusalem Roman ensigns that included a bust of Caesar. These were not used for religious purposes, nor did the Jews object on purely political grounds, since the purely symbolic ensigns used by Pilate's predecessors did not occasion such an uproar.[6] That Roman coins were engraved with a human face was likewise scandalous. Native Jewish ensigns, coins, and other artifacts would be adorned with geometric designs, floral patterns, and symbols such as the Menorah, all skillfully worked and aesthetically pleasing. This approach to art (although not always so strict in rejecting representation altogether) continued in the Diaspora and in the succeeding development of Jewish art.

That such art escaped the strictures of the commandment against graven images suggests that while the content of art might prove dangerous, aesthetic form in itself is safe. The Hebrew potter could adorn a jar by making lines, shapes, and patterns to please the eye. The only criteria were aesthetic ones. Moreover, conceiving and executing such nonrepresentational designs, which were not based on anything already existing, was a sort of creation from nothing, a shadow of what God did when He created the universe without imitating any preexisting forms.

That God's Word is preserved in writing, that the jots and tittles of the pen on paper convey direct communication from the transcendent God, provided another point of departure for monotheistic abstractionists. Calligraphy—"beautiful writing"—became an art form. Jewish scribes copying out the Torah would draw the holy letters in such a way that they bloomed into startlingly beautiful designs. Later, the Christians who had to copy out the Bible by hand in those days before printing presses lavished their devotion to the Word in illuminated manuscripts, in which writing and visual art of the highest and most intricate order merge into one (Fig. 9.2).

The Islamic tradition perhaps carried this practice of making art from words the farthest. Taking a very strict iconoclastic position, Islamic artisans would take texts from the Koran and use the shape of its Arabic letters like motifs in a Bach fugue, multiplying them and spinning off variations into stunningly complex visual patterns. The mosque in Fig. 9.3 is decorated with nothing more than written words.

This Middle Eastern heritage of monotheistic abstractionism is a rich legacy, too little appreciated in Western art. Islam's radical understanding of the prohibition of images has nourished a centuries-old tradition of the most sublime abstractionism. One need not be a follower of Islam to appreciate its art. The implications of this form for those who believe in one sovereign God—whether

FIG 9.2   *Initial page from Lindisfarne Gospels*

Islamic, Jewish, or Christian—can be illustrated by considering the design of a Persian carpet. The isolated details of the carpet will seem wild and frenzied, a riot of colors and free-wheeling shapes. Looked at from a distance, however, the chaotic individual forms harmonize into a complex but overarching pattern, one beautiful design. Such art is appropriate for believers in one sovereign God who orchestrates all of human freedom and all of the apparent randomness of life into His providential design.[7] Here is a synthesis of freedom and order in which the creativity and imagination of the artist have free

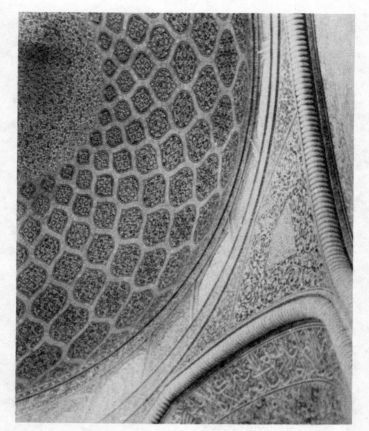

FIG 9.3   *Mosque of Shaykh Lutfullah, Isfahan, Iran*

scope, and yet every detail takes its place within a larger order, an all-embracing aesthetic design.

Monotheistic abstractionism thus reconciles form and freedom. The artist has the maximum freedom to create, bound by no requirements to imitate the external world. At the same time, the free outpourings of the imagination are orchestrated in an orderly way according to objective aesthetic principles of symmetry, balance, and harmony of form and color. According to Francis Schaeffer, one of the most crucial issues, manifesting itself in nearly every cultural sphere—in the arts, politics, law, ethics, and theology—is the problem of form and freedom. "If there is not a proper balance between form and freedom," Schaeffer observes, "then the society will move into either of two extremes. Freedom, without a proper balance of form, will lead to chaos and to the total break-down of society. Form, without a proper balance of freedom, will lead to authoritarianism, and to the destruction of individual and social freedom."[8] This balance, Schaeffer shows throughout his writings, is found in "the Christian consensus which gave us free-dom within the Biblical form."[9]

In art, the passion for form without freedom has given us the arid classicism of the Enlightenment and the hyper-realism of the scientific materialists. The passion for freedom without form has given us the self-indulgences and moral nihilism of much contemporary art. The balance of artistic freedom and aesthetic form should be a hallmark for Christian artists. That this is, in fact, a legacy of Middle Eastern art inspired by the iconoclasm of the Jews should be expected. Contemporary Christian artists might experiment with monotheistic abstractionism, thus challenging the abstractionism of modern art in its own terms while building on their own ancient legacy.

IMITATING GOD'S CREATION

At the creation, the primal moment of God's artistry, there was no question of being representational. God made everything—colors, forms, structures—solely according to His will (Revelation 4:11). God is the original abstract artist. Without models or patterns, God made all things visible and invisible from nothing. He invented colors, the laws of geometry, the shapes of animals. His works are so various and, we are just now learning, so intricate, that they are staggering.

Consider the structure of an atom, the properties of light, the existence of such things as quasars, amoebas, strawberries, the human body, blue whales—each unfathomably complex and intricately crafted. Wherever we look, on whatever scale, whether it be the vast, seething, lifeless world of the planet Jupiter or the complicated world teeming with life that exists in a drop of water, whether it be as unimaginably huge as the Spiral Nebula or as unimaginably small as the DNA molecule, we find the caring creativity of the Lord lavished on all of His works (Psalm 104).

The plenitude and magnificence of God's works are all around us. Annie Dillard has observed that God is infinitely more imaginative than we are. Pretend, she says, that "You are God. You want to make a forest, something to hold the soil, lock up solar energy, and give off oxygen. Wouldn't it be simpler just to rough in a slab of chemicals, a green acre of goo?" Instead, God creates a forest ecosystem. "A big elm in a single season might make as many as *six million* leaves, wholly intricate, without budging an inch; I couldn't make one."

> We have not yet found the dot so small it is uncreated, as it were, like a metal blank, or merely roughed in—and we never shall. We go down landscape after mobile, sculpture after collage, down to molecular structures like a mob dance in Breughel, down to atoms airy and balanced as a canvas by Klee, down to atomic particles, the heart of the matter, as spirited and wild as any El Greco saints. And it all works. "Nature," said Thoreau in his journal, "is mythical and mystical always, and spends her whole genius on the least work." The Creator, I would add, churns out the intricate texture of least works that is the world with a spendthrift genius and an extravagance of care. This is the point.[10]

Annie Dillard compares molecular structures, atoms, and sub-atomic particles to the works of specific artists. Conversely, these artists, for all of their wild abandon, can be thought of as reflecting the structures of the created universe.

When God is understood as the primal artist, depictions of His works can be a means of honoring Him. Recognizing and imitating those forms that God chose to create, even that of a pomegranate, can be a means of praise. The prohibition of images notwithstanding, Christians seem to gravitate towards representational art, and this may be one reason. Islam, in its view of God as well as its art, may be *too* abstract. God is not abstract. He affirms the physical universe He made, going so far as to become incarnate in that universe in Jesus Christ. Depictions of God's works may thus seem more satisfying than emanations of the merely human imagination.

As a matter of fact, even abstract art depends on what God has made. No artist can invent a color. Every geometric form, every phenomenon of light, every texture, no matter how it is arranged, falls within the circle of God's original creation. We speak of artists creating, but that is something of a misnomer. Only God creates. Human beings can make things too, since God graciously multiplies His creativity in His creatures, but human beings are not autonomous. We can only make use, in our faint and halting way, of what God has first given us. Abstract art makes use of colors and forms taken from God's original creation. This may be why they are sometimes visually stimulating. Even the artists of the Middle East could not be completely abstract for long—floral patterns and other innocent images from nature often intrude into their abstract designs.

Realistic artists too can reconcile form and freedom. The artist's skill in devising the illusion of reality is a mark of obedience to the forms as designed by God. The best realistic paintings suggest too the artist's personal response to the subject, the sense of awe or delight or passion or love with which the artist views what is being painted. This personal vision gives scope to the artist's own creative freedom, even in a realistic work. (Notice, for example, the range of realism in the illustrations of chapter 4 and how even a very realistic scene will express the artist's thought.)

Representational art uncovers and discloses the greatness of the Lord's works. Art draws attention to the beauty and significance of what is all around us, but which we normally ignore simply because it is so familiar.[11] By lifting up a commonplace object, removing it from its everyday context, an artist can help us see its true God-given nature. We usually have oranges at our house, but it was not until I saw a particular painting of some oranges that I really noticed and appreciated their beauty—the brightness of their color, the complex texture of an orange peel, the way light shines on them. By "defamiliarizing" experience, art can enrich our lives as it opens our eyes to the richness of God's world. Art can thus be a way to "ascribe to the Lord the glory due his name" (Psalm 96:8).

THE HEBREWS AND THE GREEKS

While the Hebrews were practicing nonrepresentational art, the Greeks were perfecting art as representation. The pagan Greeks knew nothing of the prohibition of likenesses, so in their culture representational art flourished. The Greeks believed that the essence of art is imitation.[12] Their vases show depictions of their gods and renderings of animals, plants, and people.

Although the Greeks were the great pioneers of representational art, their work was not exactly realistic. Their own philosophy of creation is reflected in their art. Whereas the Hebrews believed that the universe was created out of nothing, the Greeks believed that the universe was made out of preexistent matter, which was shaped according to transcendent ideals. The artist was not to imitate the mere appearances of physical objects—the Greeks tended to scorn the material realm. Rather, the artist should imitate the ideals. In other words, art should not present a particular human being, warts and all. Rather, art should present a representative human being, what a human being *should* look like (Fig. 9.4).

FIG 9.4   *The Discus Thrower*

No actual human being looks this good. The proportions and formal perfection are ideal. For the Greeks, beauty means coming close to that ideal, which exists in the spiritual realm as the cosmic prototype for every object in existence.

The point is, even representational art is shaped by the world-view of its maker. Just as abstract art is actually bound to the possibilities inherent in the creation, representational art has a creative dimension. All may paint the same object, but an ancient Greek, an early Christian, a Deist, a materialist, and an existentialist would each produce a different work. "Realism" depends upon what one thinks is real.

Western art derives ultimately from the Greeks. This is why we are more accustomed to statues of people than we are to Persian carpets. Like the Greeks, most of us prefer art that "looks like something." A whole complex of ideas and assumptions accompanied Greek art, and many of our own ways of thinking and imagining derive from this tradition. We Westerners can read Homer, for example, or other Greek literature with very little difficulty. The descriptions are easy to imagine, and we are oriented to the characters and actions in the way we are used to from our own literature.

The Hebrews, though, had different aesthetic assumptions, as can be seen in the poetic imagery of the Bible. I have discussed the imagery of Hebraic poetry elsewhere,[13] but the points may be worth repeating in the present context and in greater detail. The Song of Solomon provides the best examples of Hebraic imagery at its most intense and its most alien:

> Behold, you are beautiful, my love, behold, you are beautiful!
> Your eyes are doves behind your veil.
> Your hair is like a flock of goats, moving down the slopes of
>   Gilead.
> Your teeth are like a flock of shorn ewes that have come up
>   from the washing, all of which bear twins, and not one
>   among them is bereaved.
> Your lips are like a scarlet thread, and your mouth is lovely.
> Your cheeks are like halves of a pomegranate behind your veil.
> Your neck is like the tower of David, built for an arsenal,
>   whereon hang a thousand bucklers, all of them shields of
>   warriors.
> Your two breasts are like two fawns, twins of a gazelle, that
>   feed among the lilies. (4:1-5 RSV)

How are we to "picture" these things? There are many images, but they seem ludicrous, lacking unity and coherence. The poetry mixes the most extravagant and dissimilar metaphors which distract from and in no way seem to describe what they are intended to represent. In what sense do doves, goats, shorn ewes, thread, pomegranates, towers, shields, and fawns feeding upon lilies describe a woman?

The difficulty we might have with these lines, however, is due entirely to our habit of reading like ancient Greeks. The Greek imagination and our own is primarily *visual*. The Hebrew imagination, on the other hand, is not primarily visual, but draws on a wide range of senses and associations.[14] When we read "your two breasts are like two fawns," we see a picture, in this case a jarring absurdity. When we realize that the image is not visual but *tactile*, the sensuousness of the description is overwhelming. The woman's cheeks do not *look* like pomegranates (which would mean a very bad complexion). Rather the poet has made an image of fragrance and perhaps, even more sensuously, of taste.

Hebraic imagery is also associative, with an image calling to mind other images and connotations, all of which suggest a texture of meaning. The eyes-like-doves metaphor seems to refer to the timorousness but liveliness of the dove, to the woman's reticence and modesty, a sense also conveyed in the metaphor of the fawns. The hair like goats is another tactile image, with associations from the shepherd's culture of wealth and well-being. The description of the teeth is also drawn from the pastoral life. It stresses, in another highly sensuous detail, their wetness, and in the characteristic Hebrew concern for how things are built, how they match each other, how even and well-formed they are. The description of the neck refers to the way she stands, tall and aloof, proud and inaccessible. Throughout are allusions not only to her physical desirability, but also to the overpowering attractiveness, nearly forgotten in the West but still present in other cultures, of chastity.[15]

Here is poetry of the highest order, describing the Shulamite, not one-dimensionally, but richly. The lover is attracted not only by what she looks like, but what she feels like when he touches her, what she tastes like, the associations of sheep fields and battle that she calls to his mind. Not only her appearance is described. Her character is suggested in these lines of lush complexity. This is not the eroticism of the voyeur—pornography tends to stress the visual and thus creates a sense of distance and detachment from the sexual "object." Rather, this is the eroticism of marriage, conveying an overwhelming sense of closeness, intimacy, and genuine love.

Reading the Bible, one encounters other differences between the Hebraic way of writing and that of the classical tradition that began with the Greeks and with which we are most familiar. Notice that the Bible never describes what Jesus or anyone else looked like. Nor are there extended spatial descriptions of "background," the leisurely description of setting and atmosphere taken for granted in Western literature. Homer, by contrast, is full of the most vivid visual descriptions—"white-armed Hera," the red-gold hair of Achilles, the exhaustively detailed picture of his immortal shield. Writers of the Western tradition have followed Homer, so that now one of the first tasks we ask of authors is that they orient us visually to their worlds so that we can "picture" the characters and their actions.[16]

The Bible, however, works from different aesthetic assumptions. For the Hebrews, one relates conceptually to other people not by seeing them but by hearing them. Thus, to take an important example, there is little talk of *seeing* God in the Bible. Such an experience is reserved for the future life. ("Blessed are the pure in heart, for they *will* see God" [Matthew 5:8].) For the people of the Bible, a god one can see, such as the Canaanites had, would not be a real god but an idol. Although one cannot see God, one can *hear* Him. God's *Word* is the basis for relationship with Him. Our imagination today is so visual that people often have difficulty in believing in a God they cannot see. We need to encourage them to "listen" to God, to read the Scriptures, expecting from God not a "vision" but an intimate, personal voice addressed to themselves.

The peculiarities of the Hebraic imagination may well be due to the prohibition of images, which tends to subvert purely visual, imitative descriptions. This is not to say that the sense of sight is unimportant or that there are no visual images in the Bible. There is simply a different conceptual emphasis. Much of the Scripture is difficult to picture. The Tabernacle and the Temple are described in exhaustive detail, and yet they are almost impossible to visualize. The emphasis is upon how the structures were built and how the parts fit together rather than what the unified whole looked like.

The Greek mind, according to Thorleif Boman, tends to be spatial, with concern for unity and static form. This is evident not only in art but in the systematizing tendency of Greek logic and analysis, which has reached us through Plato and Aristotle. The Hebraic mind, on the other hand, assumes that form is dynamic; this mind is iconoclastic, conscious that since God alone is absolute, all human or natural forms are limited and subject to judgment and change.[17]

Whereas the Greeks envisioned time spatially, in terms of cycles and moments that could be ritually reenacted, the Hebrews understood time historically, as a sequence that both had a beginning and looked toward an end. In this respect we have followed the Hebraic imagination. The Bible's concept of historicity, so different from that of mythical cultures such as the Greeks', has been taken over into Western culture fairly completely. Even aberrant philosophies such as Marxism and Darwinism have a linear view of time, a sense of progression rather than a series of eternally repeated cycles. Try as they might, they cannot escape the influence of the Bible.

Music may be particularly Hebraic. Music is nonrepresentational, an art without images, graven or otherwise. Furthermore, it is aural rather than visual. Music is also sequential and historical rather than spatial; that is, it exists solely in time, as a series of sounds that follow one another in order. It is little wonder that music is praised throughout Scripture and that, despite all the controversies in the church over other art forms, music is universally employed in Christian worship.

The Hebraic imagination—its nonvisual imagery, its dynamic form, its nonspatial patterns of organization—would seem to have great potential, as yet untapped, in inspiring new works of art and new ways to imagine.

CHRISTIANITY AND THE MERGING OF IMAGINATIONS

With the coming of Christ and the preaching of the gospel to the Gentiles, the two streams of the Hebraic and the classical began to run together. At the same time, the momentous event of the Incarnation made a difference for the imagination of each.

"Jews demand miraculous signs and Greeks look for wisdom," says Paul, "but we preach Christ crucified: a stumbling block to Jews and foolishness to Gentiles" (1 Corinthians 1:22-23). Jews were oriented to concrete action in history; Greeks were oriented to abstract rational discourse. To both the Hebraic and the Greek minds, the message of Christ was staggering: "The Word [*Logos*] became flesh and made his dwelling among us" (John 1:14).

The Greeks knew about the *logos*, the divine pattern and source of the ideals that underlie the universe. They conceived the *logos* spatially and abstractly, a highly intellectualized philosophical principle. To say that the *logos* became flesh, became matter, a category which the Greeks in their fastidious spirituality despised, was unthinkable.[18] Some Greeks came to believe in the deity of Christ, but they taught that He was not truly a man in the flesh. The crucifixion was an illusion, since what is spiritual cannot suffer; the resurrection was a purely spiritual event, not the literal rising of a three-day-old corpse. This is the heresy of Gnosticism, which the apostles and the early church battled and which still survives in the Christian Science movement, New Age cults, and the mainline academic theology that distinguishes "the Christ event" from the historical Jesus.

The Hebrews believed in the reality and value of the flesh. But to say that the Lord of Hosts, the one God, shares His glory and His being with anyone else was blasphemy. To identify the Messiah in any literal way with the one God, much less to assert that this God-man allowed himself to be humiliated and tortured to death by the enemies of Israel, seemed, at best, a mass of impossible contradictions and, at worst, simple paganism. From this perspective, Jesus might have been a great man, a prophet and moral teacher who died for the highest principles, but he certainly was not God. The denial of Christ's divinity is the heresy of Arianism, which historic Christianity has always condemned and which is still being taught in cults and liberal seminaries.

In Christ, God makes Himself *tangible*. "That which was from the beginning, which we have heard, which we have seen with our eyes, which we have looked at and our hands have touched—this we proclaim concerning the Word of life. The life appeared; we have seen it and testify to it, and we proclaim to you the eternal life, which was with the Father and has appeared to us" (1 John 1:1-2). The "Word of life" is not an intellectual abstraction, an invisible spiritual principle. Rather, says John, we have seen it, we have heard it, we have touched it. The Incarnation means that God reveals Himself in and by means of matter.

John, as he says, actually looked on, heard, and touched the Son of God through whom all things were made. The realm of matter—Mary's womb, the Bethlehem stable, the swaddling clothes, the process of growing up, of working with one's hands, the lakes and fields of Galilee, the garden of Gethsemane, the lacerations of the flesh, physical torture, rigor mortis—has been penetrated and indwelt by God Himself in Jesus Christ. Moreover, Christ placed at the center of Christian worship two *physical* acts, one involving simple water and one involving bread and wine, as uniquely proclaiming and manifesting His relationship to His people. The physical world and human senses were thus given a significance they never had under the Greeks or the Hebrews.

This point proved to be extremely important for art. The hesitancy to depict God through imagery seemed countered now by God Himself, who deigned to manifest Himself concretely in the flesh and form of a physical human being. Christianity allowed monotheists to turn to representational art. The Hebraic tradition and the Greek tradition, despite the often unresolved tensions between them, were brought together by Christianity to constitute Western culture. The legacy for the arts ever since is one of both creation and imitation.

PART THREE

CHRISTIANITY AND THE ARTS

CONTEMPORARY CHRISTIAN ARTISTS

A study of art history reveals a curious fact—every age has its Christian artists. They usually express themselves in terms of the dominant styles of the time, even when those styles have a secular origin. This is true even of the hymns we sing at church. Isaac Watts wrote neoclassical poetry. Fanny Crosby wrote Romantic poetry. Both, while shaped by their times, were orthodox, evangelical believers. Christianity is bigger than a single style. Because the Lord's mercies "are new every morning" (Lamentations 3:23), the gospel can never be outdated but can speak to every age in a fresh way.

This does not mean that Christianity can be successfully expressed in every style. Some styles are wholly interwoven with aberrant philosophies (indeed, such styles are often nothing more than philosophical statements, which is why they are so bad aesthetically). Sometimes Christians follow a particular style uncritically without recognizing the implicit contradictions between their faith and the style they are using to express it. Such incompatibility between form and content results in bad Christian art. (Late Victorian sentimentality, heavy metal nihilism, and pop culture consumerism would not seem to accord with a Biblical sensibility, but such misbegotten hybrids fill the Christian bookstores.)

The best Christian artists manage to be contemporary while strenuously resisting the characteristic errors of their time. They may adopt a "modern" secular style, but then challenge its assumptions in its own terms. Isaac Watts wrote skillful neoclassical verse, but his compositions such as "Joy to the World" and "When I Survey the Wondrous Cross" are more passion-filled than was usual in the Enlightenment. (Fanny Crosby does not similarly counter Romantic emotionalism, but she is much less of a poet than Watts.) Similarly, Christian artists of today often adopt a modern mode while countering the assumptions of the artistic establishment.

Modern art seems particularly bereft of Christian influence. And yet God still equips individuals with "the Spirit of God, with ability, with intelligence, with knowledge, and with all craftsmanship, to devise artistic designs" (Exodus 31:3-4 RSV). This chapter will focus on one modern artist (that is, a significant twentieth-century artist well known to art historians) and several contemporary artists (artists alive and working today). They each engage the imagination of their age without selling out to it. Each is profoundly original while upholding and continuing the Christian tradition. Each draws on Scripture for inspiration, resulting not in one static formula but a multitude of Biblically informed styles. Each achieves the Biblical balance of form and freedom.

GEORGES ROUAULT (1871-1958)

In the early twentieth century, the art world of Paris was shocked by a group of artists, led by Matisse, who employed bold, bright colors in startling ways. Instead of composing their paintings in terms of quasi-mathematical design schemes and formal organization, these painters stressed the impact and orchestration of color. They drew exaggerated shapes with heavy lines and vivid primary colors. These painters had learned from Van Gogh that color could be profoundly expressive. There was something passionate about these paintings, which in turn called forth passion in their viewers. Their unusual manipulation of vibrant colors—blue trees, red ground, green shadows—not only defamiliarized their subjects but also conveyed the artist's feelings about them. Their daring approach to color scandalized the artistic establishment, which was used to the soft hues of Impressionism or the objective formalism of Cézanne. These painters were denounced as "wild beasts." The French word for wild beast is *fauves*, so their approach became known as "Fauvism."

Georges Rouault was a "wild beast"; he was also a devout Christian. Fauvism was a variety of Expressionism. Whereas other Expressionists poured out their despair, Rouault poured out his faith. In doing so, he became what many consider to be the greatest religious artist since Rembrandt.[1]

Rouault had been a nominal Catholic and a rather conven-

FIG 10.1   ROUAULT, *Christ Mocked by the Soldiers*

tional painter. He turned to Fauvism at about the same time he turned to Christ. His conversion to an evangelical Catholicism—centered in an awareness of God's grace and a personal relationship to Jesus Christ—was accompanied by a radical change in his artistic style. His transformed inner life and his new sensitivity to human sin and God's love demanded new and unconventional means of expression.

Rouault's style manages to be both modern and deeply traditional, as is evident in *Christ Mocked by the Soldiers* (Fig. 10.1). This depiction of Christ, however expressive and moving, does not attempt to be realistic in a photographic way. Its purpose is to call forth meaning and response rather than to reproduce appearances. Its degree of abstraction marks it as clearly modern.

And yet, look closer. Where else have you seen a picture formed by thick black lines that mark off fields of bright color? Think of the windows in church, with the heavy lead frames holding panes of dazzlingly bright glass and shaping them into depictions of Biblical episodes. Rouault as a young man began his artistic career as an apprentice to a restorer of stained glass windows. This work fired his love for luminous colors and would later fuel his religious imagination. The stained-glass-window quality of Rouault's style gives his work associations of holiness, even as it ties his modernism firmly into the most ancient traditions of Christian art.

As a Christian artist, Rouault did not paint only overtly religious subjects. In the first ten years after his conversion (1902-1912), Rouault painted 167 works, only six of which were explicitly religious.[2] In these works, though, his Christian sensibility is profoundly evident. Rouault got into the habit of attending courtroom trials. He would then paint the prisoners, the judges, and the moral drama that he was witnessing. Once he painted the expression on a man's face as he was condemned to be executed. Sometimes he would give the criminal and the judge the same face. He was not criticizing the judicial proceedings, nor was he merely recording what he saw like a courtroom artist for a newspaper. Rather the courtroom provided subject matter which he universalized, exploring his conviction that before God we are all on trial.

In this period, Rouault focused on the truth of human sin—our fallen nature and the consequent wretchedness of the human condition. He painted fugitives, hypocrites, the poor, and clowns. Accosted by a prostitute one day, Rouault was horrified at her plight, leading to a long (and controversial) series of paintings of prostitutes. These works are grotesque and repellent, caricatures of homely women desperately trying to be attractive so that their sexual exploitation can continue. Rouault shows in no uncertain terms the repulsiveness of sin, while at the same time conveying a deep compassion for the sinners. In doing so, he is perhaps imitating the double vision of God, whose condemnation of our sin does not negate the love He has for us.

Rouault was severely criticized even by his Christian friends for the "ugliness" of these early paintings. "Rouault agrees . . . that God is the source of beauty," observes William Dyrness. "But apart from the touch of this master-creator what is striking in this world is not the beautiful but the ugly."[3] Rouault knew the truth of human depravity, that "when one looks at man apart from God, there is only evil to be seen."[4] The faces of the soldiers mocking Christ hint at this evil (Fig. 10.1). Ernest Hello, a French Christian who influenced Rouault, remarked, "Art ought to be one of the forces that heals the imagination; it must say that evil is ugly."[5]

In the next phase of his work (1913-1932), Rouault turned to depictions not so much of human degradation but of the sufferings of Christ. More specifically, Rouault put Jesus into the scenes of human wretchedness that he had painted before. *Christ Mocked by Soldiers* (Fig. 10.1), painted in this period, acquires even more resonance when we realize that it is another one of his courtroom paintings. Rouault had shown the human condition in his courtroom scenes. We all must stand trial before God's righteous judgment, and we are all condemned by His law. Rouault's series on the trial of Christ, however, shows the Son of God taking our place in the tribunal. Jesus, in His innocence, accepts the sentence that rightfully belongs to us criminals.

Similarly, Rouault's earlier paintings of fugitives—refugees, the homeless, families running away—depict human rootlessness, the sense that we are not at home in this world. Rouault continued the motif, employing the same elements as in his earlier paintings, in several renditions of the flight to Egypt (Matthew 2:13-18). This time the fugitives were Mary, Joseph, and the Baby Jesus. Rouault continued to paint scenes of human suffering and death—but this time Jesus is there (on a crucifix over the deathbed in *De Profundis*, standing behind the abandoned children in *Christ in the Suburbs*).

Rouault's next phase (1933-1940) returned to depictions of human beings, but this time he focused not on their sin but on their significance in light of Christ. Rouault's first period explored our sinful condition under the Law; the second explored the gospel of redemption through Jesus Christ. His third period can be seen as exploring sanctification, the spiritual life put into motion by the cross. Whereas before he would paint complete human figures, now he concentrated on depicting the face. His faces of human beings, interspersed with paintings of the face of Christ, are often poignant and sometimes tragic, but they always affirm the value of his subjects, suggesting their spiritual inwardness and evoking love. Critics have commented upon Rouault's way of making the eyes come alive, in such marked contrast to the lifeless eyes in most modern portraits.[6] The difference no doubt has to do not only with technical skill but with worldview. Rouault believed in the value of personality and in the fathomless depths of the immortal soul.

Recurring subjects for Rouault, especially in this period, were circuses and clowns. Rouault loved the circus for its freedom, its play, and its laughter. It became a metaphor for life as it should be, in contrast to the degraded hopelessness of "real life" as experienced in the sinful world. Rouault became fascinated with the circus performers, who put on a joyous show but then lived their own private lives of hardship. He played with the contrast between the costume and the person. Sometimes, paradoxically, his clowns would be sad; sometimes they would be yearning for something beyond their clown suits.

This print from *Miserere* demonstrates both Rouault's clown motif and the uncanny expressiveness of his faces (Fig. 10.2).

The clown is sad, a paradox that suggests the complexities in every human being. Rouault has given the work a caption: "Who Does Not Paint Himself a Face." The clown, putting on cheerful makeup to mask his actual pain, is an emblem for the human condition—the fronts we put on, the roles we play to hide our true, vulnerable and sinful selves.

Rouault's fascination with clowns points to an even deeper Christian dimension. Life, because it ends in Heaven, is a comedy. For all of the sadness in his work, Rouault, like Dante, holds to the comic sense of life—to the joy made possible when we see ourselves in all of our foolishness from the perspective of our happy ending in Heaven.[7]

Rouault's last period (1941-1958) is characterized by serenity. He experimented with landscapes, including Biblical scenes, and returned in a different way to his earlier subjects—circuses, judges, fugitives, and Christ. The difference is the style, animated now by a sense of movement (accomplished by curved rather than angular forms) and color that is even more sumptuous than ever. All of his earlier strains come together in these last years. Studying the faces, one critic noticed how Rouault, after first portraying human depravity, next showed "Christ bearing on His visage the sin of man."[8] In this last period, "The face of sinful man, which Rouault took to give to Christ, has been given back to man by the Savior, but redeemed and appeased."[9]

Rouault's masterpiece may be his series of prints entitled *Miserere*, an allusion to the Latin title of Psalm 51, David's prayer of repentance. Ironically, for such a master of color, these fifty-eight engravings are in stark black and white. Begun soon after World War I and not finished until after World War II, the series was exe-

FIG 10.2   ROUAULT, *Who Does Not Paint Himself a Face*
from *The Miserere* Series

cuted over three of Rouault's artistic phases and includes nearly all
of his characteristic themes and motifs. The immediate subject of the
work is the horrors of war, which Rouault saw as symptoms of a
deeper spiritual sickness.

Rouault included a quasi-poetic caption for each print. These
captions often work to universalize the specific visual image, broadening its implications to apply to the human condition as a whole.
The picture of the sad clown above (Fig. 10.2), which is part of the
series, is given a greater resonance and a wider application by the

caption "Who Does Not Paint Himself a Face." Similarly, a picture of an agonized prisoner is labeled "Are We Not All Convicts?"

In *Miserere*, harrowing skeleton images of death ("Man Is a Wolf to Man"), complacency ("Upper-Class Woman Thinks to Have a Reserved Seat in Heaven"), and modern emptiness ("Street of the Lonely") are punctuated with tender drawings of Christ, who bears all of this cruelty and suffering in His own body on the cross. One print from *Miserere* depicts the suffering of a family at the wartime death of a father and husband (Fig. 10.3).

The scene is poignant—the wife's head is bowed; the child is crying. Yet on the wall the face of Jesus shines. The massive figure holding the body has angel's wings. Rouault is painting not only a picture of suffering, but of spiritual strength within that suffering. His meaning is further developed with the caption: "The Just Man, Like Sandalwood, Perfumes the Blade That Cuts Him Down." Without minimizing the pain and while affirming his outrage at human cruelty, Rouault shows death is no reason to despair, that "precious in the sight of the Lord is the death of his saints" (Psalm 116:15).

The French critic Christian Zervos has argued that Rouault's genius is in the way he balanced authority and freedom. Rouault's work exhibits great freedom in its expressiveness, subject matter, and technical experimentation. His freedom is given coherence, however, by his willingness to submit to an authority beyond himself. Such authority came not only in his adherence to Christianity, according to Zervos; it is also evident in his fidelity to the human condition, to artistic technique, and to the continuity of tradition.

With most modern artists, writes Zervos, "freedom finds itself perverted to such a degree that it is turned against itself and becomes formalism."[10] The unrestrained expressivism of modern art results, ironically, in minimalist gestures, slick cynicism, and self-conscious posing—an arid formalism drained of everything human. Paradoxically, artists who reject all authority cannot even manage to be free. In Rouault's case, shifting to Francis Schaeffer's terminology, form and freedom come together. The result is art that is richly human because it is richly spiritual.

Another mark of a Christian—one might say evangelical— artist exemplified in Rouault is his portrayal of both sin and grace. Much Christian art today of the sort sold in bookstores is "uplifting" in a sentimental and optimistic way, as if looking on the sunny side were a cure for the cancer of human sin. Today we are so obsessed with positive thinking and feeling good about ourselves, we hardly see ourselves as desperate sinners in sore need of Jesus.

FIG 10.3   ROUAULT, *The Just Man, Like Sandalwood,*
Perfumes the Blade That Cuts Him Down
from *The Miserere* Series

Evangelical artists must confront the reality of sin and awake us to the ugliness of the human condition apart from Christ. At the same time, evangelical artists must convey the reality of God's love for us sinners in Jesus Christ. Rouault's art expresses both sin and grace. His sinners may be repulsive, but they are also pathetic, clearly in need of mercy and clearly, in all of their degradation, objects of God's love. Rouault depicts the undeserved favor that is grace in his most negative-seeming work. Just as he never waters down the ugliness of sin, Rouault never compromises the specificity of the gospel. The answer to the human condition is found not in philosophical platitudes but in Jesus—incarnate, nailed, and resurrected.

CONTEMPORARY CHRISTIAN ARTISTS

Today a host of Christians are pursuing the arts. One organization of Christian artists, Christians in the Visual Arts (CIVA), has a mailing list of over 1800 names. Another organization, Christians in the Arts Networking (CAN), ties together organized groups of Christian artists that exist in nearly every major city. In many different ways, these artists are exercising their crafts and employing their God-given talents. Their faith might sometimes make them pariahs in today's art world, but despite the obstacles, many are forging successful careers.

Ironically, most Christians and the church as a whole seem almost oblivious to this large number of Christian artists in their midst. Although Christians are awakening to the need to exert a Biblical influence on our fast-declining culture, they sometimes overlook the pivotal role of Christian artists, who are on the front lines of the cultural battleground. Fighting crucial aesthetic and spiritual battles, these artists need the tactical support of the church. So often what they receive instead is disapproval ("Why don't you get a real job?"), mistrust ("There is too much immorality in the art world for a real Christian to be involved in it"), and sheer lack of understanding ("Your art is too modern"). The church needs to validate its artists, not drive them away. Artists, in turn, need to be discipled by the church. To minister to artists, the church must treat them with sensitivity and understanding, affirming their God-given vocation and utilizing their gifts.

One way of supporting Christian artists and of influencing the art world as a whole is patronage. The power of the marketplace affects the art world no less than it affects the stock exchange. The wealthy elite, large corporations, investment speculators, government grants, museums, and foundations supply the money that drives the art establishment and that helps determine its nature. By patronizing worthy artists, churches, businesses, and individuals can enable those artists to survive and their works to exert their influence on the culture as a whole.

I am not saying that art should be judged solely on the basis of the artist's religious beliefs. Christian artists can make bad art, and non-Christians can make good art. And yet the values and beliefs of the artist have a way of manifesting themselves in the work. If the aesthetic poverty of much modern art is the result of nihilistic worldviews, we might look for a richer worldview to inspire richer art.

Art should be approached with understanding and discernment. Many of the prints and sculptures we use to decorate our homes and that are sold in Christian bookstores reflect worldviews that have nothing to do with Christianity. The figurine that gives us a warm feeling because of its cuteness and emotionalism may have more to do with Romanticism than Biblical Christianity. The wildlife art may owe more to the naturalism of Charles Darwin than to a Biblical view of nature. Christians are free to enjoy these works if they wish, but they should do so while discerning their implications. They should certainly not set up such works as standards for all Christian artists to follow. Those who do wish to support a Biblically informed art should be prepared to accept a more complex and comprehensive aesthetic.

What follows are discussions of four contemporary Christian artists. These are by no means all of the Christians who are expressing their faith and their art in interesting and sophisticated ways. The problem in coming to grips with contemporary art of any kind is that there has been no winnowing, no test of time, no way even to know all of the work currently being done. What is contemporary, by definition, is what is happening now, at the present moment, encompassing multitudes of artists who are not widely known and myriads of works that few people have seen yet. My own knowledge of contemporary Christian art is woefully incomplete. I offer these four as representative examples of what contemporary Christian artists are doing today and of the sophisticated ways Biblical truth can be expressed artistically.

EDWARD KNIPPERS

Edward Knippers is a Christian artist who has been attracting the attention of the secular art world, with exhibitions in major museums that have attracted important critical attention.[11] He has done so, interestingly enough, not by following the secular trends (the path taken by more timid artists), but by flying in their face.

Whereas conventional Modernist theory holds that art must be "pure," far above the need to "tell a story," Knippers's work is unabashedly narrative. Whereas conventional modern art tends to the abstract or the ethereal, Knippers's work is blatantly physical. Whereas contemporary art might affect "spirituality" in a vague, mystical, New Age sort of way, Knippers's art is explicitly, confrontationally Biblical.

In a paper given to a Christian artists' conference, Knippers wrestles with the question of what makes a work of art Christian.[12] Reacting against the minimalism and nihilism of Abstract Expressionism, many Christian artists have felt that simply being realistic or asserting a meaningful content are ways of being Christian in one's art. Attending to God's creation and to the possibility of meaning are indeed important, according to Knippers, but today non-Christian artists are also rediscovering realism and the communication of meaning in art.

Nor is a concern for "spirituality" enough for a truly Christian art. Non-Christian artists are also experimenting with "spiritual" art, employing eerie images, symbolism from the world's religions, and evocations of meditative experiences. To be spiritual, however, Knippers insists, is not the same as being Christian. All religions are concerned with the spiritual, Knippers observes, just as all water is wet.

> But the major issue to be considered when it comes to water is not its wetness, but its drinkability. One can die of thirst in the presence of most of the world's water. As with water, so it is with religion—it is not how the religions of the world are alike (that they are spiritual) that is important, but how they are different. Which one can give life and give it more abundantly? Christianity is that life-giving religion. (Frankly, I think we have more than enough spiritual art—art that sees anything vague as somehow uplifting, and anything uplifting as life-affirming and positive, and the positive is always good, and the negative is always bad. Hogwash! We must dare to say that it is the *truth* that is ultimately uplifting and life-affirming no matter how negative it might be. Further, we can only know the truth through the One who is the Way, the Truth, and the Life.)[13]

Knippers's dismissal of vacuous spirituality and his insistence upon the particularity of the Christian message has implications for not only New Age trendiness but for much of the "uplifting" art popular with Christians.

Historically, according to Knippers, distinctively Christian art has taken three forms: symbolism (depictions of the cross, the sacramental cup, the baptismal water), icon (depictions of Christ), and narrative (depictions of Biblical events or the life stories of the saints). For Knippers, even symbols and icons point ultimately to the underlying narratives that give them their meaning. Indeed, narrative is God's chosen means of revelation:

> Although God has used other means of communication with us, the Ten Commandments for example, most often He has used narrative. From Genesis 1 through the history of the Jewish people and the prophets to the parables and Christ's passion and death on the Cross, God has made His nature plain through recountable events and stories in time and space.[14]

Because the Christian message is inextricably bound to the Word of God, the great subject for the Christian artist must be the narratives of the Bible.

Knippers is not advocating mere Bible illustration nor rote repetition of traditional subjects. He seeks to continue and revitalize what in fact Christian artists have always done. "The visual repetition of the Gospel themes—the narration of our faith—must come creatively from the vitality of the believing heart, inspired by Grace, and through skilled hands trained for the task."[15] Consider how he does so in *The Gift (Sacrifice of Isaac)* (Fig. 10.4).

This rendition of Abraham sacrificing Isaac is more than an illustration of Genesis 22:1-14. Again, it is a meditation on the passage and a communication of its meaning as we are forced to contemplate the magnitude of Abraham's faith in all of its anguish and commitment. The old man is on the verge of slaying his son. Abraham holds his son's outthrust hand—a gesture both of affection, the father holding his son's hand, and struggle, as Abraham holds him down for the knife's thrust. There are, in fact, two competing focus points. On the left they hold hands; on the right the knife is about to touch the flesh. The tangle of brush on the makeshift altar, the contorted shapes, and the tension-filled composition charge the painting with energy and intensity.

The painting captures Abraham at the moment of God's intervention in his dilemma. The angel descends, and Abraham's anguished eyes are drawn away from his victim at the sound of God's message. At the right of the painting, literally hidden in the

FIG 10.4   EDWARD KNIPPERS, *The Gift (Sacrifice of Isaac)*

underbrush (between Isaac's foot and the tree branch), is the ram that has been provided as Isaac's substitute. The painting thus points to Christ as the Lamb of God who takes away the sin of the world (John 1:29) by bearing the full brunt of this sacrificial violence. Abraham's sacrifice was interrupted, and his son was spared. God, however, did not spare His Son. The gift (in the title) is not so much Abraham's gift to God, but God's gift to Abraham and to us all.

Knippers's Biblicism is diametrically opposed to the Modernist dictum that art should divorce itself from "literary"—that is, narrative—concerns. He also opposes what he terms the gnosticism of modern thought and of modern art. Abstract art, like New Age spiritualism, is wholly cerebral and otherworldly. Christianity, on the other hand, is centered in the tangible, concrete factuality of the physical world—in the creation, in history, and, supremely, in the Incarnation, God assuming flesh in Jesus Christ. As a result, Knippers's art revels in the physical.

Knippers paints bodies—solid, massive, unclothed. That his figures are often naked might spark controversy for some Christians despite his rigorous Biblical orthodoxy.[16] Nudity, however, is not necessarily pornographic. The Venus de Milo is beautiful, but hardly sexually stimulating. Franky Schaeffer has shown that aesthetic nudity, as opposed to pornographic exploitation, has always been a legitimate subject for art.[17] The medieval church, for example, distinguished between several types of nudity and its permissible use in art: "natural nudity" (depicting Adam and Eve or other accurate portrayals of historical events or the human form); "temporal nudity" (symbolizing poverty); "the nudity of virtue" (symbolizing the forthright simplicity of truth); and "criminal nudity" (depicting sin). Pious artists of the Reformation such as Dürer, Cranach, and Rembrandt also painted naked people occasionally, as have legitimate artists ever since (including Rouault). Artists, like doctors, cannot ignore the God-designed details of the physical body. Being overly prudish may owe more to nineteenth-century Victorianism than to anything in Scripture.[18] This by no means excuses pornographic art, which has existed in every age. Such voyeuristic depictions designed for lust rather than beauty should not be confused with the nude forms that adorn the Sistine Chapel.

Knippers's paintings are typically huge. The viewer is nearly overwhelmed by these monumental bodies, which are thrown into violent and emotion-charged action. We have seen how modern art often employs shock. Knippers is not above shocking his audience, although he shocks them with Christian concepts. *The Pest House (Christ Heals the Sick)* (Fig. 10.5) is an example of how ostensibly negative images can be employed aesthetically and for the service of the gospel.

This painting of leprosy and decay is twelve feet long and eight feet tall; it assaults the viewer (especially when the sores and rot are seen in color). Even the most jaded and sophisticated will feel uncomfortable and will want to avert their eyes. As always in Knippers's works, we are confronted with physicality, in this case with diseased bodies, some of which are little more than masses of putrescence. The close quarters, the bodies piled on each other, and the guttering candle evoke a fetid, claustrophobic atmosphere.

In the midst of this repulsiveness, we see one body that is whole. Jesus is actually *touching* these loathsome figures. His right hand, strong and forceful, reaches to the man covered with sores. His left hand is not only touching the man on the table. He appears to be pushing on him. His hand seems to be reaching inside of him. Christ heals the sick, as the title of this painting proclaims. The painting manifests His sublime power—what omnipotence could make this kind of wretchedness whole? It also dramatizes, in unforgettably concrete terms, His unfathomable love. He touches people no one else would touch.

Our revulsion at this scene of suffering is countered by Christ's compassion. The charnel house makes us uneasy because it reminds us so forcefully of our mortality, the weakness and the doom of our own flesh. This painting shows how Christ enters our mortal condition in His own flesh to heal our lethal sickness—the death and decay that comes from sin. Christ is not repelled by our uncleanness, but in His grace offers healing with His touch. The painting forces us to contemplate both the desperation of the human condition and the saving grace of Jesus Christ. In that sense, for all its seeming "negativism," it is a complex, aesthetically satisfying work of art that is eminently evangelical.

THEODORE PRESCOTT

Theodore Prescott, a sculptor, has likewise employed narrative art based on Biblical episodes, although that is not his sole focus as an artist.[19] He is particularly interested in the function of art in a community. The great Biblical motifs, repeated for centuries, have special significance for the community of believers. The social dimension of art is evident in the way the church has used art in worship and in the way art can provoke discussion, interaction, and involvement among its viewers.

In one sculpture, *Descent from the Cross,* Prescott took plas-

FIG 10.5   EDWARD KNIPPERS, *The Pest House (Christ Heals the Sick)*

FIG 10.6   THEODORE PRESCOTT, *Descent from the Cross*

ter casts of his friends and colleagues, using these modern and familiar people—part of his community—to take Christ's body down
from the cross. The effect is to make that narrative leap across time
(Fig. 10.6).

The individuals he portrays are hyper-realistic—their expressions, bearing, and clothing create an uncanny sense of recognition,
as if we are seeing people whom we know tenderly taking down the
body of our Lord. Prescott reports that he had planned to use a large
wooden cross, but that seemed inappropriate for the contemporary
context. Instead, he writes,

> I made a real metal cross. By "real" I mean something that
> works. The cross in the *Descent* could actually be used. Instead
> of spikes, nuts and bolts hold the body to the cross. Given our

FIG 10.7   THEODORE PRESCOTT, *Annunciation*

century's penchant for efficient killing, I made a portable (it comes apart), adjustable (one cross fits all sizes) crucifying machine.[20]

Translating the traditional imagery into contemporary terms by no means takes away from the historicity of what is portrayed; rather it intensifies the sense that "this really happened." Medieval, Renaissance, and Reformation artists likewise painted Biblical figures dressed in the contemporary clothing of their own day. The effect was to show that these remarkable events happened to ordinary people just like those looking at the painting. Strange costumes, evocations of alien culture, and reminders of the chasm of centuries may be historically accurate, but they can distance us from the event. A true sense of history will think of a past event not merely in its remoteness, but as a moment not qualitatively different from the present, a tangible happening which we might have witnessed. Prescott's work helps us to imagine the factuality of the Crucifixion.

At the same time, it universalizes the cross, in which all Christians are in fact personally involved (1 Peter 2:24). We Christians are all implicated in the historical cross, on which Jesus bore our personal sins in His crucified body so that we could be united in a relationship with Him and with the whole Body of believers. Prescott's sculpture depicts ordinary Christians—the sort we might see at a church dinner, a Bible study, or across the pew—caring for their Lord.

Prescott also experiments with more abstract or symbolic forms and employs modern technology in his art. He has been fascinated with neon—tubes of light that can be shaped, twisted, and made into illuminated sculpture. His *Annunciation* brings together the figurative and the symbolic, the traditional and the modern (Fig. 10.7).

Mary is a real woman—in modern dress, human, and even vaguely familiar. She is working at a table; a picture (of lilies) is on the wall; she has been baking the two loaves of bread. Such details heighten the sense of the commonplace, yet they resonate with nurturing, homey associations as well as deeper symbolism (the Bread of Life; the lilies of Easter).

The angel, on the other hand, is a sketch of light. The extreme realism of Mary is countered by the stylized abstractionism of the angel. The earthiness of Mary is balanced by the high-tech symbolism of the neon angel. These contrasting styles reflect the contrasts of the original Annunciation, in which the mundane and the transcendent, the earthly and the spiritual, the human and the divine were reconciled when the angel appeared to Mary, and she conceived by the Holy Spirit.

The most moving part of Prescott's sculpture is the way the light falls on Mary's face. The Biblical symbol of light, which is used to express the person of the triune God and the power of the gospel (1 John 1:5; Matthew 4:16), here sets forth—with theological precision and with the aid of modern electronics—the beauty of God's grace, which falls on us like a beam of light, reflected back in faith such as Mary's.

Contemporary Christian art is not always narrative. Prescott's fascination with neon and other unusual sculptural materials manifests itself in nonfigurative designs which also express his faith. For some time, he has been experimenting with a series of crosses. He has commented that "the crosses have allowed me to use the 'language' of modern sculpture in a way that the narrative pieces haven't. My goal is to make crosses whose forms, materials, and processes speak about the content and experience of the cross."[21] His sculpture *Icon* is made of coal, neon, and stainless steel (Fig. 10.8).

Coal is an unlikely material for a work of art, much less paired with neon light. Yet the cross was a place of contradiction. The dark element from the earth, dirty and common, is an appropriate emblem for our sinful earthy humanness that Christ took to the

FIG 10.8   THEODORE PRESCOTT, *Icon*

cross. The vertical light—that ancient symbol of grace—intersects and embraces the piece of coal. The tangle of glass, metal, and mineral brings together the massive and the delicate, the natural and the crafted, and a range of other opposites. They are all reconciled in the sculpture by light, in which the cross is suffused, becoming a beacon that fills the room.

SANDRA BOWDEN

Sandra Bowden takes a different approach to making Biblical art. She digs beneath the Greek tradition that has dominated Western art and studies the Old Testament to draw on the aesthetic possibilities of the Hebraic tradition. As a result, although she is an evangelical Christian, her work is especially popular in Israel. In her sense of time, place, and design, and in her awareness of the way God's Word is conveyed in human writing, her work helps to recover a distinctly Biblical imagination.[22]

"I see the physical earth as a celebration by the Creator," she has commented. "I paint the earth's beauty and truth, and, to me, this is a reflection of God."[23] Her interest in "the physical earth" is different from the classical and Romantic interest in "Nature." She does not intellectualize or worship the physical order. She does not paint objects of mathematical order, nor does she paint sublime Romantic vistas teeming with life. Rather she paints soil and rock and gorges, in browns and yellows and muted reds. The texture of her works is especially striking, creating a tactile sense of stone, dust, and desert.

Such a concern for physical concreteness manifests itself in a sense of place. The "physical earth" Bowden paints is the Holy Land. The actual sites of God's saving actions in history carry great significance for her, as they always have for the Jewish people. Bowden's paintings convey not only what the land looks like but a sense of its history. Whereas the Greeks saw time as a series of repeatable cycles, the Hebrews saw time as a series of discrete, historical moments under God's design. Bowden's art manages to incorporate a sense of time as well as place and vividly suggests the historicity of what God has done as recorded in the Bible.

The *Israelite Tel Suite* is a series of four prints depicting significant archeological sites in Biblical Israel. A "tel" is a mound covering the site of some ancient settlement, generally consisting of many layers of rubble and artifacts left by succeeding civilizations. In *Tel Megiddo*, Bowden brings together earth, time, and the Word of God (Fig. 10.9).

The surface of the tel is light green; the layers below are shades of yellow, orange, and brown. Each strata has a pronounced texture—the violent brush marks in the central level, the rubble-filled dirt below, and the nearly palpable, painstakingly drawn roughness of what appears to be bedrock but is actually a stone wall from the city's ancient gate. The strata, accentuated by the horizontal lines

FIG 10.9   SANDRA BOWDEN, *Tel Megiddo*

that divide the picture into three levels, form a cross section of archaeological time.

The circled lion is a drawing of an actual artifact unearthed from Tel Megiddo.[24] Each print in Bowden's *Israelite Tel Suite* is based on an actual archaeological dig and includes a similar representation of a key find made at the tel—an ancient calendar, a

Hebrew inscription, an idolatrous image. This lion seal from Megiddo bears an important Hebrew inscription: "belonging to Shema, servant of Jeroboam." Jeroboam was the rebel who fled from Solomon and who incited ten tribes to break from Solomon's successor, Rehoboam, splitting the Hebrews into the two kingdoms of Judah and Israel (1 Kings 11:26—14:20).[25] This lion seal—besides being a remarkable piece of ancient art in its own right[26]—is a fossil of Biblical history. Not only is it tangible evidence for the Biblical account of Jeroboam; it is an object used by an official who must have known this Biblical character firsthand.

Bowden's work of art is thus a complex meditation on time. She evokes the dust and dirt of an archaeological dig, showing the strata of centuries. The passing of so much time and so many civilizations makes us look at our own day as only a moment in the vast story of human history, the sort of perspective on the shortness of our days encouraged by Psalm 90. When we get to the bottom of the strata, we find an object used by a person named Shema, an official whose political power is no more but who was a human being no less than we are. The mention of Jeroboam jolts us into a recognition of Biblical history, that this tel, this man Shema, all of this history, and our own particular transitory lives are all taken up into the Word of God. This meditation on the past is further complicated when we realize that Megiddo is the Armageddon of Revelation 16:16. This tel evokes the future as well as the past, proclaiming God's judgment and God's victory in the past, the present, and the future.

Another facet of Sandra Bowden's Hebraism and her Biblicism is her interest in calligraphy. Jewish scholars and mystics have long been fascinated by the fact that God's own Word is manifested in writing, in the marks of ink on a page. The written words of Scripture, inspired by God Himself, thus constitute a kind of divinely inspired visual art. The Jews' reverence for the sacred Torah, laboriously and lovingly copied out by the scribes, has resonance too for Christians, who are assured by Jesus Himself that "not the smallest letter, not the least stroke of a pen" of the Old Testament will remain unfulfilled (Matthew 5:18). Bowden, a student of ancient languages, makes art out of Biblical writing.

One work entitled *He Spake and It Was Done* consists of a luminous green panel, at the top of which is a light like the sun. Emanating from this light is the Hebrew text of the creation account of Genesis 1. Framing the green panel is a white border embossed with more Hebrew letters spelling out, as if carved on stone, the words of Psalm 33:6, 9 (KJV): "By the word of the Lord were the heavens made. . . . He spake and it was done."

The story of Noah in Hebrew rendered in the form and colors of a rainbow, a crucifix icon formed by the seven last words of Christ in Greek, collages of Hebrew psalms and visual imagery are provocative examples of art centered both figuratively and literally in the Word.

For all of her Hebraism, Bowden's work is generally representational rather than purely abstract. She does, however, experiment with color and form in nonfigurative ways. Her print *Aaron's Breastplate* is a good example of what I have termed "Biblical abstractionism," a nonrepresentational design that comes directly from the Bible (Fig. 10.10).

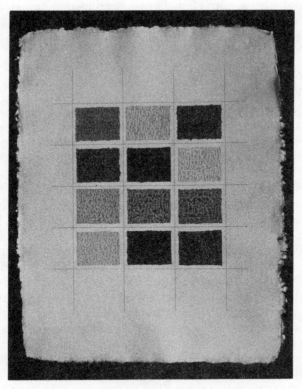

FIG 10.10   SANDRA BOWDEN, *Aaron's Breastplate*

These twelve fields of color are based on the Biblical description of Aaron's breastplate, which was to be worn by the high priest when he entered the Tabernacle's Holy Place to intercede for the people (Exodus 28:15-30). Bowden's bright colors—red, yellow, green; green, blue, white; orange, gold, purple; yellow, blue, green—correspond to the twelve precious stones that God commanded Bezalel to use in the design (Exodus 28:17-20). On these colored squares, Bowden has inscribed in Hebrew the account of Jacob giving his blessing to his twelve sons—the beginning of the twelve tribes of Israel (Genesis 49). According to the Bible, each gem was to symbolize one of the twelve tribes of Israel, so that "whenever Aaron enters the Holy Place, he will bear the names of the sons of Israel over his heart on the breastpiece of decision as a continuing memorial before the Lord" (Exodus 28:29). Aaron bearing the sign of each tribe—a precious gem, indicating their preciousness to God—is an emblem of Christ, our High Priest, bearing our names when He intercedes before the Father. This seemingly abstract work of art is not only Biblical in its meaning, but it is a reenactment of the art of Bezalel himself.

CLIFF McREYNOLDS

Not all Christian artists, of course, are working with explicitly Biblical subjects or forms. People of faith are free to paint portraits, draw flowers, carve wildlife, or enact abstract designs. God's sovereignty extends everywhere, and it is a serious mistake to limit Him or His servants to a narrowly defined sphere labeled "religious." The artists treated here work with distinctly Christian themes and subject matter, showing the continuing ability of the Bible to inspire significant works of art. Strictly speaking, however, the Bible gives a Christian dimension to all of life and to all of art.

Cliff McReynolds is hard to classify. His works are indeed forthrightly Christian, yet he does not restrict himself to the narratives of the Bible. His landscapes are astonishingly detailed and realistic; at the very same time, they are whimsical fantasies. In the vast scale of his work and in his care for the tiniest details, I see the Creator's creativity. McReynolds's is a good example of a sanctified imagination.[27]

As suggested earlier, the concept of human creativity is a legacy of the Bible's doctrine of the creativity of God. McReynolds somehow manages to honor what God has made while letting his own imagination respond with creations of its own. Consider his painting *A New Earth (2 Peter 3:13)* (Fig. 10.11).

FIG 10.11   CLIFF McREYNOLDS, *A New Earth (2 Peter 3:13)*

The Biblical text refers to the new creation God will provide to His resurrected and redeemed children after His judgment is over and the old order has been consumed. The painting is based on the Bible, but it is not a narrative. Indeed, it depicts what can scarcely be imagined—Paradise. McReynolds's favorite subjects seem to be Eden before the fall and the new creation after the Apocalypse. These subjects allow him both to revel in God's creation and to send his own imagination soaring.

The blue sky and the cirrus clouds are vividly realistic, and the moon in the sky has a hard-edged clarity (but does it now have water and an atmosphere? Or is that the old earth with its tiny continent that looks suspiciously like Africa?). In the center of the painting at a great distance, looming over the mountains and even the clouds, is what can only be the Tree of Life (Revelation 22:2).

The bottom of the painting is teeming with life of a most unusual kind. In the left-hand corner, two fish are swimming in the air, being fed by a woman. By the river, a developing unborn child is cradled in a nest. On the other side of the river, children are riding birds. We can also see pink swans, huge insects, and children doing impossible gymnastics.

McReynolds's paintings, although huge, reward the use of a magnifying glass. Every blade of grass is seemingly painted separately, and nearly hidden in that grass may be something remarkable—a giant drop of water, an infinitesimally small family walking hand in hand. What he is suggesting, of course, is the utter freedom of the resurrected body, that unimaginable state of being in which we will be free from pain, death, discord, and sin. McReynolds's imagination runs wild at the prospect, not necessarily to speculate "what Heaven will really be like," but to awaken our imaginations to the joy that is set before us, which no doubt will outdo even McReynolds's fantasies.

What interests me artistically about McReynolds's work is what he does with scale and perspective. In this painting, we see a towering waterfall in the distance, the perspective going back to mountain range upon mountain range, evoking vast size and distance—but as the perspective keeps going back, we see, dwarfing everything else, a tree! In McReynolds's new earth, size is clearly relative. Fish are the size of humans. Children are small enough to ride on birds—or the birds are large enough to carry children; it is never clear which is which.

Fig. 10.12 gives a detail from the painting. The developing life in the nest is watched over by two children, who are even smaller than the unborn baby waiting its time for life (an achingly poignant rebuke to the pro-abortion mentality). Flowers, iridescent rocks, and drops of dew—each intricately detailed though on a nearly microscopic scale—are nearly as big as the children. In McReynolds's paintings, dragonflies, pearls, and waterdrops can be larger than the human figures; sometimes trees are huge, and sometimes they are tiny. With the controlling framework of a realistic perspective, McReynolds plays with size and space.

What does this mean? Besides alluding to the mysterious nature of the resurrection body, which will be as different from our natural bodies as a plant is from a seed (1 Corinthians 15:35-49), McReynolds's shifting perspective reminds me of how God must look at the world. From a humanist perspective, enshrined in art since the Renaissance, the farther away something is, the smaller it appears. God does not perceive things in this way. He sees the life

FIG 10.12   CLIFF MCREYNOLDS, detail from *A New Earth (2 Peter 3:13)*

in the womb as intimately as He sees the Crab Nebula. He governs the farthest reaches of the universe while He attends to the silent prayers of each of His children.

Our human-centered perspective, our habit of measuring everything by ourselves, assures both our selfishness and our smallness. The sense of our insignificance in the vastness of the universe comes from measuring our worth by our size; God, to whom the infinite-seeming universe is less than an atom, perceives us differently. Each sparrow, each hair of our heads is in His care (Matthew 10:29-30). The perspective of Heaven will no doubt be very different from the perspective of earth, as McReynolds helps us realize.

The most striking feature of McReynolds's art is its sense of createdness. He works on every scale, from galaxies to blades of grass to atoms—sometimes seemingly in the same painting. His paintings often use the technique of pointillism, using tiny dots that cohere into a realistic appearance. This makes me think of God's craftsmanship, in which atoms join into molecules, which join into cells, which join into organisms. God creates on scales both enormous and minute, in each case lavishing His care upon every detail. McReynolds, in a much lesser vein, does the same thing. His art, like that of the other Christian artists, calls to mind God's art.

ART AND THE CHURCH

Granted that art is affirmed by Scripture and that Christians have always been involved in the arts, the question remains as to how the arts should be used by the church. To speak of "using" art would be questionable to many artists. Indeed, works of art exist in their own right as objects of beauty and meaning. Treating art as nothing more than a means to an end might seem to miss the point of art. Nevertheless, there is a sense in which religious art, as with all worshipers and evangelists, must set aside its usual autonomy in an act of self-effacement before God.

C. S. Lewis makes the distinction between the way a work of art can be used in devotion and the way art is normally approached:

> A crucifix exists in order to direct the worshiper's thought and affections to the Passion. It had better not have any excellencies, subtleties, or originalities which will fix attention upon itself. Hence devout people may, for this purpose, prefer the crudest and emptiest icon. The emptier, the more permeable; and they want, as it were, to pass through the material image and go beyond.[1]

In worship or evangelism, art, while remaining an aesthetic object, must go beyond aesthetics.

Worship, strictly speaking, is what Christians do, gathering as a body of believers before God to pray, praise, and receive His Word. Evangelism is the church's outreach to non-Christians with the message of the gospel. While evangelism certainly takes place in a worship service, the distinction between what Christians do among themselves and what they do to reach unbelievers may prove useful.

Traditions that restrict art in worship may not restrict secular art or the use of art in evangelism. Art that is effective in worship may not be effective in evangelism. Art that is effective in evangelism may not be appropriate in worship.

The universal church has employed art in many different ways. For all of the controversies art has occasioned, the various traditions, emphasizing different facets of Christian truth, agree more than they realize.

THE TRADITIONS OF ART AND WORSHIP

No one can deny that the church has been one of the most significant patrons of art in Western history. Art has also been a bone of contention for Christians. From the conflict in the early church between the iconophiles and the iconoclasts, through the Reformation debates about graven images, to the squabbles in churches today over the choir director's choice of music, art has been a source of division. The virulence of these debates testifies to the power of art to evoke strong feelings among Christians. Although such controversies are often petty failures to apply the church unity principles of Romans 14, in which the strong in the faith give in to the weak, important theological issues are sometimes at stake. From the Greek Orthodox adoration of icons to the Zwinglian rejection of all church ornamentation, the Christian tradition offers a wide range of stances to church art, reflecting the various interpretations of Scripture held by the different denominations.

In discussing the use of art in worship here, I will not presume to challenge the practices of the different theological traditions. Rather I hope to explain them and to show that each does have room for art of a particular kind. I will also offer some suggestions of my own, which should apply to each of the traditions.

Denominations that have a high view of the liturgy—a formal, historic order of worship—tend to employ art the most in their worship. Because their worship centers around a sacramental spirituality—in the notion that God manifests Himself by means of tangible objects, i.e., the bread and wine of communion, the water of baptism—they are particularly open to the way the senses can stimulate devotion. Crucifixes vividly impress upon their minds what Christ suffered on the cross. Paintings or stained glass depictions of Bible stories recall the events recorded in the Word of God. In these worship services, if your attention wanders, everywhere you look is something to draw you back.

Greek Orthodoxy makes the most extensive use of art in worship. Paintings of Christ or the saints, following strict canons of representation and technique that go back to the most ancient traditions, are integral to worship and devotion. Icons fill the churches, are carried in procession, and serve as the focus for private prayer. (I met a Greek Orthodox student who had a laminated icon in the back of his class notebook to help him with prayer between classes.) These icons reflect not only Greek Orthodox sacramentalism, but also their strong emphasis upon the Incarnation—God dwelling in human flesh. Greek Orthodoxy goes so far as to interpret their icons in sacramental terms, as holy images charged with real spiritual power, as physical objects that, by serving as "windows into Heaven," become means of grace.[2]

Roman Catholics do not go this far. Their churches are typically full of art, but they do not see it as a quasi-sacrament (at least officially, although in popular piety the adoration of particular images is common). Art is valued for its devotional effect and its educational function—inspiring the people to greater love for Christ at the contemplation of His wounds, instructing the faithful about Mary's suffering through images of her Sacred Heart (bound by thorns and burning).

Catholic art, concerned to create powerful devotional impressions in its viewers, is often highly emotional. Greek Orthodox art, on the other hand, is highly objective. Catholic art, though, is freer precisely because it has less theological status.

Greek Orthodox icons may not be sculpted, as these would be "graven images." Rather icons must be drawings on a two-dimensional plane. The style must follow the ancient patterns with no hint of humanist perspective or Romantic subjectivity. The artist is not to express his own individuality or to create an original work, but he must execute his craft in solidarity with the living tradition of the church. Prayer and personal holiness in the artist are intrinsic to the making of an icon.

Catholic art, in contrast, is relatively unrestrained. Roman Catholic churches include painting and sculpture executed in a plethora of artistic styles. It has medieval icons (similar to those of Greek Orthodoxy) and also works of Renaissance humanism, Mannerist eeriness, Baroque mysticism, sentimental nineteenth-century madonnas, and modern kitsch (plaster garden statues, ceramic Marys, dashboard ornaments of Jesus). Although, theology aside, I find the Greek Orthodox austerity particularly satisfying as religious art, the Roman Catholic tradition has historically employed art in all of its exuberance.

Protestants usually find the visual barrage encountered upon entering an Orthodox or Catholic church unnerving. Protestants are oriented to the Word, not to visual images. The Reformers, with good reason, saw the religious images that filled the medieval church as signs of superstition, false doctrine, and idolatry. The Reformed churches of Calvin and Zwingli eschewed visual images in church altogether, centering worship exclusively upon the Word. Churches in this Reformed tradition are not always as strict in avoiding art as they once were, but their legacy of imageless worship is significant.

I once visited a hyper-Calvinist church. Its extreme *lack* of ornamentation spoke as eloquently as the profusion of art in a cathedral. The sanctuary was utterly void of imagery. There were no paintings, no stained glass windows, no decorative molding, no woodwork, no wallpaper. There were no crosses, no altar. The walls were painted a blank white. The floor was plain uncarpeted wood. There was no choir or organ or piano. Instead of the usual hymnbook was a book of psalms set to music. In place of carved pews were simple folding chairs. In place of an elaborate pulpit was a simple podium for the pastor's Bible. The emptiness of the room was dramatic, its lack of even the most simple decorations setting it apart from ordinary secular space, creating thereby a sense of holiness. The rejection of all symbolism and all tangible imagery underscored the utter transcendence of God. This emphasis on God's transcendent glory and unfathomable sovereignty was in fact the distinctive theological emphasis of this church.

Ironically, what is true of the Roman Catholic cathedral, crowded with religious images, is also true of the Calvinist church, with its conspicuous emptiness. The decor of each church visibly expresses its theology. In its strenuous iconoclasm, the Calvinist church was making a visual—that is to say, an artistic—statement. Paradoxically, the very lack of art can function artistically.

The Reformed iconoclasts did not by any means forbid all art. Music, an aural rather than a visual art form, was a universal part of worship. (The heirs of Zwingli did not employ musical instruments, but did stress singing—music accompanied by the Word. The Calvinist church I visited sang only psalms, instead of hymns of merely human origin.) Churches would often be decorated with framed texts of Scripture. Paintings and sculpture were permitted— as long as they were not in the church building. Calvin and Zwingli even permitted religious art, such as pictures of Christ and Biblical narratives, as long as it was not set up in a place of worship. We have already discussed how Reformed iconoclasm led to the flowering of portraiture, to the opening up of secular subjects to the arts, and to artistic geniuses such as Rembrandt.

In between the extremes of Greek Orthodox veneration of icons and Zwinglian iconoclasm is the view of Martin Luther. As mentioned in chapter 9, Luther came out of hiding to calm down the iconoclastic riots with their wholesale destruction of church art. But he also opposed those who venerated images. In Luther's reforms, art that distracted attention from Christ was removed; art that proclaimed Christ was retained.

The Lutheran university where I teach acquired a new campus that was formerly a Roman Catholic institution. We reformed the chapel in exactly the manner Luther altered the churches in the sixteenth century. A monumental crucifix was the focal point of the chapel, next to which was a large statue of Mary, symbolizing her intercession between the people and her Son. We removed Mary but left the crucifix. A magnificent stained glass window at the back of the sanctuary showed the ascension of Mary. We removed her head and replaced it with the countenance of Christ, so that it now depicts Christ's triumphant ascension. We removed the numbers on the Stations of the Cross, changing them from a penitential "good work" to a narrative sequence of Christ's passion. Much of the old art was removed; much was retained; much was changed or simply reinterpreted.

Luther stressed both Word and sacrament. He favored liturgical worship, not because he believed in ritualism, but for the same reason the Calvinist church sang only psalms. The liturgy consists wholly of the Word of God, which is the sole basis and means of worship. On the basis of his Biblical literalism, Luther did believe that God is at work in the sacraments. He agreed that our human senses can help us to contemplate God, which is why he welcomed the arts. At the same time, Luther rejected any veneration of images or any use of the arts that interfered with or distracted from God's Word.

Luther's position draws from the insights of both the iconophiles and the iconoclasts while avoiding the extremes of each. Episcopalians for the most part would probably agree with Luther, although some are more "Catholic" and some are more "Reformed." Some Christians, such as Presbyterians and many Baptists, are on the Reformed side, but to varying degrees, perhaps allowing crosses but no body on the cross, allowing stained glass windows but with nonrepresentational designs. Many evangelical churches show great flexibility. Some employ art that is decorative, though not particularly symbolic. Some employ art more freely. Those who do not have paintings might employ banners; those who bridle at statues may not be averse to electronic music.

My point here is simply to stress the wide range of approaches to the arts found in Christian congregations. The various positions and the theological fine points they represent could be debated, but that is not my concern here. I contend that artists and those interested in art can thrive in any of these traditions. The kind of art and the way it is used in worship will vary greatly. The artistic literacy in a local church is likely to be as little developed as that of contemporary society as a whole. There is, however, nothing intrinsically hostile to art in any form of the Christian religion.

This point is important. Christian artists may be Baptist, charismatic, or Calvinist. Their local church may not employ art in their worship services, but this should not be misread—by the artist or by the church leadership—as a rejection of art altogether. What is not done inside the church (such as eating, playing, doing business, or enjoying art) may well be done outside (and done better). Few artists today have much of an interest in liturgical art to begin with. Traditions that are leery of art in worship can still support their Christian artists. Rembrandt and the Dutch masters have proven that.

Furthermore, I am of the opinion that theological traditions should not change their worship practices simply to accommodate cultural or aesthetic trends. I have seen Baptists try to be liturgical, and I have seen Lutherans try to be informal. Believe me, in either case, it was not a pretty sight. Neither side can quite pull it off. The free-wheeling spontaneity of a revival service fits perfectly a spirituality built around religious experience and "decisions for Christ." The intense concentration, timelessness, and sense of the holy in a traditional Lutheran service corresponds to their emphasis on the objectivity of grace and to the spiritual efficacy of the Word of God. Both styles of worship have an integrity of their own. The style fits the theology, a congruity of form and content which, whether or not visual images are employed, is essentially "artistic."

A Baptist preacher dressing up in vestments and swinging an incense burner is ludicrous, as is a Catholic priest conducting mass in jeans and a T-shirt while playing a guitar. The sense of absurdity comes from an aesthetic contradiction—the form and the content do not go with each other. The problem is not with the clothes or the artistic accessories. The preacher could get away with the guitar and maybe even the T-shirt. The priest could handle the vestments and incense. An individual might come to believe that a particular theological position is correct and, on that basis, change to another mode of worship. Changing the styles without changing the theology, however, is more than discordant. The form communicates the content, so that changing the style changes the message, whether it is intended to do so or not.

Changing churches out of theological conviction is certainly legitimate. One should never switch churches, however, purely on the basis of aesthetic preference. To choose or reject a church on the basis of how good a choir it has, the attractiveness of the sanctuary, or the aesthetic impact of its liturgy is to trivialize that church and to misapply its art. Churches are not to be concert halls, museums, theaters, or entertainment centers. The focus should be on the content of what that church teaches—its understanding of the Word of God and its faithfulness to the gospel. Art can express that understanding and that faithfulness to varying degrees, but art should not be confused with or take the place of theology.

Christians interested in the arts are sometimes impatient with their particular tradition and are tempted to join a tradition that is "more open to the arts." If they truly accept the teachings of the other church and disagree with the theology in their present fellowship, then they should change. Barring such theological conviction, it is usually better to plumb the depths of what one already has. If you are an Anglican, stick with your prayer book; if you belong to the Church of Christ, do without an organ. "As the Lord hath called every one, so let him walk" (1 Corinthians 7:17 KJV).

SUGGESTIONS FOR ART IN WORSHIP

Worship services do tend to employ art to some degree, if only inadvertently. Even supposedly nonliturgical services tend to follow a predictable order (with the sequence of greetings, prayer, songs, Scripture reading, offering, sermon, and altar call constituting a genuine liturgy). Everyone uses music, whether Gregorian chants or contemporary Christian music, accompanied by an organ, electrical guitar, or nothing at all. From bulletin covers to the color scheme of the paint and the design of the furniture, churches are saturated in art whether they realize it or not. What follows are some suggestions for art in worship that should be applicable to every tradition.

Art should aid the worship of God, not be distracting. The best art calls attention to itself, to its own artfulness and the skill of its maker. The best liturgical art, on the other hand, calls attention to God, sacrificing its artfulness in the self-abnegation of worship. One of the great religious paintings is Caravaggio's *The Conversion of St. Paul,* an enigmatic Mannerist depiction of Paul knocked off his horse. The horse in fact dominates the painting; darkness is at its center; Paul, blinded, is writhing at the bottom of the painting bathed in the light of grace. This painting is profound, complex, and endlessly fascinating. It is located not in a museum but above the altar in an Italian church. For all of the greatness of the painting—indeed because of the greatness of the painting—I would find it hard to pray at that altar. My attention would be riveted to that painting.

We must be careful about confusing the aesthetic for the spiritual. I know of a church renowned for its magnificent choir. Its one hundred resplendently robed singers fill the front of the sanctuary, dwarfing the altar and the pulpit. Going to this church is like going to a concert. The congregation does not sing much, preferring simply to listen to these semiprofessionals intone their perfect harmonies. I know of other churches whose sanctuaries look like recording studios, replete with mike stands, drums, and amps cranked up to full volume. I have heard soloists in church working the crowd like a lounge singer, striding into the audience with a Las Vegas patter, crooning into the mike, costumed for a screen test.

Entertainment is not the purpose for going to church. Indulging ourselves in aesthetic pleasure is not the same as worshiping. Churches dare not choreograph their worship services to add entertainment value, even to attract nonbelievers. Evangelistic art, addressed to those outside the faith, might combine entertainment with instruction. To do so in worship, however, risks undercutting the Christian message. Ours is a culture wholly centered upon the self. The church must counter this egotism, not give in to it.[3] The Bible calls us to repentance, faith, service, and self-denial—qualities utterly opposed to the entertainment mentality. In Christian worship, the congregation is not the audience; God is the audience.[4]

If good art and entertaining art can be distracting (the two are by no means the same), bad art can be even more distracting. I know of a church that has at the front of the sanctuary a huge picture of Christ that is so unbecoming, so grotesquely misshapen, such a travesty of religious art, that I could hardly pay attention to the service. This was unspiritual of me, I admit, and yet the distraction was real. Other people complain about music, not necessarily out of aestheticism, but because wrong notes and off-key singing call attention to themselves and thus break the devotional mood.

If good art is distracting and bad art is distracting, what is left? Am I saying that mediocre art is best for the church? Not at all. The point here is that in worship art assumes a different function than in the concert hall or the museum. Liturgical art exists not for aesthetic contemplation but for the contemplation of God. Such self-effacing concentration of the attention of the worshipers on the subject matter of the art takes consummate artistic skill.

A good choir glorifies God and in doing so sweeps up the congregation into an attitude of adoration. The skill of their singing allows the composer's music to do its work and presents the text most powerfully. The self-sacrifice evident in a well-practiced choir—in which each voice blends with the whole—is a rigorous spiritual as well as aesthetic discipline.

Although I honor church musicians who insist on offering God nothing less than their very best, it is also true that technical perfection is not always necessary in worship if the ardor is there and if the sense of devotion is palpable. Furthermore, while a good choir is priceless, they should not have to do all of the singing. Because worship is to be performed by the entire body of believers, everyone in the congregation should sing, even if many of them do it badly, though the best they can, out of a desire to praise God.

Christian worship should focus on the Word of God. Songs should be chosen very carefully. If they are to be used in worship, they must proclaim the Word of God. Top-forty love songs are not appropriate for a church wedding, not because there is something wrong with them, but because they do not say anything about Jesus Christ. The texts of the hymns should be taken seriously and reflect the teachings of the church. A good tune should not excuse bad theology.

Since the focus is to be upon the message, not the medium, the words of the songs should be understandable. (Making thirty people sing together in such a way that the words are crisply enunciated takes great artistic skill and is one of the many under-appreciated achievements of a good choir.) Foreign texts sung by the choir should be translated in the bulletin.

The visual arts used in worship should also serve the Word. Narrative images from Scripture, whether in paintings, banners, or stained glass, can piercingly remind their viewers of Biblical history. Symbols, insofar as they are understood by the congregation, can encapsulate complex truths and can rivet attention to their meaning. Many visual images are inescapable—bulletin covers, architectural layout, furniture design, decorative details. They might as well be used when possible to draw the worshipers' attention to Christ. Crosses, sacramental images (the cup, the vine, water), or Biblical figures (the staff, the lamb, the angels) can be effective. Churches leery of visual representations can employ written texts of Scripture—in simple or calligraphic designs—to achieve the same end.

We are told to "worship the Lord in the beauty of holiness" (Psalm 29:2 KJV). The art of the church worshiping, from the decor to the symbols, from the music to the artfully composed sermon, should exhibit this "beauty of holiness." To be holy means to be set apart, to be distinct from the world. The fashions of the mass culture, the cultural trends and latest fads, must therefore be largely irrelevant to worship, which should be self-consciously different from ordinary life.

This means that old art will always speak to the church. Church worship employs ancient symbols, archaic paintings, and "old-fashioned hymns." The continued popularity of hymns that are centuries old is significant. This is not arid traditionalism. The old styles have a powerful resonance for Christians precisely because they are different from the styles of the current culture. We have discussed how art "defamiliarizes" experience. Although brand-new styles can help us break out of the deadening glaze of familiarity, old styles can do the same, insofar as they are different from the modern styles we are accustomed to. The classic hymns—whether from the Middle Ages, Reformation, Enlightenment, or Romantic eras— ironically address us in a new way, mired as we are in the provincialisms of the twentieth century. Of course, we are also told to "sing to the Lord a new song" (Psalm 149:1). The alternation of old and new, the preservation of a living heritage that embraces all styles, does in fact characterize the worship of most churches, exemplifying a richer artistic texture than most people give them credit for.

THE BRAZEN SERPENT

Worship services also include the proclamation of the gospel. Not only the sermon but the hymns, confessions, sacraments, and liturgical responses are saturated with the message of salvation, the good news that Christ died for our sins. Worship is evangelistic, although evangelism takes place outside the walls of the church as well. The ability of art to communicate the gospel is perhaps its most important religious function, whether in a worship service or in a secular setting. The ever-present cross in a church building is a sign of the gospel, calling both believers and nonbelievers to a consciousness of Christ's sacrifice.

The Bible gives examples of art that communicates the gospel. One used in worship is the Ark of the Covenant, picturing the sacrificial blood covering the tablets of God's Law. One used outside the context of worship is the brazen serpent. The book of Numbers describes how the children of Israel, miraculously delivered from Egypt and sustained in the wilderness, rebelled against the life of freedom and faith. God saved them from His wrath with a snake made out of bronze:

> They traveled from Mount Hor along the route to the Red Sea, to go around Edom. But the people grew impatient on the way; they spoke against God and against Moses, and said, "Why have you brought us up out of Egypt to die in the desert? There is no bread! There is no water! And we detest this miserable food!"
> Then the Lord sent venomous snakes among them; they bit the people and many Israelites died. The people came to Moses and said, "We sinned when we spoke against the Lord and against you. Pray that the Lord will take the snakes away from us." So Moses prayed for the people.
> The Lord said to Moses, "Make a snake and put it up on a pole; anyone who is bitten can look at it and live." So Moses made a bronze snake and put it up on a pole. Then when anyone was bitten by a snake and looked at the bronze snake, he lived. (Numbers 21:4-9)

The people disliked their freedom. Although God was actually present in their midst in the pillar of cloud and the pillar of fire, guiding them and sustaining them, the people were dissatisfied. The desert was uncomfortable. They wanted to be entertained. Every morning God worked a miracle, providing them with manna, the bread of heaven, which "tasted like wafers made with honey" (Exodus 16:31). The children of Israel, though, turned up their noses at this miracle. "We detest this miserable food." They thought it was boring. God punished this monstrous ingratitude by a plague of poisonous snakes. (Soft, sensation-craved moderns, who have more material blessings and an even shorter attention span than these Israelites, should feel uneasy at this point.)

Terrified by the severity of God's judgment, the people turned to Moses to intercede for them. God's response was to have Moses make a work of art through which the people could experience divine deliverance and healing. Why, though, did God choose to work in such a roundabout manner? Why did He not just heal them if that was His purpose? Why was their healing connected with looking at a bronze replica of a snake, of all things?

Here Scripture gives a profound example of how art can be used to create in its audience a conviction of sin and an intimation of salvation by grace through faith. What God wanted the people to feast their eyes on (the bronze snake) was an image of the very punishment He was inflicting on them. He wanted them to truly look at

His judgment and the reality of their sinfulness. But did they not know this already? Could they not see this judgment all around them in the real snakes that slithered through the camp? Why was looking at a representation, a work of shining bronze, more convicting than actual snakes of flesh and blood and venom?

Scripture here suggests something that modern theorists are just noticing about how art functions. Art is powerful because it heightens perception. It does this by lifting an object or experience out of its normal context so that it can be apprehended freshly and more fully. Human faces are everywhere, but a portrait causes us to see a human face as a special object of contemplation. Part of the joy of reading good fiction comes from the sense of recognition as our own experiences are called forth and intensified by the work of art which, in a sense, reveals what we have already known but never thought about before. Art can take a common object or a universal experience and, by aesthetic techniques of form and distancing, lift it up, disclosing that object or that experience in a compelling way and drawing out its meaning. Art enriches life because it can make us aware of meaning.

When the Israelites were looking at the bronze snake glittering in the desert sun, they were seeing it in a different way than they saw the vipers swarming through their tents. The bronze snake had a meaning that enlightened them about the meaning of the real snakes all around them. In looking at the image, the people were gazing at God's wrath against their sin. The real snakes were not simply vipers of the desert, a natural disaster, but instruments of God's anger, a fact the metallic statue forced them to understand by virtue of its divinely proclaimed *meaning*. The bronze serpent is a paradigm of how art can communicate and can awaken people to truth.

God wanted the people to look at this image of a snake, lifted up out of the context of their suffering, to make them fully and deeply recognize both His wrath and their sin that provoked it. That is, He was using the artifact to bring His people to repentance. When they looked on the brazen serpent, when they recognized where they stood under God's judgment, then they could receive forgiveness and be healed.

The brazen serpent had another meaning as well. "Just as Moses lifted up the snake in the desert," said our Lord, "so the Son of Man must be lifted up, that everyone who believes in him may have eternal life" (John 3:14-15). Speaking of His imminent crucifixion, Christ said, "Now is the time for judgment on this world; now the prince of this world will be driven out. But I, when

I am lifted up from the earth, will draw all men to myself" (John 12:31-32).

The brazen serpent symbolizes the lifting up of Christ on the cross, in whom sin and Satan, "that ancient serpent" who seduced us from Paradise and who continues to plague us (Revelation 12:9), are annihilated. Christ on the cross, in the mystery of the atonement, actually *became* sin: "God made him who had no sin to be sin for us, so that in him we might become the righteousness of God" (2 Corinthians 5:21). The sin of the Israelites in Moses' day, along with the sins of the entire world through all time, were nailed to the cross in the innocent body of our Lord, who then bore all the judgment and wrath that such sin deserves. It was through this atonement that the repentant Israelites in the desert and all other sinners throughout time are really forgiven.

The brazen serpent brought healing because it represented sin in the depths of its meaning, as rejection of God's grace, as provoking God's wrath, as originating in Satan. At the same time, it represented God's provision for sin, to be fully manifested in Jesus Christ. Looking to this image in the midst of judgment typifies what it means to look to Christ for salvation, and it is through this act of faith that God's people, poisoned in their inmost being and dying from the sting of the serpent, receive healing. The brazen serpent is a model for other evangelistic art. It provokes a knowledge of sin, leading to repentance, and it depicts Christ's provision for that sin, leading to faith.

ART AND THE MORAL LAW

Luther distinguishes between law and gospel in the Scriptures and in the process of evangelism. God's law, the moral absolutes codified in the Ten Commandments and other passages in the Bible, shows us how we should live—what it means to love our neighbor and to live a God-pleasing, righteous life. The moral law, significantly, is universal. Revealed perfectly in Scripture, God's principles of justice and ethical behavior inhere in human nature itself:

> When Gentiles, who do not have the law, do by nature things required by the law, they are a law for themselves, even though they do not have the law, since they show that the requirements of the law are written on their hearts, their consciences also bearing witness, and their thoughts now accusing, now even defending them. (Romans 2:14-15)

Those who do not know the Scriptures nevertheless know "by nature" (their creation in God's image and the testimony of the created order) what the law demands. The conscience, although it can be seared by continual sin, bears testimony to the moral dimension of life. Furthermore, principles of right and wrong make human communities possible.

The concept of a "natural law," that is, a set of moral absolutes built into the universe itself and applicable in all religions and in all cultures, has been a commonplace of moral and legal theory for centuries. Only today has this foundational principle been lost. Many people oppose the teaching of morality in schools in the name of the separation of church and state. Lawmakers insist on excluding moral considerations in the abortion debate as "religious intrusions into public policy." Morality, though, has never been seen as simply a matter of religion. Ethical concerns are secular as much as they are religious. Although God is the ultimate ground of the moral law, it is applicable universally, even to those who do not know Him.

Moral teachers from every culture and religion, if they teach truly, will tend to promulgate God's law. Because morality is not exclusively the property of Christians, even non-Christians can sometimes teach us something about God's law. The early church honored the "virtuous pagans" (such as Socrates, Aristotle, and Virgil) as teaching valid moral principles even though they did not know Christ.

Art can have a moral function. Aesop's *Fables*, Goya's anti-war paintings, Dickens's novels, Dorothea Lange's photographs of the poor—such works of art are frankly didactic. Art's moral impact comes not so much from teaching abstract ethical principles (which most people already know intellectually). Rather art can *move* its audience to a moral response. Artistic images can appeal powerfully to the emotions, kindling pity at human suffering or outrage at evil. Art that is ostentatiously didactic, having no other merit than that of the lesson it teaches, generally fails both as art and as teaching. This is often because it starts preaching or lecturing in propositional terms instead of moving its audience by artistic means.

Serious art does tend to have a moral dimension. It works in the context of moral realities, the theme emerging from the aesthetic form and provoking its audience to reflection and action. Conversely, utterly immoral art—such as pornography—can scarcely have aesthetic merit.

The capacity of art to expound and explore ethical truth is part of its religious ministry. Telling people to be good, however, is not evangelism. We cannot be saved by our good works. In fact, self-righteousness, trusting in our own ethical behavior to get us into Heaven, is a serious spiritual danger, shutting out our need for Christ. "You who are trying to be justified by law have been alienated from Christ; you have fallen away from grace" (Galatians 5:4). Paradoxically, some of the most spiritually dangerous works of art may be those that seem most moral—self-help books that teach that anything is possible if we just try hard enough; models of complacent respectability that make us content with a facade of virtue; pop psychology tracts that teach us to feel good about ourselves no matter what we do; optimistic works that suggest that we really are not so bad, that virtue is easy. Such works may have an appearance of rectitude, but they can encourage us to trust in ourselves for salvation and anesthetize us from our true sinful nature and from our aching need for Jesus Christ.

The evangelical function of the law, according to Luther, is to awaken us to our moral failures. "Through the law," says Paul, "we become conscious of sin" (Romans 3:20). The proper response to this self-knowledge is repentance, whereupon sinners, broken by the realization of their lostness, can cling to Christ, who offers free forgiveness and a new life in the Holy Spirit.

Works of art can challenge our moral complacency and puncture our self-satisfied egos, thereby applying the moral law in an evangelical way. Tragedy, for example, will show a hero with boundless aspirations who is forced to realize human limits when pride leads to self-caused catastrophe. Comedy, although in a lighter vein, discloses similar human limits, revealing the absurdity of human beings, especially when they operate under delusions of grandeur. Satire, critics have observed, assumes the strictest standards of morality, against which the target of the satire is measured and found wanting. The satirist exposes and ridicules hypocrisy and evil, using laughter as a cutting offensive weapon. (True satire is not the same as mockery, which can operate outside moral law, ridiculing virtue as well as evil.) Both the tragic and the comic modes of art— and this holds true not only for literature but also for "tragic" paintings such as Picasso's *Guernica* and "comic" paintings such as those by Breughel or Daumier—can be applications of the law.

Much art, especially of this century, projects a bleak view of the world. Images of ugliness, emptiness, and absurdity seem almost obsessions of modern art. They also can be found throughout Christian art—from the grotesqueries of Breughel and the gruesomeness of Grünewald around the time of the Reformation to the black comedy of Flannery O'Connor's fiction and the desolate landscapes of T. S. Eliot's poetry. What do such depressing and pessimistic images have to say to Christians? Should not Christians resist this morbid concentration on the negative and project a more positive outlook on life?

Christians do have a hope and a joy that set them forever apart from the nihilists. Yet that hope and joy reside in Christ alone, not in worldly success, not in fallen human beings, certainly not in any kind of optimism that looks on only "the sunny side" of life. "The Scripture declares that the whole world is a prisoner of sin, so that what was promised, being given through faith in Jesus Christ, might be given to those who believe" (Galatians 3:22). Contemporary Christians perhaps have neglected the radical implications of the doctrine of sin. Human beings are *depraved*; nature is under a *curse*. Negative-seeming art and literature, far from contradicting Scripture on this point, actually confirm it. People need to awaken to the desperateness of their condition and their need of Christ, in whom alone is salvation. We are often so comfortable in our pleasures and so complacent in our self-satisfaction that we need to be forced to see the absurdities of our condition according to transcendent standards. Art can help us—even make us—to do just that.

It has always seemed to me a great evidence for the Christian faith that those who reject it acknowledge, if they are honest, that without God they have no hope in the world (Ephesians 2:12). Great unbelieving artists generally do not pretend that the absence of God in their lives is in any way fulfilling or a cause of rejoicing. Lacking God, they express their own emptiness. Looking outward, they probe and find that everything—other people, their society, nature itself—is a sham and a cheat. Is not their experience exactly what the Christian would predict? Is not their cry of "meaninglessness" a recognition of the same futility proclaimed in Scripture (Romans 8:20)? Those who are complacent in their worldliness need to realize the message of Ecclesiastes, that in the world considered apart from God, "Everything is meaningless" (Ecclesiastes 1:2). This unsettling truth of the law may be a necessary prelude to the good news of Jesus Christ.

In suggesting that even secular art can speak to us of law and thus be part of the work of the gospel, some cautions are in order. Not all works of art speak of the law; some openly flout it, promoting immorality or moral relativism. Some artists in their despair and negativism attack God along with everything else. Such works may deserve a hearing, but Christians will discern their tragic spiritual emptiness. Although Elijah provides a model for satire when he mocks the idolatrous priests (1 Kings 18:27), not all targets are fair game. Scripture forbids us to mock the legitimate messengers of

God, the poor, our parents, or God Himself (2 Chronicles 36:16; Proverbs 17:5; 30:17; Galatians 6:7).

Art can uphold moral values and reprove moral failures. Even art by non-Christians, insofar as it agrees with God's universal law, can be of enormous social and spiritual benefit. Even the most moral art, however, cannot of itself communicate salvation.

ART AND THE GOSPEL

Although the law to a certain extent is universal, the gospel is inextricably tied to the specific, revealed person of Jesus Christ. The gospel partakes of what has been called the "scandal of particularity." Salvation is contingent on faith in the transcendent but also historical Jesus Christ. "Salvation is found in no one else, for there is no other name under heaven given to men by which we must be saved" (Acts 4:12). This particularity is sometimes embarrassing to Christians who want to be sophisticated and tolerant, but the specificity is essential to the gospel. Christianity is not a vague cosmic optimism, a utopian vision of everyone loving one another, a formula for success and happiness, or even a belief in a benevolent deity. It is rather the scandal of Christ crucified (1 Corinthians 1:23).

Art can convey this gospel, the word of the cross. This message, however, is highly specific, unlike the message of the law, which is broad and universal in its scope. The evangelistic impact of a gospel-bearing work is not contingent on the skill or eloquence of the artist. It is God who acts in the gospel, calling people to Himself, and He is not thwarted by human limitations. He can speak through inferior art—a cheap tract, a badly written song, a gospel comic book—as well as through an aesthetic masterpiece. Having said this, and remembering that art need not be evangelistic in order to please God, we may consider *how* art can convey the gospel of Christ.

First, it needs to maintain the "scandal of particularity." That is, it must present directly or indirectly the person and the name of Jesus Christ. An evangelistic work cannot present the gospel by vague intimations or moralizing. It must point explicitly or symbolically, but always clearly, to Jesus of Nazareth and His work. This does in a sense limit the artist who also desires to be an evangelist, but this is the same limitation given to any other preacher or witness and, considered rightly, it is scarcely a limitation. Christ is the most profound and inexhaustible of subjects. What can send the imagination reeling like the doctrine of the Incarnation, the infinite concealed in the finite, or the Atonement, the tragedy of sacrifice and the comedy of resurrection and the forgiveness of sins? All of human nature and the divine nature are present and accessible in Christ, who experienced and suffered the whole range of human experience, including the entire weight of the world's sin.

This is not to say that evangelistic art must always depict Bible stories. To be sure, the Biblical narratives must hold a privileged place. The Nativity, the adoration of the Magi, the Virgin Mary with the Christ-child, the Crucifixion, the burial, the Resurrection—such set pieces of Christian art have proven inexhaustible sources of inspiration for the greatest artists.[5] They exalt the Christ of the Scriptures in a very explicit and powerful way. Christ may also be presented in other contexts, showing the ascended Christ as He relates to all of life and to individual needs.

In art, symbols are ways of penetrating beneath a surface appearance to explore and present *meanings*. A painting of Christ may appear to some people as the painting of any other man. A painting such as Van Eyck's *Adoration of the Lamb* that depicts Christ through the symbol of a lamb pouring out its blood into a chalice, a lamb slain yet alive, explores and communicates the meaning, not just the appearance of the Christ. Religious art nearly always resorts to symbolism, which simply involves expressing trans-sensory ideas through concrete images. The most narrative of Biblical paintings are apt to include symbolic details: the trampled serpent, the skull, the crown, the halo, the beaten gold.

The Bible makes clear that Christ underlies all of existence:

> He is the image of the invisible God, the firstborn over all creation. For by him all things were created: things in heaven and on earth, visible and invisible, whether thrones or powers or rulers or authorities; all things were created by him and for him. He is before all things, and in him all things hold together. And he is the head of the body, the church; he is the beginning and the firstborn from among the dead, so that in everything he might have the supremacy. For God was pleased to have all his fullness dwell in him, and through him to reconcile to himself all things, whether things on earth or things in heaven, by making peace through his blood, shed on the cross. (Colossians 1:15-20)

Thus Christ underlies *everything*, from the physical universe (the "visible") to the realm of ideas and spiritual truths (the "invisible"). In Him is everything that is fully human and everything that is fully divine. Indeed, "in him all things hold together."

Christ is the center, the ultimate meaning of every entity. To one who knows Him, practically everything can be seen in light of

Christ. When the poet Gerard Manley Hopkins writes of a hawk in "The Windhover," he sees in that hawk the qualities of "Christ our Lord." The most common, ordinary actions can be made to speak to us of spiritual realities, of Christ Himself, as artists continually reveal.

The simple act of eating, for example, images in the most profound way the basic unquestionable truth that there can be no life apart from sacrifice. Every life depends upon the sacrificial death of some other living thing. When we eat, we are nourished through the death of another creature. The sacrificial nature of eating meat is fully recognized in the Old Testament dietary regulations. The gentlest of animals depends upon the tearing and eating of plants, whose life is given to nourish it. (Vegetarians cannot escape their dependence upon sacrifice, try as they might, since plants are every bit as alive as animals.) If we spurn the sacrifice, whether of animals or of plants, we starve to death.

In a fallen world, this is a matter of violence. And yet there is something wonderful about this truth, as life is literally transformed into other life. The magical fish in George MacDonald's *The Golden Key* take joy in being chosen to be eaten, willingly sacrificing their lives for others. The point is, the seemingly arcane and primitive idea of sacrifice—that life is made possible by the death of another living being—is reenacted every time we sit down to a meal. What is true physically—life's dependence upon sacrifice—is also true spiritually.

Behind all of this is the person of Christ, who made Himself the sacrifice, dying so that we might live, expressing what He has done for us by establishing a holy meal:

> The Lord Jesus, on the night he was betrayed, took bread, and when he had given thanks, he broke it and said, "This is my body, which is for you; do this in remembrance of me." In the same way, after supper he took the cup, saying, "This cup is the new covenant in my blood; do this, whenever you drink it, in remembrance of me." For whenever you eat this bread and drink this cup, you proclaim the Lord's death until he comes. (1 Corinthians 11:23b-26)

Sacramental images—bread, wheat, grapes, the vine, the cup—are evident throughout Christian art. Another powerful gospel-bearing image set forth in the Bible and occurring everywhere in the arts is that of water. It cleanses, brings life to parched ground, and thus expresses the mystery of death and rebirth. Christian baptism employs simple water to convey the gospel of Christ. The wealth of

sacramental imagery throughout Christian art—indeed, the sacramental imagination, which tends to see the works of grace in the
most ordinary physical objects and events—is particularly important
in symbolizing and proclaiming Christ and His work.

THE CENTRALITY OF THE WORD

According to the Scriptures, the gospel is communicated by means
of human language:

> How, then, can they call on the one they have not believed in?
> And how can they believe in the one of whom they have not
> heard? And how can they hear without someone preaching to
> them? And how can they preach unless they are sent? . . .
> Consequently, faith comes from hearing the message, and the
> message is heard through the word of Christ. (Romans 10:14-
> 15, 17)

Technically, it is the *Word* of God that communicates the gospel.
Faith comes from *hearing*, from responding to a message discerned
through language. A person may learn of Christ by hearing God's
Word preached in a sermon, by conversation with a Christian, by
perusing a gospel tract, or by reading the Scriptures. Hearing, rather
than seeing or feeling, is the main way we relate to God, and it is
God's *Word* that is the normal means of grace.[6]

This priority of the Word means that, for art to convey the
gospel, it must be in some sense propositional. It must be connected
directly or indirectly to language. Again, pure art need have no particular propositional content to be pleasing to God; its main purpose
is to embody aesthetic forms. To give or receive aesthetic pleasure is
a worthy and exalting goal in itself, but aesthetic delight as such cannot lead anyone to Christ. The preaching of Christ involves propositional, linguistic statements about the person and work of Christ.
Art can convey such statements, but "the word" is necessary for
evangelism.

Christianity is sometimes criticized for being "word-centered"
and thus insufficiently oriented to visual images or to emotional subjectivity. This, however, cannot be otherwise and is nothing to apol-
ogize for. The Word is at the essence of the Christian faith. The faith
of the ancient Hebrews was based on God's revelation in language;
the faith of their pagan neighbors was based on gods revealed in
graven images. This basic conceptual conflict between the priority
of language and the priority of images continues. The media critic

Neil Postman worries that the image-dominated mind-set of the TV generation has eroded thought and trivialized the culture.[7] The theologian and social critic Jacques Ellul insists that the church must resist what he terms "the humiliation of the word" that is occurring everywhere else in modern society.[8] Christianity's emphasis on the Word need not negate the visual arts; it simply means that visual images and language must mutually support each other.

Zwingli makes an important point on the priority of "the word" in religious art, as summarized by Charles Garside:

> To begin with, men can learn nothing of the content of God's Word from an image. "Why," Zwingli rhetorically asks, "do we not send images to unbelievers so that they can learn belief from them?" Precisely because we would be required to explain what they mean, which in turn requires knowledge of the Word. "If now you show an unbelieving or unlettered child images, then you must teach him with the Word in addition, or he will have looked at the picture in vain." For if "you were newly come from the unbeliever and knew nothing of Christ and saw Him painted with the apostles at the Last Supper, or on the Cross, then you would learn nothing from this same picture other than to say 'He who is pictured there was a good-looking man in spite of it all.'"
> . . . One may have images of Christ, but they are powerless; the "story must be learned only from the Word, and from the painting one learns nothing except the form of the body, the movements or the constitution of the body or face." [9]

This does not mean that visual art is incapable of communicating the gospel. The physical elements of bread, wine, and water become sacramental, according to the theologians, when they are connected to the Word of God. A work of art, by analogy, may be "connected" to the Word.

It is probably true that a mere picture of the Crucifixion would be no substitute for missionaries who could explain in language what the Crucifixion means. Alongside the explanation, though, the painting might well help the people to realize and to imagine the extent of Christ's suffering for them. To someone who knows nothing of the New Testament, a painting of Christ may be simply another figure of a bearded man in a robe. But to someone who has had at least some exposure to the Word and thus knows whom the painting represents, the picture of Jesus might reawaken a sense of the love of God.

It is easy to become complacent with things familiar to us. We may take concepts such as grace, sacrifice, incarnation, and salvation for granted, so that we no longer "hear" them. A work of art can help us come to grips with these concepts in a fresh, concrete way, revitalizing their meaning for us. A great painting of the Crucifixion can help us imagine with vividness and specificity what Christ did for us, reminding us that the Atonement is no mere set of abstract ideas but an actual moment of physical history. The word may be in our minds, half-buried or forgotten, but a work of art can throw that word in high relief.

Just as a picture can illuminate a word, a word can illuminate a visual image and charge it with meaning. The title of a work of art, for example, can be very important. The Scriptures describe two monoliths, huge bronze pillars decorated with nets and pomegranates, which were to adorn the Temple complex (1 Kings 7:15-22). They were imposing aesthetic objects, but their specific *meaning* was conveyed by their names: Jakin ("God establishes") and Boaz ("He comes with power"). The pillars embodied a specific meaning: God's establishing power. The connection between form and meaning is perfect, but without "the word" the pillars would never communicate such a meaning. They would simply be two huge pieces of bronze.

Some modern aesthetic theories minimize the importance of language. Some artists go to great lengths to avoid language, refusing to title their works and instead giving them numbers. This may be legitimate when the artist seeks to create a work that is purely aesthetic and nonreferential, although the artist's "theory," which legitimizes the piece, is inevitably a matter of language.

Art in fact depends upon language. People need to talk about art, to read and write about art. We can take pleasure from seeing paintings in a gallery, but reading the catalog of the collection, listening to a lecture by an art historian, or reading a review by an art critic increases the impact of any work of art.

This is why literary or aesthetic criticism is important. A critic's explanations and scholarship literally connect the work of art to "words"—to contexts, patterns, and meanings mediated through language. Criticism can cause the various meanings of a work to unfold so that they can be noticed more fully. Christian criticism can thus be a gospel-bearing activity, as the Word of God is connected to the work of art. The depths of a work's symbols, the patterns of death and rebirth, the figures of sacrifice and grace—these often need to be pointed out and explained before they can be fully perceived in a work of art. Writing about art, or talking about art in an informal conversation after a movie or a play, can often bring out explicitly what the gospel says and means.

Because the gospel is a function of the Word as expressed in Scripture and in Jesus Christ, it is objective. This means, interestingly, that an artist does not necessarily have to be a Christian to be working with images that express the gospel. The Jewish painter Marc Chagall's *The White Crucifixion* is a moving meditation on Christ's suffering. Frank Lloyd Wright's church designs are often symbolically precise and effective, although he himself was not a Christian. Literature is filled with Christ symbolism, patterns of death and rebirth, and emblems of forgiveness and redemption. Any time artists deal honestly with sin, suffering, sacrifice, love, and forgiveness, they may find themselves following the pattern engraved on the foundations of the world, the drama of redemption fulfilled by Jesus of Nazareth and revealed in the Scriptures.

If art can convey the gospel, has anyone come to faith through art? The examples I know best come from literature (art consisting wholly of words). A student told me that in her reading of Graham Greene's novel *The Power and the Glory*, she came to realize what Christ's bearing of our sins really means. The novel enabled her to believe. Another person I know never really understood God's grace until she found it in the poetry of John Donne and George Herbert. C. S. Lewis's spiritual autobiography *Surprised by Joy* is largely a record of the books he read and the music he listened to, the growth of his imagination, which in his case served to "prepare the way of the Lord." I know of others, in turn, who have come to faith through the works of C. S. Lewis—not only through his apologetic works but also through his fiction, through his characters such as Screwtape and his symbols such as Aslan.

The gospel, of course, is not dependent upon the skill of the artist or the aesthetic greatness of a work, but on the Holy Spirit working in the hearer's heart. I have known people who have been converted to faith in Christ through gospel comic books and apocalyptic novels about a worldwide dictator who takes over and tattoos "666" on everybody's forehead. Others have been introduced to Christ through contemporary Christian music. Such gospel-bearing art may not be artistic masterpieces. It might be utterly inappropriate for worship. Nevertheless, if the objective gospel is there, God has promised that His Word "will not return to me empty, but will accomplish what I desire" (Isaiah 55:11).

This holds true also for the visual arts. I have heard of people who have had to consider the claims of Christ because they were overwhelmed by the cathedrals and museums of Western Europe which testify so strongly, by aesthetic means, to the power of the Christian faith. Constantine was converted by a vision of the cross. One young nobleman in the eighteenth century was going through the art gallery in Dusseldorf on the "grand tour" of Europe that was customary for eighteen-year-olds of his rank. He found himself staring at a painting by the Baroque artist Domenico Feti. Entitled *Ecce Homo,* it depicted Christ—scourged, bound, and crowned with thorns. At the bottom of the painting, Feti had added a Latin inscription: "This I have done for you, but what have you done for me?" Haunted by the expression of Jesus in the painting and by the words of the inscription, the young man dedicated his life wholly to Christ. Thus began the career of Nicholas Von Zinzendorf, founder of the pietist movement, whose emphasis on missionary work and personal spirituality was to have a major impact on American Christianity.[10]

Notice how Count von Zinzendorf's response was both to the image and the word. The word gave the image its full meaning, convicting him of sin ("what have you done for me?") and setting forth the gospel ("This I have done for you"). The image dramatized the word, seizing his attention, making the abstractions come alive and moving him in a personal way.

The church has expressed itself in art as naturally as breathing—both in its worship and in its outreach. The Tabernacle and the Temple were full of artifacts that lifted the worshipers into an attitude of praise and impressed upon them God's sacrificial provision for their sins. Worship, to be sure, is different since Christ fulfilled all of the sacrifices in His cross; we have a legacy of freedom. Evangelism is also different now that the Holy Spirit has been poured out into the world and God's Word has been put into our hands. Art does not always have to be at the service of the church— we have a legacy of freedom here also. And yet, art, like all human gifts, can be offered back in service to God's Kingdom.

The Scriptures name aesthetic categories in connection with the impulse to proclaim God's salvation to the nations:

> O sing to the Lord a new song; sing to the Lord, all the earth!
> Sing to the Lord, bless his name; tell of his salvation from day
>   to day.
> Declare his glory among the nations, his marvelous works
>   among all the peoples!
> For great is the Lord and greatly to be praised; he is to be
>   feared above all gods.

*For all the gods of the peoples are idols, but the Lord made
   the heavens.*
*Honor and majesty are before him; strength and beauty are in
   his sanctuary. (Psalm 96:1-6 RSV)*

The lover of God, in whose sanctuary is all beauty, can scarcely
refrain from "telling of his salvation." The psalmist gives two reasons: first, because the Lord is great in Himself, intrinsically deserv-
ing all praise and exaltation (the perspective of worship); and
second, because "all of the gods of the peoples" are false, so that the
nations are in desperate need of Him (the perspective of evangelism).
The psalmist exhorts us to declare God's glory and His saving works
by writing a song about them—by composing music, a "pure" aesthetic form, and by putting words, God's words, to that music.

CONCLUSION

*T*he arts have a solid foundation in Scripture and are part of a living tradition in the Christian church. That some art today is morally, spiritually, and aesthetically bankrupt is a sign of the barrenness of our times. Art itself is not to blame. Christianity has proven uniquely hospitable to great art, inspiring giants such as Giotto, Michelangelo, Rembrandt, Shakespeare, Bach, and scores of later artists. Contemporary secularism has inspired Andy Warhol, Robert Mapplethorpe, and Andrés Serrano. It is fair to ask which has proven more hospitable to the arts, Christianity or contemporary secularism.

Christians are often criticized for their narrow anti-aesthetic attitudes, but I have never understood why they need to be open to this charge. Surely Christianity, with its affirmation of both the physical and the intangible, offers a stronger basis for the arts than the competing worldviews of modern times.

Materialism can hardly value art. There is no room for the pursuit of beauty in a totally mechanistic universe. If Darwin is correct, what is the survival value of art? Existentialism does give high status to art as a human creation of meaning in a meaningless world. And yet, if the existentialists are right, why pay attention to anyone else's art? If meaning is private and relative, someone else's art can have nothing to say to me. New Age paganism might value art in the same way the ancient Canaanites did. Yet seeing art as a sacred totem is not the same as enjoying it aesthetically. The ancient pagans saw their Baal figurines as objects of power, not beauty. The new pagans value their crystals and their pyramids not as art but as sources of mystical power.

The real reason for Christian indifference towards the arts, a relatively modern phenomenon, seems to derive from two other indifferences. Our society as a whole is indifferent to art, and art is indifferent to society.

Our contemporary culture as a whole knows little about art and cares less. I comfort Christian artists who complain to me that the church does not understand art by saying that the secular world does not understand art either. Our mass culture, although increasingly visually oriented because of television, encourages instant responses and superficial entertainment value rather than subtle contemplation of objective qualities. Contemporary Christians, like everyone else, have been caught up in this mass culture, although the Bible can show them something far better.[1]

Part of the blame for this rupture between the fine arts and the broader society must fall on the art world. In a healthy culture, art is part of the texture of everyday life. Today's art world has become elitist, scorning ordinary people and their concerns, becoming a status symbol for the wealthy, the intellectual aristocracy, and those yearning to be a part of these inner circles. The art world has turned art into something esoteric, an arcane mystery that demands initiation rather than enjoyment. The artistic establishment seems more interested in excluding rather than educating, preferring to shock or ridicule the less sophisticated rather than creating works that might enrich their lives.

Instead of constantly being on the defensive, Christians might assert their heritage in all of its vigor and vitality. Christians might go on the offensive by reclaiming art for themselves.

THE BRAZEN SERPENT REVISITED

The brazen serpent made by Moses was a great evangelistic work of art. It communicated God's law and gospel, symbolizing Christ on the cross and bringing healing to thousands. As one might expect, it was kept and treasured. Eventually, however, this historical instrument of God's grace was turned into an idol.

In the third year of Hoshea son of Elah king of Israel, Hezekiah son of Ahaz king of Judah began to reign. He was twenty-five years old when he became king, and he reigned in Jerusalem twenty-nine years. His mother's name was Abijah daughter of Zechariah. He did what was right in the eyes of the Lord, just as his father David had done. He removed the high places, smashed the sacred stones and cut down the Asherah poles. He broke into pieces the bronze snake Moses had made, for up to that time the Israelites had been burning incense to it. (It was called Nehushtan.) (2 Kings 18:1-4)

This God-ordained work of art, ironically, had become another idol—just like the sacred stones and the pillars devoted to the fertility goddess. How could this have happened? How is it that even Biblical art can be turned into a means of spiritual corruption?

For one thing, the serpent was probably interpreted according to the prevailing intellectual climate. Baalism also used images of snakes. The meaning of the bronze figure had changed for the Israelites. Instead of symbolizing sin and grace, it came to symbolize the idea that God was equivalent to Baal. Syncretism, the urge to combine religions, to select parts we like from a smorgasbord of incompatible worldviews, has always been a threat to Biblical faith. The bronze snake would be especially insidious since it was made by Moses, a fact which could persuade a wavering Israelite to participate in such idolatry on the assumption that it was sanctioned by the messenger of God.

Many people say that while religions may differ in their outward forms, they are identical in their essential content. As Chesterton has observed, this view is precisely backward. The forms of religion often *are* the same—patterns of worship and sacrifice, shared symbols such as blood and serpents. The difference is the content, what these forms *mean*.[2] A statue of a woman with a child might represent an actual family, a fertility goddess, or the Virgin Mary, who, in turn, might be thought of as a heavenly intercessor or simply as a Biblical example of faith. Problems generally inhere not in the work of art—Jeremiah says of the physical objects that had been turned into idols, "Do not fear them; they can do no harm nor can they do any good" (Jeremiah 10:5). Interpretation is always necessary, as is careful theological reflection.

Scripture affirms that Hezekiah was right to destroy the bronze serpent. The principle is important. No matter how successful a practice has been in the past, no matter how God has used a particular method or technique, it is possible to turn it into an idol, to pursue it for its own sake until it becomes an obstacle to true faith. At that point, the practice, no matter how venerable, must be changed. Hezekiah's action is especially important for a Biblical view of art. Art *is* sanctioned by God; it can even communicate the gospel. Yet we must not "burn incense to it."

Art should not be turned into an object of worship. The Israelites in the desert received the Word of God from the bronze image; the movement was from God through the image to the viewers. The later Israelites reversed these spiritual vectors. They were not receiving anything from the image in faith. Rather they were giving their prayers, offerings, and allegiance *to* the image. They were not receptive to the intended meaning; they projected their own meanings onto the image. They were worshiping and praying to the creature rather than the Creator (Romans 1:25).

It is possible to turn even the most theologically correct work of art into an idol. I have known Shakespearean critics whose religion is Shakespeare. They are so wrapped up in the aesthetic experience of the great plays that their lives are focused on them. Although Shakespeare always points outside himself to the world he is exploring, many scholars never notice that, so intent are they on his poetic genius. Aberrant critical approaches they treat as heresies, exhibiting all the intolerance and self-righteous zeal that they accuse the church of having. I have known of artists who dedicate themselves exclusively to their art, sacrificing everything—their marriages, their children, their morals—to their artistic careers.

This sort of idolatry is what C. S. Lewis explores in *The Great Divorce*. In the story, souls from hell are allowed to come to Heaven, but they are so caught up in themselves and so intent on refusing grace that they refuse to stay. Among them is an artist who cannot enjoy the beauties of Heaven because he is so intent on painting them. A blessed spirit, on earth a fellow artist, tries to explain to him that "if you are interested in the country only for the sake of painting it, you'll never learn to see the country."

> Every poet and musician and artist, but for Grace, is drawn away from love of the thing he tells, to love of the telling till, down in Deep Hell, they cannot be interested in God at all but only in what they say about Him. For it doesn't stop at being interested in paint, you know. They sink lower—become interested in their own personalities and then in nothing but their own reputations.[3]

The artist learns that in Heaven he will drink the waters of forgetfulness from the river, whereupon he will forget all proprietorship in his works. In doing so, he will be free to enjoy his own art without pride or modesty. All reputations, he is told, are the same in Heaven. When the artist learns that his works are now out of fashion on earth, he storms back to Hell to write a manifesto.

DEMYSTIFYING ART

There is another sense in which we can "burn incense" to a work of art. We can overmystify it, ascribing to it supernatural or religious functions. The passage on the destruction of the serpent image says that "it was called Nehushtan." The Hebrew is rather ambiguous here, but the *King James Version,* in what scholars agree is a legitimate reading, translates the passage "and *he* [that is, Hezekiah] called it Nehushtan," which means a piece of brass. Hezekiah's reform, in other words, was not only to destroy the image but to demystify it. He broke the image and said that it was nothing more than a piece of brass.

One way to defeat idolatry is to demystify the idol. This is what Isaiah does, showing how an idol is made as a way to persuade the people that there is nothing supernatural about it:

All who make idols are nothing, and the things they treasure are worthless. Those who would speak up for them are blind; they are ignorant, to their own shame. Who shapes a god and casts an idol, which can profit him nothing? He and his kind will be put to shame; craftsmen are nothing but men. Let them all come together and take their stand; they will be brought down to terror and infamy.

The blacksmith takes a tool and works with it in the coals; he shapes an idol with hammers, he forges it with the might of his arm. He gets hungry and loses his strength; he drinks no water and grows faint.

The carpenter measures with a line and makes an outline with a marker; he roughs it out with chisels and marks it with compasses. He shapes it in the form of man, of man in all his glory, that it may dwell in a shrine. He cut down cedars, or perhaps took a cypress or oak. He let it grow among the trees of the forest, or planted a pine, and the rain made it grow. It is man's fuel for burning; some of it he takes and warms himself, he kindles a fire and bakes bread. But he also fashions a god and worships it; he makes an idol and bows down to it. Half of the wood he burns in the fire; over it he prepares his meal, he roasts his meat and eats his fill. He also warms himself and says, "Ah! I am warm; I see the fire." From the rest he makes a god, his idol; he bows down to it and worships. He prays to it and says, "Save me; you are my god." (Isaiah 44:9-17)

By understanding the *technique* of artistry, by understanding the raw materials and the process of creation, one is less likely to worship the work of art or the artist.

Consider Shelley's exalted view of the poet (a title he extends to all artists):

> Poets . . . are not only the authors of language and of music, of the dance and architecture and statuary and painting; they are the institutors of laws, and the founders of civil society and the inventors of the laws of life and the teachers, who draw into a certain propinquity with the beautiful and the true that partial apprehension of the invisible world which is called religion.[4]

Shelley practically deifies artists, ascribing to them not only the creation of civilization, but the creation of the moral law and of religion itself. This romantic view of the artist, naturally enough, led to the bohemian myth, the idea that artists are far superior to ordinary people and are not bound by the same rules.

Against this view, Isaiah observes that "craftsmen are nothing but men" (44:11). Artists have the same limitations, obligations, and needs as anyone else. Their God-given talent exempts them from nothing and gives them no special moral or spiritual status. The truth of this is borne out in the history of art. The greatest artists have never been those who think themselves superior to the rest of the human race. The greatest artists are those who are most fully human. They show in their art that they share and understand the everyday struggles and demands of life.

The picture Isaiah gives of the artist praying to what he has made is poignant and tragic. The craftsman laboriously gathers his materials, plans his design, works and works to the point of exhaustion. Finally, at his point of need and despair, he falls down before his art, imploring it to "save me; you are my god" (44:17). There can be nothing more futile than such a prayer, yet this scene is played out again and again in the world of the arts, as artists devote their lives to their craft, but find out too late that their art cannot save them.

Isaiah continues, giving the answer to his despairing artist and to everyone in need of salvation:

> Remember these things, O Jacob, for you are my servant, O Israel. I have made you, you are my servant; O Israel, I will not forget you. I have swept away your offenses like a cloud, your

sins like the morning mist. Return to me, for I have redeemed
you. (44:21-22)

The description of the artist making a god is immediately countered
by God's statement, "*I* have made *you*." The artist does not make
God; God makes the artist. We, for all of our talents, are the intran-
sigent raw material that *He* forms by refining, breaking, and molding into works of art—He is the potter; we are the clay (Isaiah 64:8).
God, "who hates nothing that He has made,"[5] crafts us into "vessels of mercy" (Romans 9:23). He does so by sweeping away our
sins like mist through the redemption accomplished in Jesus Christ.

Ironically, seeing artists as mere human beings and understanding the techniques of their artistry can free us to respond aesthetically to their work. At one time in my life I was unusually taken
with the poetry of Walt Whitman. He seemed to me inspired, a
prophetic bard whose insights revealed the spiritual dimensions of
ordinary life. Not only did I admire his poetry, but I took him as an
oracle, an authority.

Some time later I was engaged by a professor to help edit
Whitman's notebooks. In the course of this project I began to see the
poet in a different way. I could see how my favorite poems were
actually written—the crossovers, the false starts, the constant revi-
sions, the labor that went into them. I began to see the poet as a real
person, his insecurities, his self-doubts, his ordinary family and business concerns, even his efforts to create an image of himself for his
public.

Whitman was demystified for me. And yet—and this is the
important point—this knowledge of the real Whitman and the real
processes of his art caused me to appreciate his poetry even more. I
could see its artistry, its createdness. I no longer view "The Song of
Myself" as an authoritative oracle of the transcendental ego, but as
a human product, something *made*. It is not religion but art.

THE LIBERATION OF THE ARTS

Surely nothing stifles art more than the insistence that it be a religion. Such a view, for example, would resist artistic change for its
own sake. It might promote change, but only because the prevailing
art is "wrong." When the new style becomes established, it resists
anything else and becomes as totalitarian as any of its predecessors.
This is the view that issues manifestoes and personal attacks. This
view is responsible for the sanctimony, self-pity, and politics in the
art world. Academic heresy hunters, bored but obedient audiences,

backstabbing in the name of a higher and higher culture are every-where in the world of the arts. When people think they are the unac-knowledged legislators of humanity, they tend to become elitist and arrogant and thus cut off from authentic artistic sensitivity.

The Bible does not permit us to take art so seriously; it liber-ates art to be itself. This is certainly true historically. Tribal and pagan art is seldom evaluated aesthetically by their cultures. The images are so tied into the culture and the religion that they are eval-uated solely according to their cultural and religious function. "It was the Christians," observes Werner Jaeger, "who finally taught men to appraise poetry by a purely aesthetic standard—a standard which enabled them to reject most of the moral and religious teach-ing of the classical poets as false and ungodly, while accepting the formal elements in their work as instructive and aesthetically delightful."[6] Herbert Schneidau credits the Bible, which demythol-ogized art and other cultural institutions, for the unprecedented artistic and cultural change that marks the history of Western civi-lization.[7]

This freeing of the aesthetic dimension has many implications. We are freed to appreciate the beauty of a work of art, even though we may reject the overt concepts that the art expresses. That is, we can approach a work of art not simply for propositional knowledge but for aesthetic understanding, so that we can perceive the depths of what the artist is communicating without confusing the creative expression for absolute truth. We may enjoy art from all ages in a multiplicity of forms. We are freed from the need to attack people personally because of their artistic tastes. We are freed from the obli-gation to be overly awed in the presence of works of art or, better yet, artists.

C. S. Lewis demonstrates this freedom. As a critic, he enjoys art in an infectious way without sanctimonious seriousness. For all of his commitment to Christian orthodoxy, he approaches art pri-marily in terms of its aesthetic impact. His book *An Experiment in Criticism* is a model of a truly catholic and far-ranging taste. Lewis here and elsewhere in his critical works is not afraid to challenge the literary establishment. He treats such sacrosanct figures as Eliot and Donne (both Christians) with some irreverence and defends others who have fallen out of favor, such as Shelley (an atheist). He also defends the "less serious" genres such as adventure stories and sci-ence fiction, forms beloved by children and the masses but scorned by the high priests of culture. He exults in fictionality:

A story which introduces the marvellous, the fantastic, says to the reader by implication, "I am merely a work of art. You must take me as such—must enjoy me for my suggestions, my beauty, my irony, my construction, and so forth. There is no question of anything like this happening to you in the real world."[8]

One might say that Lewis, the great apologist for "mere Christianity," is arguing here for "mere art"—art accepted for what it is, stripped of pretension so that it can be received with zest and pleasure.

"Mere art" liberates also the artist. Styles, forms, and movements are not sacred; therefore they can be used or changed at will. The gospel always brings liberty. The Christian artist is liberated from the exhausting role of the "doomed genius," from the pressures of bohemianism and egotistic introspection. If art is not religion, then the artist can go elsewhere and find a real religion, a faith that can give genuine substance to one's art. When art *is* religion, it tends to be simply about art—which soon becomes horribly, horribly boring. When art and religion are distinct, they can reflect each other.

Art is not only less important than God, it is less important than people. Lewis gives some helpful touchstones: "The Christian knows that the salvation of a single soul is more important than the production or preservation of all the epics and tragedies in the world."[9]

There are no *ordinary* people. You have never talked to a mere mortal. Nations, cultures, arts, civilizations—these are mortal, and their life is to ours as the life of a gnat. But it is immortals whom we joke with, work with, marry, snub, and exploit—immortal horrors or everlasting splendours.[10]

To use artistic taste as a means of snubbing other people, to use art as a means of exploiting or debauching other people, is a common perversion that a Christian must guard against. True art will be open to human beings; instead of lording it over them, the best art will serve them.

THE VALUE OF BEAUTY

Having been warned against the dangers of aestheticism, we may now focus upon the truly positive and salutary effects of art. I would argue that the aesthetic dimension is valuable in itself, apart from its use or religious content. I admit, beauty can be a lure that can lead people astray. The problem lies in what it leads to. Mere beauty, however, is always safe and God-pleasing.

To say that aesthetic pleasure is always good may sound like an overstatement. Surely some pleasure that art gives may be sinful. Some art is pornographic, for example. Some works give pleasure by creating in us sinful fantasies, whether they have to do with sex or anger or power. Some works pander to our prejudices and reinforce our worst qualities. Such illicit pleasures, though, are not *aesthetic* pleasures.

The ancient philosophers and theologians are helpful in distinguishing between the different pleasures and different faculties of the mind.[11] According to classical thought, beauty is perceived by the *mind*, which contains two faculties—rationality (*ratio*) and intellect (*intellectus*). *Ratio* is the mind's ability to be logical, mathematical, and analytical, to perceive truth by a process and by effort. *Intellectus* is the faculty of immediately perceiving truth, intuitively and directly. The old theologians taught that angels are pure intellect; that is, they perceive God and all things immediately and fully.

Fallen humanity, though, at present depends upon *ratio*. We can apprehend truth, but we must do so indirectly and piecemeal, through experiments, logical analysis, and the accumulation of knowledge through time (as in working one's way through a book, as you have been doing here). Because we are fallen, our minds do not function as they should, so that we are utterly dependent upon God's revelation to discern spiritual truth. The higher power of the intellect is still operative to a certain extent. When we see something, our perception and our knowledge are instantaneous. When we finally grasp the truth of an idea, our intellect experiences a flash of illumination. That our intellects can be deceived through false appearances is more evidence for the fall.

According to the ancients, beauty is perceived by the intellect. It is common today to say that art appeals to the emotions. Our vocabulary is rather more clumsy than the ancients'. Their view of intellect was holistic and would include much of what we mean by "emotions," including love and joy. (Intellect includes feelings, but it does not include logic, which is a function of *ratio*.) They would insist, however, that beauty is perceived by the mind, not by the more physical "passions," which can give occasion to other, sometimes sinful, pleasures.

When we see something beautiful, our intellects experience a flash of satisfaction and joy. Classical aesthetics understands our perception of beauty on earth as a glimpse of that total and direct apprehension of the essence of things that the angels and saints in Heaven always experience. "For now we see through a glass, darkly; but then face to face: now I know in part; but then shall I know even as also I am known" (1 Corinthians 13:12 KJV). Now we cannot even understand earthly things without the cumbersome instruments of scientific rational analysis. But when we stand before God, we shall know directly, face to face. This fuller perception is not merely abstract knowledge, but it is concrete and personal, partaking of the experience of beauty.

This point helps us to understand something of the felicity of Heaven. The Beatific Vision, the direct perception of God enjoyed forever by the redeemed in Heaven, is described by the old theologians as an experience of ultimate beauty. The beauty of God, the source of all secondary beauties which so enrapture us on earth, permeates Heaven, as imaged by the Biblical figures of music, song, and dazzling light. The blessed, their intellects freed, can now see *everything* in its divinely intended beauty, a beauty which before was obscured by their fallenness and physical limitations. The divinely appointed beauty that inheres in all existence is now largely veiled from us. The freeing of the intellect means that we will perceive this beauty; that is, we will see how everything that God has made is "very good" (Genesis 1:31).

If beauty is perceived by the intellect, the highest faculty of the mind as shared with angels, it follows that aesthetic pleasure involves a kind of intuitive "knowing" of the highest status, and that it is distinct from other kinds of pleasures. We can see then why pornography is not only a moral fault but also an aesthetic fault. Pornography appeals not to the intellect but to the sexual passions. One may read Updike, say, and respond to his great aesthetic skill. But when he begins vividly describing sexuality, the reader's sexual passions can be so engaged that the aesthetic spell is broken. Certainly fallen human beings may experience greater pleasure from the passions than from the intellect. Passions, though, whether they are sexual, violent, or sentimental, have nothing to do with beauty, even though it too is perceived through the senses.

This is why the Greeks banned explicit violence from the stage. Such titillation breaks the aesthetic unity of the work, as is evident in modern cinema. One can become involved in the plot and characters of a film; but when one of the actors takes a chain saw to the others, the aesthetic response of the intuitive intellect is interrupted by physical revulsion. This is also why sentimentality is an aesthetic fault. Sheer emotionalism may give a certain pleasure, but it is not the pleasure of beauty. It is, literally, a lower pleasure than that of aesthetic satisfaction.

This is not to say that such pleasures are not good in their places. Sexual pleasure is a great good in marriage. Art, however, is not the appropriate means for such pleasure. It may be perfectly correct to weep when a puppy is run over, but a poem, a country-western song, or a Norman Rockwell-style print on the subject is apt to be derided as sentimental if its effect is "tear jerking" rather than aesthetic. Thus there are aesthetic reasons for avoiding the pornographic, the overly violent, and the sentimental. The experience of beauty, however, in all of its complex forms is always good and even exalting.

Beauty is valuable in itself because it is a quality of God (Psalm 27:4). Furthermore, He expresses this quality in His creation. Human beings can both perceive and create beauty because they are made in the image of God.[12] Augustine says that "those beautiful patterns, which through the medium of men's souls are conveyed into their artistic hands, emanate from that Beauty which is above our souls, which my soul sigheth after day and night."[13] In the context of this quotation, Augustine was warning against being ensnared by mere worldly beauties, using them as idolatrous substitutes for God. The source of the beauty, though, is God, who works through the artistic hands of human beings (in this case, even of those who do not know Him).

George MacDonald observes how aesthetic experience can elevate the mind:

> Whatever it be that keeps the finer faculties of the mind awake, wonder alive, and the interest above mere eating and drinking, money-making and money-saving; whatever it be that gives gladness, or sorrow, or hope—this, be it violin, pencil, pen . . . is simply a divine gift of holy influence for the salvation of that being to whom it comes, for the lifting of him out of the mire and up on the rock. For it keeps a way open for the entrance of deeper, holier, grander influences, emanating from the same riches of the Godhead. And though many have genius that have no grace, they will only be so much the worse, so much nearer to the brute, if you take from them [their art].[14]

This is to say that the arts shield us from mere materialism and dull insensitivity. They cannot save of themselves, but they are still exalting. They make us more human, more what God created us to be, and less animal-like. They involve a perception that transcends the narrow, empty world of materialism and brutishness.

If the perception and creation of beauty are gifts of God, it follows that the proper use of the arts is a matter of stewardship. Any of God's gifts can be used or abused. They can be twisted into sin; they can be buried in the ground; they can be multiplied. We dare not despise art. If God gives us artistic talent, we are obligated to develop that talent. If God gives us an aesthetic experience—a glimpse of a sublime landscape, the satisfaction of a good novel, the pleasing forms of a painting or sculpture—we must not cover our eyes, spurning God's gift of beauty. We are obligated to linger over it, to enjoy it fully, and to glorify God.

GOD'S ARTIST

Bezalel was called by name. God empowered him with the gifts necessary to make designs "for glory and beauty." These gifts—the Spirit of God, ability, intelligence, knowledge, craftsmanship, and the inspiration to teach—are rare and precious and are to be honored wherever they appear. Scripture honors them in five successive chapters, not only in the calling and equipping of Bezalel, but in the detailed account of the variety and magnificence of his works. Nearly every verse in Exodus 36—39 repeats the litany, referring back to Bezalel, that "he made . . . and he made," a phrase repeated fifty-five times in the four chapters:

> And he made loops of blue. . . . And he made fifty clasps of gold. . . . He made eleven curtains. . . . Then he made the upright frames for the Tabernacle of acacia wood. . . . And he made the veil of blue and purple and scarlet stuff and fine twined linen; with cherubim skilfully worked he made it. . . . Bezalel made the ark of acacia wood. . . . And he made a mercy seat of pure gold. . . . And he made two cherubim of hammered gold. . . . He made the holy anointing oil also. . . . And he made the laver of bronze and its base of bronze, from the mirrors of the ministering women. . . . The onyx stones were prepared, enclosed in settings of gold filigree. . . . Bezalel the son of Uri, son of Hur, of the tribe of Judah, made all that the Lord commanded Moses. (Exodus 36—39 RSV)

Such passages may seem tiring to some—descriptions of artifacts that have been lost for thousands of years, details of a mode of worship long superseded, blueprints of incomprehensible designs. Yet it pleased God to include these passages in Holy Scripture, all of which He declares to be "profitable for teaching, for reproof, for correction, and for training in righteousness" (2 Timothy 3:16 RSV). What we are to learn from these passages is that God loves craftsmanship and design, that He exults not only in His own creation but also in the creations and the aesthetic satisfaction of His children.

RESOURCES

*T*he following are resources that may prove helpful to Christians interested in the arts. It includes not only books but also organizations, since knowing people is sometimes as valuable as knowing information, especially for artists in need of fellowship and support. This list is by no means complete. It can be supplemented by the sources mentioned in my notes and in bibliographies listed in the works that follow.

ORGANIZATIONS

CHRISTIANS IN THE ARTS NETWORKING (CAN). An organization devoted to tying together the hosts of artists' fellowships, arts ministries, and individual Christian artists. CAN offers a newsletter, a directory, a data base, and personal contacts that can connect people with Christian artists throughout the world. Write to Philip Griffith, Christians in the Arts Networking, Inc., P.O. Box 1941, Cambridge, MA 02238-1941, or call him at (617) 783-5667.

CHRISTIANS IN THE VISUAL ARTS (CIVA). A national organization of Christian painters and sculptors. CIVA publishes a newsletter and a directory and sponsors national and regional conferences and exhibitions. For more information and a free copy of the newsletter, write to *CIVA Newsletter*, P.O. Box 10247, Arlington, VA 22210.

AUDIO-VISUAL

Colin Harbinson, *The Arts: A Biblical Framework* and *The Artist: A Spiritual Foundation*. Eight audio tapes. A series of lectures by a

wise and experienced dramatist who has spent many years in arts
ministry. The discussion of artists' specific spiritual needs and their
spiritual pitfalls is invaluable. Available from Tri-HarDur
Productions, P.O. Box 1324, Cambridge, Ontario, Canada N1R
7G6.

Francis Schaeffer, *How Should We Then Live?: The Rise and Decline
of Western Thought and Culture.* Ten-episode film series. Schaeffer
makes provocative use of the arts in his dissection of Western culture. Produced by Franky Schaeffer and available from Gospel
Films, P.O. Box 455, Muskegon, MI 49443.

BOOKS

Rookmaaker, H. R. *Modern Art and the Death of a Culture.*
Downers Grove, IL: InterVarsity Press, 1970. A hard-hitting critique of modern art, demonstrating how artistic styles reflect
changes in worldviews.

Ryken, Leland. *Culture in Christian Perspective: A Door to
Understanding and Enjoying the Arts.* Portland, OR: Multnomah
Press, 1986. A wide-ranging discussion of the arts by a preeminent
Christian critic.

Sayers, Dorothy L. *The Mind of the Maker.* San Francisco: Harper &
Row, 1941. A stimulating application of the doctrine of the Trinity
to art.

Schaeffer, Francis. *Art and the Bible.* Downers Grove, IL: InterVarsity
Press, 1973. A small but influential book on what the Bible implies
about the arts.

Schaeffer, Franky. *Sham Pearls for Real Swine.* Brentwood, TN:
Wolgemuth & Hyatt, 1990. An impassioned plea by a Christian
artist (and son of Francis Schaeffer) for understanding on the part
of the church.

Seerveld, Calvin. *Rainbows for the Fallen World: Aesthetic Life and
Artistic Task.* Toronto: Tuppence Press, 1980. A sophisticated but
engaging treatment of art and aesthetics by an important Christian
philosopher.

Wolterstorff, Nicholas. *Art in Action.* Grand Rapids, MI: Eerdmans,
1980. A sophisticated discussion by a Christian aesthetician of
"high art" as opposed to art that is a part of life.

NOTES

CHAPTER ONE: *The State of the Arts*

1. This would be an example of the logical fallacy known as "the undistributed middle premise." The conclusion is fallacious because other things shock people besides great art.
2. Franky Schaeffer, *Sham Pearls for Real Swine* (Brentwood, TN: Wolgemuth & Hyatt, 1990), pp. 12, 17. The entire book is an impassioned, sometimes vitriolic, indictment of the contemporary church's misunderstanding and neglect of its artists.
3. *See*, for example, Jacques Ellul, *The Humiliation of the Word*, trans. Joyce Main Hanks (Grand Rapids, MI: Eerdmans, 1985) and Neil Postman, *Amusing Ourselves to Death: Public Discourse in the Age of Show Business* (New York: Penguin, 1985).

CHAPTER TWO: *The Scope of the Arts*

1. For a sophisticated discussion of art as a part of life as opposed to a strict "high art" perspective, see Nicholas Wolsterstorff, *Art in Action* (Grand Rapids, MI: Eerdmans, 1980).
2. *See* "The Nicomachean Ethics," bk. 6, sect. 4, in *The Pocket Aristotle*, ed. Justin D. Kaplan (New York: Washington Square Books, 1958), p. 227.
3. Dante Alighieri, *Inferno*, cantos 11, 14.
4. Dante Alighieri, *Inferno*, canto 11, lines 106-12. Trans. Dorothy L. Sayers, *The Comedy of Dante Alighieri* (New York: Penguin Books, 1949), 1:137.
5. Quoted from *How Should We Then Live?* in *The Complete Works of Francis A. Schaeffer* (Wheaton, IL: Crossway Books, 1982), 5:203.
6. *Ibid.*
7. *See* Edith Schaeffer, *The Art of Life* (Wheaton, IL: Crossway Books, 1987).
8. *See* Luther's discussion of the Sabbath in "The Large Catechism," in *The Book of Concord*, trans. Theodore G. Tappert (Philadelphia: Fortress Press, 1959), p. 377.
9. For the difference between a quilt used as an object of art and as a part of

ordinary life, see Alice Walker's short story "Everyday Use," in *In Love & Trouble* (New York: Harcourt Brace Jovanovich, 1973).

CHAPTER THREE: *Understanding Art*

1. *See* Sir Edmund Burke's classic essay "A Philosophical Enquiry into the Origin of Our Ideas of the Sublime and the Beautiful" (1739). The Grand Canyon and other vast or even terrifying objects that partake of the infinite, Burke terms "sublime." The dogwood blossom and other orderly, regular objects that create a feeling analogous to love, Burke terms "beauty." I am using beauty in a larger sense to embrace the whole range of positive aesthetic experiences.
2. *See* Aristotle, "Poetics," in *Criticism: The Major Statements*, ed. Charles Kaplan (New York: St. Martin's, 1985), p. 377. *See* also my discussion of tragedy in *Reading Between the Lines* (Wheaton, IL: Crossway Books, 1990).
3. *See* Edgar Allan Poe's essay "The Philosophy of Composition." The most effective subject, he concluded, was the death of a beautiful woman. Poe's frightening tales are often seen as expressions of a morbid and unstable personality. Judging from his critical writings, however, Poe emerges as a very rational formalist. Poe may well have been cold-bloodedly experimenting with formal techniques rather than "expressing himself" in his fiction. Certainly, what makes his tales so good, in contrast to those of the typical horror writer, is his impeccable craftsmanship.
4. For a searching discussion of St. Augustine's aesthetics, see William H. Pahlka, *St. Augustine's Meter and George Herbert's Will* (Kent, OH: Kent State University Press, 1987).
5. Calvin Seerveld, *Rainbows for a Fallen World: Aesthetic Life and Artistic Task* (Toronto: Tuppence Press, 1980), p. 63.
6. *Ibid.*
7. *See* Kenneth Myers, *All God's Children and Blue Suede Shoes* (Wheaton, IL: Crossway Books, 1989).
8. Seerveld, *Rainbows for a Fallen World*, pp. 63-64.
9. *See* Stanley E. Fish, *Self-Consuming Artifacts* (Berkeley, CA: University of California Press, 1972).

CHAPTER FOUR: *A Walk Through the Museum*

1. *See* J. R. R. Tolkien, "On Fairy Stories," in *The Tolkien Reader* (New York: Ballantine Books, 1966), pp. 46ff.
2. *See* Francis A. Schaeffer, *How Should We Then Live?* in *The Complete Works of Francis A. Schaeffer* (Wheaton, IL: Crossway Books, 1982), 5:104-5.
3. John Calvin, *Institutes of the Christian Religion*, trans. Ford Lewis Battles, ed. John T. McNeill (Philadelphia: Westminster Press, 1960), bk. 1, chap. 11, sect. 12.
4. Quoted in Charles Garside, *Zwingli and the Arts* (New Haven, CT: Yale University Press, 1966), p. 171.
5. Quoted in *ibid.*, p. 182.
6. The Reformation began in the early 1500s. Rembrandt painted a hundred

years later. He and Bach are generally classified under the Baroque style. Their connection to the spirituality of the Reformation is clear, although I am violating chronological order in discussing them before the Renaissance artists. Cranach, though, was a contemporary of Luther, as was Dürer.

7. See Wylie Sypher, *Four Stages of Renaissance Style: Transformations in Art and Literature, 1400-1700* (Garden City, NY: Doubleday, 1955), for further discussions of these styles and for their interdisciplinary implications.

8. Strictly speaking, the term Expressionism refers to a school of German and Nordic painters such as Gustav Klimt and Edvard Munch. I am broadening the definition somewhat to include Gauguin and Van Gogh, who are very different, yet who are likewise expressing their inwardness in their art. Expressionism is a convenient label to put in opposition to Impressionism.

9. See A. M. Hammacher, *Van Gogh* (New York: Paul Hamlyn, 1967), p. 22, and J. Grant Swank, Jr., "The Not-quite Reverend Van Gogh," *Christianity Today*, 16 July 1990, p. 57.

10. William Wordsworth, "The Tables Turned," line 28, in *Lyrical Ballads (1798)*, ed. W. J. B. Owen (New York: Oxford University Press, 1969).

11. See Kathleen J. Regier, ed., *The Spiritual Image in Modern Art* (Wheaton, IL: Theosophical Publishing House, 1987). Theosophy teaches that God, nature, and the self are all one. Unity with God—defined as the Self that underlies and unites all selves—is reached through an inward-looking mysticism based on meditation, psychic experimentation, and esoteric spiritualism.

CHAPTER FIVE: *The Abdication of the Arts*

1. See Leland Ryken, *Culture in Christian Perspective: A Door to Understanding and Enjoying the Arts* (Portland, OR: Multnomah Press, 1986), pp. 235-38.

2. Tom Wolfe, *The Painted Word* (New York: Farrar, Straus, Giroux, 1976), pp. 97-103.

3. *Ibid.*, p. 104.

4. See Rowland Evans and Robert Novak, "The NEA's Suicide Charge," *The Washington Post*, 11 May 1990, p. A27; George Archibald, "Explicit Shows Rejected by NEA," *The Washington Times*, 14 May 1990, pp. A1, A12; Joyce Price, "Artists Outraged by NEA 'Denial' of On-Stage Sexual Performances," *The Washington Times*, 15 May 1990, pp. A1, A8.

5. Wolfe, *Painted Word*, p. 26.

6. *Ibid.*, pp. 26-27.

7. *Ibid.*, pp. 21-22.

8. Tom Strini, "Art Groups Unite to Fight NEA Restrictions, but Still Skirt Real Issue," *Milwaukee Journal*, 27 May 1990, p. E6.

9. *King Lear*, act 1, sc. 1, lines 252-55. Quoted from William Shakespeare, *The Complete Works*, ed. Peter Alexander (London: Collins, 1970).

CHAPTER SIX: *The Vocation of Bezalel*

1. For the comprehensive scope of Christian thought, see G. K. Chesterton, *Orthodoxy* (Garden City, NY: Doubleday, 1973). *See also* my book *Loving God with All Your Mind* (Wheaton, IL: Crossway Books, 1987), pp. 131-41.

CHAPTER SEVEN: The Works of Bezalel

1. *Art and the Bible* in *The Complete Works of Francis Schaeffer* (Wheaton, IL: Crossway Books, 1982), 2:378.
2. *Ibid.*, p. 381.
3. According to the notes in the NIV.
4. André Lemaire, "Probable Head of Priestly Scepter from Solomon's Temple Surfaces in Jerusalem," *Biblical Archaeology Review*, 10 (January/February 1984), pp. 27, 29.
5. The Temple in Ezekiel's vision is not necessarily identical with Solomon's Temple, which had been destroyed. The prophet is describing the restored spiritual Temple.
6. Schaeffer, *Art and the Bible*, p. 380.
7. *See* Dorothy L. Sayers, *Introductory Papers on Dante* (London: Methuen, 1954).
8. The connection between the "signifier" and the "signified" may be arbitrary, but, contrary to many contemporary theorists, it is nevertheless real.
9. The Reformers had some useful advice in interpreting Biblical symbols: Scripture must interpret Scripture. Medieval Catholics interpreted the story of Esther as symbolizing and therefore giving evidence for the intercession of the Virgin Mary. The Reformers stressed that no symbolic meaning can be valid unless it is affirmed literally elsewhere in the Bible. Because the doctrine of Mary's intercession is nowhere stated in the Bible, Esther should not be read as symbolizing it. The Temple rituals, on the other hand, do symbolize the work of Christ because the book of Hebrews says that they do.
10. For the differences between the Hebrews and their neighbors, see Herbert N. Schneidau, *Sacred Discontent: The Bible and Western Tradition* (Berkeley: University of California Press, 1977).
11. *See* Schneidau, *ibid.*, who argues that our Western culture is open to change precisely because our Biblical heritage prevents us from making any cultural form absolute, in marked contrast to civilizations based on "myth."
12. *See* Psalms 33:3; 40:3; 96:1; 98:1; 144:9; 149:1. *See* also Luke 5:36-39.

CHAPTER EIGHT: The Idolatry of Aaron

1. "The Study of Poetry," in *Poetry and Criticism of Matthew Arnold*, ed. A. Dwight Culler (Boston: Houghton Mifflin, 1961), p. 306.
2. Certainly art can deal with pain and even horror—it is not always "pleasant." A great tragedy may be devastating, but it still gives its audience a sense of satisfaction, a positive aesthetic enjoyment deriving from its form, which is distinct from the "pity and fear" created by its content. Aesthetic pleasure and satisfaction can encompass a wide, complex range of emotional responses.
3. Flannery O'Connor, *The Violent Bear It Away* (New York: Farrar, Straus & Giroux, 1955), p. 8.
4. Kierkegaard develops these distinctions in *Either/Or*, trans. W. Lowrie, 2 vols. (Princeton, NJ: Princeton University Press, 1944) and *Stages on Life's Way,* trans. W. Lowrie (New York: Oxford University Press, 1940).
5. For a profound poem on creation's refusal to take the place reserved for God, despite human desires, see Francis Thompson's "The Hound of

Heaven," *Hound of Heaven & Other Poems* (Boston, MA: Branden Publishing).

6. Francis A. Schaeffer, *Art and the Bible* in *The Complete Works of Francis Schaeffer* (Wheaton, IL: Crossway Books, 1982), 2:380.

7. King Ahaz went so far as to build in the Temple a new altar that was specifically modeled after one used by the pagan Assyrians (2 Kings 16:10-16). The significance of the passage is not clear. Although Ahaz was an apostate king and a notorious idolater and although his slavish devotion to all things Assyrian was contemptible, there is no indication that the Lord refused the sacrifices performed on this altar.

8. A Christian might even be an Abstract Expressionist or a minimalist or a conceptualist or a performing artist. My earlier criticism of these movements is based on my belief that they are bad art, that they lack artistic form. They also grow out of an insufficient worldview, which a Christian artist slinging paint against a canvas might not realize. In a sense, abstract art, which conveys no "content" as such, is safe for an artist afraid of contradicting the Scriptures. On the other hand, random abstractionism does have an implicit content—the meaningless of life. In art that is pornographic or blasphemous, again, the problem is its content, not its form.

9. *See*, for example, W. H. Auden's Kierkegaardian perspective on the question in his essay "Postscript: Christianity and Art," in *The Dyer's Hand*, reprinted in the anthology *Religion and Modern Literature: Essays in Theory and Criticism*, eds. G. B. Tennyson and Edward C. Ericson, Jr. (Grand Rapids, MI: Eerdmans, 1975), pp. 114-18.

10. We should remember that Aaron repented of his idolatry and was received back into his sacred ministry. That Aaron's gross failure as a priest and as an artist was fully forgiven should be a comfort to the rest of us.

CHAPTER NINE: *Creation and Imitation*

1. Elizabeth A. Douglas, "Art: The Genesis Basis," *Christians in the Visual Arts Newsletter*, Summer 1988, pp. 1, 4.

2. *Ibid.*, p. 4. The entire discussion of light, space, and unity is drawn from Professor Douglas's article.

3. *See* the discussion in Leland Ryken's *Culture in Christian Perspective* (Portland, OR: Multnomah Press, 1986), pp. 66-69.

4. Walter Wangerin, Jr., Plenary Address, Midwest Conference on Christianity and Literature, Concordia University-Wisconsin, 29 September 1989.

5. G. K. Chesterton, *The Everlasting Man* (Garden City, NY: Doubleday, 1974).

6. *Antiquities of the Jews*, bk. 18, chap. 3, sect. 1; from *Josephus: Complete Works*, trans. William Whiston (Grand Rapids, MI: Kregel Publications, 1960), p. 379.

7. *See* Henry James's short story, "A Figure in the Carpet."

8. *The Great Evangelical Disaster* in *The Complete Works of Francis A. Schaeffer* (Wheaton, IL: Crossway Books, 1982), 4:309.

9. *Ibid.*, p. 310.

10. Annie Dillard, *Pilgrim at Tinker Creek* (New York: Bantam, 1975), pp. 114, 129-30, 132.

11. *See* my article, "Defamiliarizing the Gospel: Shklovsky and a Theory of Religious Art" in *Christianity and Literature*, 28 (1979), pp. 40-47.

12. *See* Plato's *Republic*, bk. 10.

13. Gene Edward Veith, Jr., *Reading Between the Lines* (Wheaton, IL: Crossway Books, 1990), pp. 86-89.

14. This discussion is indebted to Thorleif Boman, *Hebrew Thought Compared to Greek*, trans. Jules C. Moreau (Philadelphia: Westminster Press, 1960).

15. *See ibid.*, pp. 77-81.

16. *See* Eric Auerbach, *Mimesis: The Representation of Reality in Western Literature* (Princeton, NJ: Princeton University Press, 1953), pp. 3-23, for a close analysis of the difference between Biblical and classical narration.

17. *See* Herbert N. Schneidau, *Sacred Discontent: The Bible and Western Tradition* (Berkeley: University of California Press, 1977).

18. *See* Augustine's *Confessions*, bk. 7, sect. 9. Augustine, a Roman citizen steeped in Greek philosophy, describes his difficulty with the concept of the *logos* becoming flesh. His conversion and subsequent writings are profound examples of the new synthesis of Greek and Hebrew thought made possible by Christianity.

CHAPTER TEN: *Contemporary Christian Artists*

1. William A. Dyrness, *Rouault: A Vision of Suffering and Salvation* (Grand Rapids, MI: Eerdmans, 1971), p. 16. My discussion of Rouault is indebted to this excellent book, which is worth reading not only for its scholarly study of Rouault, but for its wider relevance to Christian aesthetics.

2. *Ibid.*, p. 89. The following discussion of the phases of Rouault's work is based on chapter 7 of Dyrness's book.

3. *Ibid.*, p. 102.

4. *Ibid.*, p. 108.

5. Quoted in *ibid.*, p. 106. Dyrness also discusses Léon Bloy, Joris-Karl Huysmans, André Suarés, and Maurice Denis as other Christian intellectuals who influenced Rouault.

6. *Ibid.*, p. 200. Dyrness cites Waldemar George on this point.

7. *See* my discussion of the comic sense of life in chapter 6 of my book *Reading Between the Lines* (Wheaton, IL: Crossway Books, 1990).

8. Dyrness, *Rouault*, p. 94.

9. Michel Hoog, quoted in *ibid.*, p. 94.

10. Quoted in *ibid.*, p. 49.

11. Those interested in Knippers' work could contact him through his studio at 2408 Washington Blvd., Arlington, VA 22201.

12. Edward C. Knippers, Jr., "Statement for the 1989 CIVA Conference Panel on Narrative," Typescript, Christians in the Visual Arts Conference, 22 June 1989.

13. *Ibid.*, p. 4.

14. *Ibid.*, p. 9.

15. *Ibid.*, p. 10.

16. That he sometimes paints Jesus unclothed may be particularly disconcerting. In a telephone conversation, Knippers stressed that this treatment of Christ is designed to stress the full implications of the Incarnation, that in Christ, God became a physical human being. Furthermore, Knippers is con-

cerned to rebuke feminist theology, seeing their genderless, androgynous Christ—an image prevalent also in images of Christ that came out of nineteenth-century Romanticism—as being dangerously contrary to Scripture.

17. *See* Franky Schaeffer's important discussion of this issue in terms of the Bible, church history, and the canons of religious art in *Sham Pearls for Real Swine* (Brentwood, TN: Wolgemuth & Hyatt, 1990), pp. 109-21.

18. *Ibid.*, pp. 112-17.

19. Those interested in Prescott's work could contact him through Messiah College, Grantham, Pennsylvania 17207.

20. Ted Prescott, *"Making the Descent from the Cross," Festival Quarterly,* (Winter 1987), p. 15.

21. Letter to the author, 27 July 1990.

22. Those interested in obtaining prints of her work may do so through the Sandra Bowden Studio, 237 Moe Road, Clifton Park, New York 12065.

23. Quoted from a flyer from Sandra Bowden studios.

24. The archaeological details cited in this discussion are based on notes Sandra Bowden includes with the prints.

25. Another King Jeroboam reigned in the time of Jonah (2 Kings 14:23-29), but the Megiddo ruins seem to be from the era of Solomon.

26. That the lion is clearly an example of representational art does not negate our earlier discussion of the Hebrew preference for nonrepresentational art. Both Jeroboams are described in Scripture as being evil and idolatrous kings (1 Kings 12:28; 2 Kings 14:24). Their servants would not feel obliged to cling to the orthodox Mosaic prohibition of images. In any event, the Biblical sanctions against idolatry did allow for representational figures. Solomon's palace featured carvings of lions (1 Kings 10:20).

27. Prints of McReynolds's works are available from Pomegranate Publishers, P. O. Box 808022, Petaluma, CA 94925.

CHAPTER ELEVEN: *Art and the Church*

1. C. S. Lewis, *An Experiment in Criticism* (Cambridge: Cambridge University Press, 1961), pp. 17-18.

2. For the Greek Orthodox position on these and other issues, see Anthony Ugolnik, *The Illuminating Icon* (Grand Rapids, MI: Eerdmans, 1988).

3. *See* Kenneth Myers, *All God's Children and Blue Suede Shoes: Christians and Popular Culture* (Wheaton, IL: Crossway Books, 1990).

4. I am indebted to Rev. Timothy Maschke for this observation.

5. *See,* for example, Frederick Buechner's compilation of paintings of Jesus in his book, *The Faces of Christ* (San Francisco: Harper & Row, 1989).

6. The sacraments, following St. Augustine, are often described as "visible words," presenting the gospel in tangible signs so that Christ's promises can be literally tasted and experienced as well as verbally apprehended. Even here, the elements must always be accompanied by the *words* of consecration.

7. *See* Neil Postman, *Amusing Ourselves to Death: Public Discourse in the Age of Show Business* (New York: Penguin, 1985). *See* also my discussion of this point in the first chapter of my book *Reading Between the Lines* (Wheaton, IL: Crossway Books, 1990).

8. See Jacques Ellul, *The Humiliation of the Word,* trans. Joyce Main Hanks

(Grand Rapids, MI: Eerdmans, 1985).

9. Charles Garside, *Zwingli and the Arts* (New Haven, CT: Yale University Press, 1966), pp. 172-73.

10. See John Rudolf Weinlick, "Moravianism in the American Colonies," in *Continental Pietism and Early American Christianity*, ed. F. Ernest Stoeffler (Grand Rapids, MI: Eerdmans, 1976), pp. 125-26. *See* also Weinlick's *Count Zinzendorf* (Nashville, TN: Abingdon, 1956).

CHAPTER TWELVE: Conclusion

1. See Kenneth Myers, *All God's Children and Blue Suede Shoes: Christians and Popular Culture* (Wheaton, IL: Crossway Books, 1990).

2. G. K. Chesterton, *Orthodoxy* (London: The Bodley Head, 1908), p. 220.

3. C. S. Lewis, *The Great Divorce* (New York: Macmillan, 1946), p. 81.

4. Percy Shelley, "A Defence of Poetry," in *The Norton Anthology of English Literature*, ed. M. H. Abrams *et al.*, 4th ed. (New York: W. W. Norton, 1979), 2:784.

5. The phrase is from the Ash Wednesday Collect, the traditional liturgical prayer for the first day of Lent.

6. Werner Jaeger, *Paideia: The Ideals of Greek Culture*, trans. Gilbert Highet (New York: Oxford University Press, 1935, 1965) pp. xxvii-xxviii.

7. Herbert N. Schneidau, *Sacred Discontent: The Bible and Western Tradition* (Berkeley: University of California Press, 1977).

8. C. S. Lewis, *An Experiment in Criticism* (Cambridge: Cambridge University Press, 1961), p. 56.

9. C. S. Lewis, "Christianity and Literature," in *Christian Reflections*, ed. Walter Hooper (Grand Rapids, MI: Eerdmans, 1967), p. 10.

10. C. S. Lewis, "The Weight of Glory," in *The Weight of Glory and Other Addresses* (Grand Rapids, MI: Eerdmans, 1965), p. 15.

11. The following discussion draws on Augustine and Thomas Aquinas, who in turn are indebted to Plato and Aristotle.

12. See Dorothy L. Sayers, *The Mind of the Maker* (San Francisco: Harper & Row, 1941).

13. Augustine, *Confessions*, sect. 34, in *Basic Writings of St. Augustine*, ed. Whitney J. Oates (New York: Random House, 1948), 1:174.

14. George MacDonald, *Robert Falconer* (New York: Rutledge, 1870), p. 88.

SCRIPTURE INDEX

GENERAL INDEX

Iconoclasts, 21-22, 24, 58-59, 63, 159,
196, 198-199
Iconophiles, 21-22, 24, 196-197
Idolatry, 21, 22, 25, 58, 127-128, 133-
143, 148, 159, 222-224
Illuminated manuscripts, 32, 57-58
see also *Calligraphy*
Imitation, 57-58, 145, 148-149, 153-157,
161
Impressionism, 53, 76-77, 166
Islamic art, 150-152, 154

Jaeger, Werner, 228
James, Henry, 241
Johnson, Samuel, 110
Josephus, 149-150
Jud, Leo, 59

Kafka, Franz, 43
Kandinsky, Vasili, 84
Kierkegaard, Søren, 139-140, 241
Kitsch, 47-51, 100, 197
Klee, Paul, 84, 154
Klimt, Gustav, 239
Knippers, Edward, 175-180, 242

Lange, Dorothea, 208
Language, 147, 214-217
Lascaux, cave paintings, 21
L'Engle, Madeleine, 58
Lewis, C. S., 58, 125-126, 195, 217, 224,
228-229
Lewitt, Sol, 92
Literature, 131-132, 217
Luther, Martin, 37, 62, 63, 199, 207,
209, 237, 239
Lutheranism, 199-200.

MacDonald, George, 58, 213, 232
Mannerism, 66-67, 197, 201-202
Mapplethorpe, Robert, xv, 19-21, 50, 94,
99, 221
Marx, Karl, 73, 96-97, 159
Marxism, 96-97
Maschke, Timothy, 243
Matisse, Henri, 85, 97, 122, 166
McReynolds, Cliff, 190-193, 243
Medieval Art, 54-58, 183, 204
Michelangelo, 21, 63, 66, 99, 113, 221
Milton, John, 69
Minimalism, 50, 92-93, 97, 115-116,
149, 172, 176, 241
Miro, Juan, 84
Modern Art, 79-86
Monet, Claude, 76-77
Morality, 207-211

Mulder, Karen, xiii
Munch, Edvard, 79-80, 239
Music, 37-38, 40, 41, 62-63, 69, 130,
159-160, 165, 198, 199, 201-204, 217,
219
Myers, Kenneth, 49

Narrative art, 57, 176-177, 179-180,
190, 203, 212
National Endowment for the Arts, 98-
100
Naturalism, 73
Neoclassicism, 70, 165
New Age movement, 84, 176-177, 179,
221
Nudity, 179, 242-243

O'Connor, Flannery, 139, 209
Op art, 84
Orthodoxy, Greek, 196-199

Performance art, 19, 93-94
Perspective, 64-65, 77, 81-82, 192-193
Photographic realism, 85, 122, 129
Picasso, Pablo, 43, 81-83, 113, 209
Plato, 64, 159, 244
Poe, Edgar Allan, 42, 238
Poetry, 131
Pointillism, 193
Pollock, Jackson, xv, 50, 84, 86, 89, 113,
116
Pomegranate, from Solomon's Temple,
117-119
Pop art, 85
see also *Warhol, Andy*
Pornography, 179, 230-232, 241
Portraiture, 59-60
Postman, Neil, 215, 237
Presbyterians, 199
Prescott, Theodore, 180-186, 243
Pre-Raphaelites, 73-75

Raphael, 64-65
Reformation, 58-63, 183, 204
Reformed worship, 198
Rembrandt, 44-47, 51, 59-60, 88, 94,
166, 179, 198, 221, 238
Renaissance, 63-66, 183, 192-193, 197
Representational art, 117-123, 129, 148-
149, 155, 161
Rockwell, Norman, 232
Romanticism, 53, 71-76, 165-166, 175,
186, 204, 226, 243
Rookmaaker, H. R., 236
Rossetti, Dante Gabriel, 73-75
Rouault, Georges, 166-174, 179, 242